MW00817607

THE HAPPY PEAR 20

RECIPES AND LEARNINGS FROM THE FIRST 20 YEARS

DAVID AND
STEPHEN FLYNN

GILL BOOKS

Gill Books
Hume Avenue
Park West
Dublin 12
www.gillbooks.ie

Gill Books is an imprint of M.H. Gill and Co.

9781804581032

Designed by www.grahamthew.com
Collages by Bartek Janczak
Edited by Emma Dunne
Photography by Joanne Murphy
Other photography: © Alan Rowlette: 336B; © Sean Cahill: 88, 89, 90T, 91B, 93, 134-135, 191B, 259, 336R, 337, 338L
Styling by Charlotte O'Connell
Printed and bound by Printer Trento, Italy
This book is typeset in Clarendon URW and Mundial in 9pt.

The paper used in this book comes from the wood pulp of sustainably managed forests.

A CIP catalogue record for this book is available from the British Library.

5 4 3 2 1

To the friends, family and community who have helped us on our journey. Thanks for your kindness and support.

Contents

Introduction 1
Breakfasts 10
The evolution of our food philosophy 42
Soups 50
20 things we've learned after 20 years 68
Salads 74
The farm and what it means 88
Sandwiches and burgers 96
Quick midweek dinners 112
What we've learned about failure 130
Dinners our kids actually eat 138
20 ways to eat more veg (and to get your kids to eat more veg!) 166
Steve's meals to impress 174
What we have learned from our community 190
Desserts and cakes 198
5-ingredient cakes 220
20 ways to pick yourself up when feeling down 234
Breads 240
20 learnings from our podcast 256
Dips and savoury delights 262
Snacks 280
20 foods we couldn't live without 288
Fermentation 294
20 dreams we have 316
Our number ones 322
(More than) 20 people who have made The Happy Pear what it is 336
Index 340

The Happy Pear
The Happy Pear™

Introduction

In one sense it's hard to imagine it's been 20 years since, as 24-year-olds, we opened the doors of our little veg shop, which we called The Happy Pear – but then we look in the mirror and two grey-haired, lined-faced 44-year-old men look back! We started The Happy Pear in 2004 with the dream of creating a happier, healthier world and building community. Today, this dream is as relevant as it was on that first November day.

Now The Happy Pear consists of the same veg shop, a café, a supper club, a coffee roastery, two organic farms, a production facility, an app that has had more than 100,000 people through its courses, six bestselling cookbooks that have sold nearly 500,000 copies and 80 food products that have sold 20 million units. Each of these parts of the business performs the same function, albeit in different ways: to help people EAT MORE VEG!

We never trained as chefs. When we started the café all those years ago we were both plant based, so we weren't drawn to formal chef training, as much of it would have been about butchery, fishmongery and dairy, which we naturally had no interest in. Instead, once we started our plant-based café in the small town of Greystones, we hired Dorene Palmer, who had been teaching vegetarian cooking for over two decades. She was our 'chef mother' who worked with us for nearly a decade, and we learned a huge amount from her. We cooked in our café kitchen in Greystones for most of the first 10 years and developed our craft. In the most recent ten years, social media and the opportunity to write cookbooks emerged. In 2015, we got an invitation from Jamie Oliver to join his YouTube family, FoodTube, and this led to us producing over 700 recipe videos on YouTube and gaining nearly 50 million views. This really helped us to hone our recipe-creating skills, as we were constantly generating new dishes that pushed limits and explored frontiers. This book you are holding is our greatest hits, in a sense – it has our best recipes from the thousands we have created over the last two decades, as well as stories of the adventure thus far! Each of these recipes has been trialled by thousands of people and stood the test of time.

From potatoes to pomegranates

Potatoes, 10kg bags of them, were the most popular item when we first opened the doors of our veg shop in 2004. We sold literal tonnes of them every week and usually had a pallet out the front piled high with them. We sold lots of different varieties, such as Maris Pipers, Kerr's Pinks, Golden Wonders, Queens and many others. Some people only bought them dirty, and others liked them washed. Our customers really knew their potatoes, and they schooled us on what was the best chipping potato, the best to boil or mash and the best for roast potatoes. The first new potatoes of the year, which would usually be ready for Easter, would sell for mad money and be auctioned off in the fruit and veg market in Smithfield in Dublin. Cabbages and turnips were also very popular, and we remember many a customer in search of a York cabbage with a 'good heart'! We'd have to throw out aubergines and peppers most weeks, as not many people bought them or knew what to do with them, and we never stocked mangoes or pomegranates, as they just didn't sell.

Today we don't even sell 10kg bags of potatoes or York cabbages. We do still sell potatoes, but the demand for 10kg just isn't there – most

customers are just looking for a few washed potatoes and rarely ask about the variety. The top items we now sell in our veg shop are avocados and lemons! We sell a lot of berries and plenty of produce from our own organic farm too.
For the first decade, every morning at 4.30 we would go to the market in Smithfield to pick our produce for the day. From early in the morning it was alive with energy, and there was a real buzz with forklifts flying around the place and trucks and lorries competing for the best parking spots to load their stock into. Sadly, the Dublin fruit market in Smithfield closed its doors in 2019, likely due to supermarkets getting bigger and so few independent greengrocers being left. It was a special place, which we remember fondly.

Writing our first cheque!

A 20-year adventure

We started The Happy Pear to create positive social change. It has always been about inspiring and enabling people to EAT MORE VEG and live a fun, positive life. At its inception, Steve was adamant that The Happy Pear would be a charity, to be super-explicit that we had higher intentions than personal wealth creation. It has been a constant challenge to balance the social mission with the commercial aspect of being financially responsible.

A key milestone was in 2023 when, as a community business, we decided to see if our community wanted to become owners in The Happy Pear. We loved the idea of a community crowdfunding campaign, where a business literally sells off a piece of itself to raise money for growth and get its own followers and supporters to become owners – and hopefully new advocates and emissaries for the business. In June of 2023, we did an equity crowdfund, where we sold off 18 per cent of The Happy Pear to the public, our community, to raise €2.5 million to expand into the UK (not for ourselves!). It was the first time we had put ourselves out there like that, selling a piece of what we had put our hearts and souls into creating. We were incredibly nervous. It felt a bit like organising a party and not knowing if anyone would show up! Within the first 24 hours, more than €2.5 million had been pledged as an investment, and within the first week over €4.5 million was pledged, which was overwhelmingly reassuring. We only took €2.5 million in the end, and at the time of writing we are in the process of launching our food products in the UK with the funds raised.

When our hair was plentiful ...

We like to think of the last 20 years in business as the epitome of an adventure. There have been huge highs, and many dreams of ours have come true – like opening multiple cafés, having bestselling books and food products, starting a farm and having millions of followers on social media. And, just like any adventure, there have been just as many lows and challenges – like nearly going out of business many times, having large losses in terms of trading for a number of years, having to close down three cafés permanently and having to lay off tens of our team multiple times as we went through difficult periods. We have found the game of business to be incredibly fulfilling. It has required everything we have to really bring it to life, and what more could you ask for from any adventure?

Within each meal is an opportunity

Food is one of the great joys of life. We all need to eat for nourishment, but for most of you reading this book, food is more than nourishment: it is one of life's true pleasures. Over the last two decades, plant-based food has become more mainstream and less in the wings and on the fringes of society. Usually in an introduction to one of our books we would be espousing the benefits of a plant-based diet and affirming that it is not lacking in any way. However, you likely know this already.

We have dedicated the last 20 years and our careers to making healthy plant-based food tasty and attractive. Our goal is to ensure a bright future for our children and the next generations, with a wonderful planet to live on. It may not be obvious, but your food choices carry significant personal responsibility and opportunity. By opting for local and organic plant-based foods, you actively support the environment. We've never been into politics, but we believe that 'politics begins on your plate' through your food choices. These choices have a tremendous impact on your personal health and well-being. But they are also among the most impactful actions you can take to combat climate change.

This book holds our learnings of more than two decades of cooking and eating a wholefood plant-based diet. The recipes have been tried by people from all over the world. They work. Changing your diet can be hard – food is entwined with every aspect of life. We have foods that we eat when we are stressed or overwhelmed, comfort foods, celebration foods and family-favourite foods. However, within each meal you choose to eat lies a massive opportunity, not just for your own health but also for a sense of meaning and purpose.

As we reflect on the past 20 years and the incredible journey we've embarked on, we are filled with a deep sense of gratitude and awe. The Happy Pear started as a simple dream to create a happier, healthier world, and it has grown into a movement fuelled by the support and enthusiasm of our incredible community. Each recipe in this book represents more than just a delicious meal: it carries the potential for personal transformation, for positive change at so many levels and for a brighter future. Every meal we choose is an opportunity for change. By embracing the nourishing power of plant-based food, we can create a better world for ourselves, our loved ones and the planet we call home. Together, let's savour the joy of healthy eating and make a positive impact that will ripple through for the generations to come.

Cooking notes

Sometimes we specify the kind of oil you should use, but when we don't, you can just use whatever type you have. If you're using spray oil, a tablespoon is about five sprays. And remember that all fruit and veg should be washed if you aren't peeling them.

We had Happy Pear 'army jumpers' for our veg revolution!

MONDAY
SUNDAY
SUNDAY

LEARN AND SHARE
A SIMPLE dream to create a HAPPIER, HEALTHIER world

SMALL
CHANGES,
BIG
RESULTS
COMMUNITY
family
Nettle
kimchi

BREAK

FASTS

MEXICAN BREAKFAST BOWL

Serves 4

Tortilla chips

4 wholewheat or corn tortillas

Refried beans

1 × 400g tin of red kidney beans
1 tsp ground cumin
1 tbsp tamari or soy sauce
100ml water

Quick-fire guacamole

5 cherry tomatoes or 1 tomato
2 ripe avocados
juice of 1 lime
½ tsp chilli powder or cayenne powder

Tofu scramble

200g firm tofu
1½ tsp tamari or soy sauce
¼ tsp onion or garlic powder
¼ tsp ground turmeric
50ml non-dairy milk of choice
1 tsp black sulphur salt or salt of choice
1 tbsp peanut rayu

Garlic spinach

1 clove of garlic
1 tsp oil
100g baby spinach
2 tbsp water

6 vegan sausages

salt and ground black pepper

Growing up in Ireland, the most indulgent and comforting of breakfasts was an Irish fry – not the most healthy but a real treat! This is a healthier, Mexican-inspired version of a fried breakfast, low in added fat, for a morning when you have a little more time. The colours of this dish really pop, so it's a pretty breakfast too, particularly if you have guests over!

Preheat: Preheat the oven to 200°C fan/425°F/gas 7.

Cook the vegan sausages: Cook the sausages as per the instructions on the packet, and keep warm while you prepare the rest of the dish.

Make the tortilla chips: Stack the 4 tortillas and cut them into quarters, then cut each quarter in half, giving you lovely triangles. On two baking trays, spread out the tortilla triangles, sprinkle with a pinch of salt and bake for 7 minutes. Turn them over and bake for another 7 minutes. Once they're nice and golden and going crispy, remove and cool on wire racks, where they can release their steam, otherwise they will get soggy.

Make the refried beans: Drain and rinse the beans. Put a pan on a high heat and add the beans with a good pinch of salt. Leave to heat up for 1 minute. Start to mash them using the back of a wooden spoon or a potato masher then add the ground cumin and ½ teaspoon of ground black pepper. Slowly add the tamari or soy sauce and water to make it nice and paste-like. If it seems sloppy, stir and cook for a minute or two to evaporate the excess water and until it reaches your desired texture. Taste and adjust the seasoning to your liking.

Make the quick-fire guacamole: Chop the cherry tomatoes or tomato into small pieces. Cut the avocados in half, remove the stones and, using a spoon, scoop the flesh from the skin. Chop into small pieces. In a bowl, add the avocado, lime juice, chilli powder, ½ teaspoon salt and a pinch of ground black pepper. If you prefer smooth guacamole, mash everything well with a fork or use a blender. If you like more texture, simply stir together. →

Make the tofu scramble: Drain the tofu to remove any liquid, then put in a bowl and mash well. Mix together the tamari or soy sauce, onion or garlic powder and ground turmeric in a small bowl, then add to the crumbled tofu, stirring just until the tofu is evenly coated. Heat a frying pan on a high heat. Once the pan is hot, turn the heat down to medium and add the tofu mixture. Cook gently and slowly for 3 to 4 minutes, stirring with a spatula, until it has slightly browned and firmed up. Add the milk and cook for 1 to 2 minutes to incorporate it. Season with black sulphur salt or the salt of your choice. The sulphur salt adds an eggy taste that tends to diminish when cooked, so add just before serving to maintain the flavour. Finish with a tablespoon of peanut rayu.

Cook the garlic spinach: Peel and finely chop the clove of garlic. Put a pan on a high heat, and once it's hot, reduce to medium. Add 1 teaspoon of oil as well as the garlic, cook and stir for 1 minute. Add the spinach along with 2 tablespoons of water and a pinch of salt. Put the lid on and leave to sweat for 2 minutes. Remove the lid and allow the water to evaporate. Turn the heat off.

To serve, divide everything between four plates, making it as pretty as you can!

dry
TM

GRANOLA 3 WAYS

Makes approx. 1 kg

	Chocolate nut crunch	**Crispy coconut granola**	**Maple and vanilla granola**
OATS 50%	500g regular oats	500g regular oats	500g jumbo oats
SEEDS 10%	50g sesame seeds 50g sunflower seeds	50g sesame seeds 50g ground flaxseeds	50g pumpkin seeds 50g sunflower seeds
NUTS 10%	50g flaked almonds 50g cashew nuts	50g desiccated coconut 50g ground almonds	50g almonds 50g walnuts
SWEETENER 10%	130g maple syrup	100g agave syrup	100g maple syrup
FAT 10%	120g coconut oil	100g coconut oil	100g sunflower oil
DRIED FRUIT 10%	50g raisins 50g dried apricots	50g raisins 40g dried figs 10g freeze-dried raspberries	50g goji berries 30g currants 20g dried mango
FLAVOUR ENHANCER	25g cocoa powder 1 tsp almond extract pinch of salt	pinch of salt	1 tsp vanilla extract pinch of salt

We make tons of granola – literally! We sell three different types all around Ireland and the UK. You can make your own granola at home using the following basic framework: 50% oats, 10% nuts, 10% seeds, 10% liquid sweetener, 10% fat and 10% dried fruit. The three recipes here are based on that formula, but the chocolate nut crunch granola is a bit different because cocoa powder is a little bitter, so we increased the sweetness and fat to balance it out.

Preheat: Preheat the oven to 160°C fan/350°F/gas 4.

Mix the dry ingredients: Place the oats, seeds, nuts and a tiny pinch of salt in a large bowl and mix. Leave the dried fruit and any other extras aside (including the cocoa powder for the chocolate nut crunch), as they will be added at the very end once the granola is cool.

Mix the wet ingredients: In a separate bowl or jug, mix the liquid sweetener, oil and extra flavours (such as vanilla or almond extract) together. (If you are using coconut oil, melt it first by heating it in a pan.)

Combine wet and dry ingredients: Add the wet ingredients into the dry-ingredients bowl and mix thoroughly so that everything is evenly coated.

Bake: Divide the granola mix between two large baking trays lined with parchment, and spread out in a thin, even layer. If it is not spread evenly, it will steam as well as bake and result in some soft and some crunchy bits in your granola. Put the trays in the oven and bake for 25–30 minutes, or until golden brown, making sure to mix once or twice during baking to ensure it's evenly cooked. (You can leave it in a little longer if you want it really crunchy, but keep an eye on it and make sure you take it out before it starts to burn.) While your granola is baking, place your dried fruit and extras in a large mixing bowl. Chop the dried apricots, figs and mango into smaller bite-sized pieces if using.

Leave to cool and assemble: Once the granola is baked, leave it to cool for at least 20 minutes. Then add it to the mixing bowl with the dried fruit and extras. Granola is great with your non-dairy milk or yoghurt of choice, with some fresh fruit, on porridge, or just as a healthy snack. Store in an airtight container – it will last for 3–4 weeks.

TIP: If you like your granola chunkier, then prepare it just as in the recipes above. But before baking, when you've put it in the trays, using your hands, or the back of a clean cup, press down the granola into a flat, tight layer – this will make the oats, sweetener and fat stick together, a little like baking a flapjack. Once baked, the layer of granola can be broken up into smaller clusters.

Regular oat flakes cluster much better than jumbo oat flakes, and thicker sweeteners, such molasses, dark date syrup or really dark coconut blossom syrups, tend to be more sticky, so using one of those will also help the clustering effect.

OVERNIGHT OATS 3 WAYS

Overnight oats are easy to make, delicious and a nutritious solution for busy mornings. You can make them in 15 to 20 minutes or prepare them the night before and by morning you'll have a tasty, creamy breakfast waiting for you! Here are three of our favourite varieties.

SALTED CARAMEL OVERNIGHT OATS

Serves 4

Salted caramel
300g pitted dates
4 tbsp almond butter
1 tsp vanilla extract
140ml water, to blend
pinch of salt

Overnight oat mix
250g oat flakes
40g raisins
20g chia seeds
600ml oat milk
pinch ground cinnamon

Caramelised pecans
30g pecan nuts
2 tbsp maple syrup

To serve
350g coconut yoghurt or yoghurt of choice

A decadent, delicious creamy breakfast that will leave you salivating for more!

Soak the dates: Put the dates in a bowl, cover them with boiling water and leave to soak for 5 minutes.

Prepare the oats: Add all the ingredients for the overnight oat mix to a bowl, mix well and leave to soak for about ten minutes, or as long as it takes to make the other components, or overnight in the fridge.

Caramelise the pecans: Place a pan on medium heat. Once hot, add the pecans and cook for about 4 minutes until they start to turn golden, stirring regularly to avoid burning. Remove the pan from the heat then add the maple syrup, stirring quickly to ensure you coat each nut. Continue to stir for a minute or so, until the maple syrup has started to harden.

Make the salted caramel: Drain the dates and add to a food processor with the almond butter, vanilla extract, 140ml of water and a pinch of salt. Blend until it reaches a smooth caramel-like texture (you may have to add a little more water if the dates you've used are very hard). This will take approximately 3 minutes.

Serve: We like to serve this in four drinking glasses (about 400ml each) to see the layers really clearly. Divide half of the caramel between the four glasses and smooth it out. Give the overnight oats a good mix and then divide it between the four glasses. Add another layer of caramel by dividing the remaining caramel between the glasses and smooth it out. Add a generous dollop of yoghurt to each glass, then top with some caramelised pecans and enjoy!

TIRAMISU OVERNIGHT OATS

Serves 2

Overnight oat mix

100g oat flakes
250ml oat milk
3 tbsp chia seeds
2 tbsp maple syrup
½ tsp vanilla extract
pinch of salt

Coffee chocolate caramel

100g dates, soaked for 5 minutes
50g almond butter or peanut butter
2 tbsp cacao powder
150ml cold black coffee

To serve

100g coconut yoghurt
cacao powder, for dusting

These oats are an incredibly tasty start to the day or a perfect pick-me-up at any time. The coffee chocolate caramel layer is a great way to eat your coffee rather than just drinking it!

Prepare the oats: Place all the ingredients for the overnight oat mix in a bowl, mix well and leave to sit for 15 minutes or overnight in the fridge.

Make the caramel: Add all ingredients for the coffee chocolate caramel to a food processor or high-speed blender and blend till super smooth – this will take about 5 minutes, depending on your machine.

Serve: You're going to be making six layers here, so take two 250ml glasses and start with a quarter of the overnight oats in each glass, followed by a quarter of the caramel, then a quarter of the coconut yoghurt. Repeat, dividing the rest of the remaining overnight oats, caramel and coconut yoghurt between each glass, then sieve some cacao powder on top!

BROWNIE OVERNIGHT OATS

Serves 2

Overnight oat mix

50g oat flakes
1½ tbsp cocoa powder
1 tbsp almond butter or nut butter of choice
100ml oat milk
1 tsp vanilla extract
2 tbsp maple syrup
pinch of salt

To serve

200g coconut yoghurt or yoghurt of choice
2 tbsp chocolate chips or cocoa nibs

This tastes really indulgent but it's actually pretty healthy. Steve's kids adore it and thought it was a dessert!

Prepare the oats: Place all the ingredients for the overnight oat mix in a bowl and mix well with a fork. Leave to sit for 20 minutes or overnight in the fridge.

Serve: Divide the oat mix between two tall glasses, leaving about half free for the yoghurt. Divide the yoghurt between the two glasses, smooth out, and top with the chocolate chips or cocoa nibs.

HEALTHY CHIA PUDDING 3 WAYS

Chia seeds are packed with omega-3s, fibre and protein. They also absorb up to 10 times their weight of liquid so are a great way of keeping you hydrated. The texture puts some people off, so adding enough milk to reach your desired consistency is key.

CHIA PUDDING WITH FRUIT

Serves 2

Base chia pudding

90g chia seeds
2 tbsp ground flaxseeds
1 tbsp cacao nibs (optional)
300ml oat milk or milk of choice, plus a little extra

Fruit topping

Use whatever fruit you have and like (we try to have 1 to 2 pieces of fruit or a punnet of berries with this recipe, for example: apple, pear, raspberries, blueberries, banana, kiwi)

Optional toppings

nut butter of choice
coconut yoghurt
nuts
seeds
chocolate chips

You can make a triple batch of the base pudding recipe here and leave it in the fridge, but you will need to add a little milk each morning to get the consistency right.

Make the base pudding: Place all the base chia recipe ingredients in a bowl and give it a good mix with a fork.

Prepare the fruit: While the pudding is thickening, get your fruit ready – for example, peel and slice banana or kiwi, finely chop apple or pear.

Serve: Give the another stir with a fork, add a little oat milk (about 50ml) and mix well to loosen it. You don't want it too thick and stodgy – it should be light and wet, but not like soup! Divide between two bowls, then add the fruit on top and any other additional toppings.

STRAWBERRIES AND CREAM CHIA PUDDING

Serves 2–3

60g chia seeds
1 tbsp beetroot powder
2 tbsp ground flaxseeds
1 tbsp maple syrup
300ml oat milk or milk of choice
200ml coconut yoghurt or yoghurt of choice (preferably white for a cream-like look), plus a little extra
1 punnet of strawberries

Beetroot powder gives this pudding its vibrant pink colour. It's reasonably inexpensive, compared to other superfoods, and you use very little of it so it lasts ages. But without it, it still looks well classy!

Prepare the pudding: Mix the chia seeds, beetroot powder, ground flaxseeds, maple syrup and oat milk, and leave to sit for 5 minutes.

Prepare the strawberries: Cut the green tops off and quarter the strawberries.

Serve: After 5 minutes, give the pudding another stir with a fork, add a little oat milk or milk of your choice (about 50ml) and mix well to loosen it. You don't want it too thick and stodgy – it should be light and wet, but not like soup! Add half the yoghurt and fold it through the chia pudding. Stir through half the strawberries, then add the rest on top with the remaining yoghurt.

DATE AND VANILLA VELVET CHIA PUDDING

Serves 2–3

60g chia seeds
250ml coconut yoghurt
200ml oat milk
1 tbsp cacao nibs (optional)
1 tsp vanilla extract
30g chopped, pitted medjool dates

Serving suggestion
fresh fruit of choice, granola or frozen berries

This is a really creamy, indulgent chia pudding – the dates give it an almost toffee-like note.

Prepare the pudding: Mix all the ingredients and leave it to sit for 10 minutes. Give the pudding another stir with a fork, add a dash of oat milk (about 50ml) and mix well to loosen it. You don't want it too thick and stodgy – it should be creamy, light and wet, but not like soup!

Serve: Divide between 2 to 3 bowls. Top with some fresh fruit of your choice – fresh or frozen berries go great with this.

CHIA PUDDING WITH FRUIT

STRAWBERRIES AND CREAM

DATE AND VANILLA

PANCAKES 3 WAYS

We've been making plant-based pancakes for our kids for decades. They've reached the stage where they can make them for themselves now! Dave even designed his kitchen with a hob on an island so he can make pancakes for his kids while watching them rather than having his back to them.

RASPBERRY RIPPLE PANCAKES

Serves 2 (makes 6–8 small pancakes)

120g self-raising flour
210ml oat milk or milk of choice
2 tbsp peanut or almond butter
2 tbsp maple syrup
small pinch of salt
½ tsp vanilla extract
250g raspberries, fresh or frozen
a little oil for the pan

To serve
maple syrup
a handful of fresh raspberries
peanut butter

These fluffy crepe-style pancakes are a twist on the classic peanut-butter-and-jelly flavour. Served with more peanut butter and some maple syrup, they make an amazing treat!

Make the batter: Whisk all the ingredients (except the raspberries and oil) together well in a bowl, or use a blender to get it super smooth.

Cook the pancakes: Heat a pan on high heat, and once hot, reduce to medium. Coat the bottom with a little oil. Pour on a light coating of batter, add 5–6 raspberries on top and lightly press into the batter. Cook the pancake on one side, and once bubbles start to appear and the edges start to dry out, flip and cook on the other side. Once cooked, remove to a warm plate, and repeat with the rest of the batter to make a big, beautiful stack.

Serve: Drizzle with some maple syrup, peanut butter and fresh raspberries and enjoy!

TIP: To make pancakes healthier, use half brown and half white flour. The more brown (wholemeal) flour you use, the more milk you will need to add.

HIGH-PROTEIN PANCAKES
RASPBERRY RIPPLE PANCAKES
CHOCOLATE ORANGE PANCAKES

HIGH-PROTEIN PANCAKES

Serves 2 (makes 4 pancakes)

120g gram flour
1½ tsp baking powder
210ml oat milk or milk of choice
2 tbsp maple syrup
small pinch of salt
½ tsp vanilla extract
a little oil for the pan

We have never been fans of protein powders. Here we use gram flour, a type of chickpea flour that is naturally high in protein. Gram flour is great for pancakes too, as it has a natural eggy consistency and a yellow hue. You can find it in most health food stores or buy it online.

Make the batter: Sieve the flour and baking powder together into a bowl, as the gram flour can be clumpy. Add the remaining ingredients (apart from the oil) and whisk until it forms a smooth batter, or put in a blender and blend till super smooth.

Cook the pancakes: Heat a pan on high heat. Once hot, reduce to medium. Coat the bottom with a little oil, then pour in a light coating of batter and spread evenly. Cook the pancake on one side, and once bubbles (air pockets) start to appear and the edges begin to dry out, flip the pancake using a silicone spatula and cook the other side. Once cooked, remove to a warm plate, and repeat with the rest of the batter to make a big, beautiful stack.

Serve: Add whatever you fancy – we like peanut butter, berries, coconut yoghurt (or yoghurt of choice) and maple syrup!

CHOCOLATE ORANGE PANCAKES

Serves 3–4 (makes 6–8 pancakes)

120g wholemeal or brown flour (use buckwheat for GF option)
270ml non-dairy milk
1 tbsp ground flaxseeds
2 tbsp cacao powder
¼ tsp salt
1 tsp vanilla extract
3 tbsp maple syrup
1 tsp baking powder
zest of 1 orange
a little oil for the pan

To serve
50g chocolate of choice
2 oranges

These easy pancakes are sweet and crispy, topped with some chocolate, orange zest and a squeeze of juice. We use wholemeal flour to make them a little healthier but they're still a total treat!

Make the batter: In a blender, add all the ingredients for the batter (apart from the oil) and blend till smooth. If you don't have a blender, mix all the ingredients well in a bowl, and leave to sit for 3–4 minutes for the flax to thicken the batter.

Cook the pancakes: Heat a pan on a high heat. Once hot, reduce to medium. Coat the bottom with a little oil. Pour in a light coating of batter and spread evenly. Cook on one side until bubbles start to form and the edges start to dry out. Turn the pancake (a silicone spatula works best) and add a few small pieces of chocolate and a squeeze of juice from the orange and cook until the chocolate has melted and the bottom is golden. Remove to a warm plate and repeat with the rest of your batter.

Serve: Use a spoon to spread the melted chocolate, sprinkle with some more orange zest, then serve.

A LOVE LETTER TO PORRIDGE

We have given away free plain porridge in our café for nearly 20 years now – probably enough to cover Greystones in a thick layer of it!

Our pimped-up fancy porridge is one of the most popular items on our breakfast menu in our café. We serve it with berry compote, fresh fruit, granola, almond butter and coconut yoghurt. It has just the right balance of crunch (granola), sweetness (fruit), creaminess (yoghurt), richness (almond butter) and a touch of sharpness (berry compote). It goes down very easily, particularly after a morning dip in the cold Irish Sea!

QUICK AND EASY PORRIDGE

Serves 1

1 mug (100g) of porridge oats
1 mug (250ml) of water
1 mug (250ml) of non-dairy milk of choice

Use jumbo oats for a more textured porridge and standard quick-cook oats for a more homogenous or smooth porridge.

Cook the porridge: Add all ingredients to a saucepan and put on a high heat. Bring to the boil, stirring occasionally. Once boiling, it's good to go! Add more milk if you prefer a looser porridge, or leave to boil and reduce while stirring if you prefer a thicker porridge.

Serve: If desired, add a little nut butter, maple syrup to sweeten and some fruit compote or caramelised banana (see page 35).

TRANSFORMING THE HUMBLE PORRIDGE …

The toppings are really where porridge is won or lost. By itself it can be a bit stodgy and bland.

- **Granola** (see page 15) will add crunch, which is key to a satisfying porridge.
- **Fresh fruit** helps lighten the heavy gruel-like consistency of porridge. Use whatever fruit you like, have and can afford. We have a fruit shop so are generally able to use local seasonal fruits.
- **Yoghurt can be divisive.** Dave's kids and wife don't like any plant-based yoghurt through their porridge, yet Dave loves some coconut yoghurt in it. It adds lightness as well as a slight acidic note to it. Steve loves berry or cherry soya yoghurt.
- **Berry compote** is a real treat, and it adds a crimson antioxidant-rich colour, which is such a strong contrast to the white of the porridge.
- **Caramelised banana** really elevates your porridge – particularly if you're having family or friends around for breakfast!
- **Sweeteners:** maple syrup is our go-to sweetener when it comes to porridge. However, we do minimise it and tend to use fruit, berry compote and caramelised banana to bring most of the sweetness.

FRUIT COMPOTE

Makes 600g

600g frozen berries (strawberries, raspberries or blueberries)
4 tbsp of water
1 tsp cinnamon (optional)
2 tbsp maple syrup

We love fruit compote – it adds colour, sweetness and a touch of sharpness too! This recipe makes enough for a few days and will last for at least a week in your fridge.

Put the frozen berries and water in a medium pot over a high heat. Bring to the boil, then reduce the heat to a simmer. Add the cinnamon and maple syrup, then simmer for 15–20 minutes, or longer if you have time – the longer you cook it, the thicker and sweeter your compote will become (it will also thicken as it cools).

CARAMELISED BANANA

Serves 1

1 ripe banana

This is a really simple way to immediately elevate your porridge!

Peel and slice the banana in half lengthwise. Place a pan on a high heat. Once hot, reduce to medium and add the slices of banana to the pan face down. Leave to cook for a minute or two, until they start to brown and caramelise. Turn (using a silicone spatula is easiest) and repeat on the other side. Best served hot!

CINNAMON SWIRLS IN 30 MINUTES

Makes 8

Dough
200g self-raising flour
35g icing sugar
¼ tsp salt
80g cold vegan butter, cut into cubes, plus extra for the tin
100ml oat milk

Cinnamon filling
2 tbsp vegan butter
90g brown sugar
1 tsp ground cinnamon

Cream cheese icing
4 tbsp vegan cream cheese
65g icing sugar
¼ tsp vanilla extract
1 tsp oat milk

We make hundreds of cinnamon swirls every weekend in our bakery. They are our most popular treat by a distance! This version is so practical and quick to make. We have simplified the process so they don't require any proofing, as they have no yeast. You can bake these in the oven or even in an air fryer.

Preheat the oven and grease the tin: Preheat the oven to 180°C fan/400°F/gas 6, or the air fryer on bake function to 160°C. Grease and line a 2lb (900g) loaf tin.

Prepare the dough: Add the self-raising flour, icing sugar and ¼ teaspoon of salt to a mixing bowl, and stir together. Add the butter, and use your fingers to rub the butter into the flour mixture until it looks like damp sand or breadcrumbs. Stir in the milk. Using your hands or a wooden spoon. bring the dough together into a rough ball. Coat the dough in a little flour so it is easy to handle.

Dust your counter with flour, place the dough on it and knead for 2–3 minutes. Using a rolling pin, roll out into a rectangle roughly 45cm × 30cm.

Prepare the filling: Melt the butter. In a separate bowl, mix the cinnamon and sugar together. Using a pastry brush, spread the melted butter over the dough, bringing it right to the edges. Then sprinkle over the cinnamon sugar as evenly as you can.

Roll and cut the dough: Starting at the long end of the rectangle, roll the dough up tightly into a log. Cut the log in half, then halve both pieces, and then halve each remaining piece – you should have 8 evenly sized swirls. Place them in the loaf tin face up, so you can see the cinnamon layers.

Bake: Place the loaf tin into the preheated oven and bake for 25 minutes, or bake in the air fryer for 18–20 minutes.

Make the icing: While the rolls are in the oven, place the cream cheese in a bowl, then add the icing sugar, vanilla and milk. Use a fork to break it down and stir until smooth and super creamy.

Ice and serve: When the rolls are ready, remove them from the oven or air fryer and drizzle the glaze over the top. They'll keep for 2–3 days in an airtight container.

RASPBERRY BAKEWELL BREAKFAST MUFFINS

Makes 12

2 tbsp ground flaxseeds
6 tbsp water
180g oats (use gluten-free for GF version)
50g flour (use gluten-free for GF version)
160g ground almonds
1 tsp baking powder (use gluten-free for GF version)
1 tsp baking soda
150g coconut oil
150g maple syrup or date molasses
1 tsp vanilla extract
1 tsp almond extract
125g punnet of fresh raspberries
20g flaked almonds

These were a very popular breakfast muffin or snack on our first gut-health course. They can be easily made gluten-free and are very easy to eat! We've adjusted them slightly to make them more of a summer Bakewell-flapjack-muffin.

Preheat: Preheat the oven to 180°C fan/400°F/gas 6.

Make the flax egg: Mix the flaxseeds with the water in a small bowl, and leave to sit while you prepare the other ingredients

Mix the dry ingredients: In a large bowl, mix the oats, flour, ground almonds, baking powder and baking soda.

Add the wet ingredients: Melt the coconut oil by heating it in a small pot. Add it to the dry ingredients along with the maple syrup or date molasses, vanilla and almond extract and the flax egg and mix thoroughly. Stir through ¾ of the raspberries and ¾ of the flaked almonds.

Divide and decorate: Line a 12-hole muffin tray with paper cases and divide the muffin mixture evenly between them. Decorate the tops of the muffins with the remaining flaked almonds and raspberries.

Bake and serve: Bake in the preheated oven for 25 minutes, then remove and leave to cool.

TOASTIES 3 WAYS

It's been tough to pin down our three favourite toasties over the last 20 years – particularly when one of our specialities is dips, which are the foundation of a good toastie!

SMASHED AVOCADO, TOMATO AND OLIVE

Makes 2

2 slices of bread, ideally sourdough
1 avocado
1 ripe tomato
handful of good olives, like Kalamata
½ lime
salt and ground black pepper

Our all-time favourite, a classic that we have been serving in the café and eating in our own homes for two decades, this toastie has it all!

Toast the bread. Cut the avocado in half and remove the stone. Use a spoon to scoop out the flesh, and then slice. Slice the tomato and remove the pits from the olives. Using a fork, mash the avocado onto the slices of bread. Sprinkle with a generous pinch of salt, and squeeze over the juice of ½ lime. Add 2–3 slices of tomato to each toastie in an even layer. Sprinkle some olives on top, followed by a small pinch of salt and some black pepper.

BUTTERY HUMMUS WITH A POP

Makes 2

2 slices of bread, ideally sourdough
60g buttery hummus (see page 264)
30g pink sauerkraut (see page 296)
1 tsp lacto-fermented chilli sauce (see page 303) or your fave store-bought chilli sauce

Bright, colourful and banging with flavour – the hummus is oh-so creamy, and with the vibrant sauerkraut and the chilli sauce this toastie is a fermenter's dream. A treat for your taste buds as well as your gut!

Toast the bread, and spread a generous layer of buttery hummus on each slice. Spoon over the sauerkraut, followed by a drizzle of the chilli sauce.

DOWNTOWN FLAVOUR BOMB!

Makes 2

This toastie lives up to its name. There's nothing subtle about it – it's creamy, spicy, savoury, sweet and even has that umami note too.

2 slices of bread, ideally sourdough
50g pesto
30g kimchi (see page 300)
4 gherkins or about 35g pickled cucumber
2 tbsp peanut rayu (see page 273)

Toast the bread, and spread a generous layer of pesto on each slice. Add a layer of kimchi on top. Thinly slice the gherkins and add a layer on top of the kimchi. Finish with a generous drizzle of the peanut rayu.

The EVOLUTION of our FOOD PHILOSOPHY

Plant-based living and the pursuit of perfection

Back in 2002, when we were just a couple of 22-year-old meat-loving, beer-swilling jocks, we shocked ourselves and everyone around us by going vegan. We were the last people anyone expected to ditch carnivorous ways and embrace a plant-exclusive diet. It was a total plot twist!

When we shifted to a plant-based diet, we turned into full-blown evangelists. Passion and enthusiasm were practically oozing out of us. No need to ask if we were vegan – trust us, we'd make sure to tell you! When we started hosting cooking classes and health courses above the veg shop in 2008, we were so righteous and preachy we probably scared people away with our intensity. Our message was anything but subtle: we were on a mission to convert everyone to the plant side of the table.

But we soon discovered that our approach was a total flop – it was much too extreme. We quickly learned that real change takes time and needs to be sustainable, particularly around eating habits. We also came to the realisation that a plant-exclusive diet isn't everyone's cup of tea, and that's absolutely fine. It's not about chasing perfection; it's about making steady progress through small, lasting changes.

During the initial years of our own plant-based journey, we went all-in, striving for dietary perfection. We meticulously followed the advice of every health guru, pushing ourselves to the extreme. Our diets consisted mainly of raw foods, accompanied by copious amounts of green juice and wheatgrass shots. We practically lived on alfalfa and broccoli sprouts, and we wouldn't dream of indulging in a slice of pizza – not even if it was vegan and made from sourdough. Yep, we were those annoying vegans who always turned every meal into a discussion about food and why what was on our plate was better than what was on yours!

However, everything changed when we had kids at the age of 30 in 2010 (we both had kids only two months apart!). Unsurprisingly, our approach to food became more balanced and socially acceptable. While we continued to embrace a wholefood plant-based diet, we let go of the pursuit of perfection. We realised that our food choices were just one aspect of leading a healthy and happy life, and they couldn't continue to take as much focus as they had up until then.

Our food philosophy

Our food philosophy can be summed up in three words: EAT MORE VEG! We strive to make it inclusive and accessible for everyone. When we say 'veg', we really mean 'eat more whole plant foods' – plant-based foods in their natural, unprocessed state, just as you would find them in nature, such as:

- **Fruit** – all kinds
- **Veg** – a wide variety
- **Legumes** – lentils, chickpeas, butter beans and more
- **Whole grains** – oats, brown rice, wholemeal pasta, quinoa, wholemeal couscous, wholegrain flours or breads
- **Nuts and seeds**

Until the 1950s, whole plant foods were the norm, and ultra-processed foods (UPFs) didn't really exist. Whole plant foods are rich in fibre – a crucial nutrient. Fibre not only aids in digestion, but it also nourishes healthy strains of microbes in the gut, where over 70 per cent of our immune-system cells reside.

Surprisingly, over 80 per cent of people in high-income countries like Ireland and

Travelling in America in 2001

the USA are deficient in fibre and fail to meet the recommended daily intake. Fibre is derived from plant cellulose and is primarily found in whole plant foods. There is no fibre in meat, cheese, fish or eggs and virtually none in UPFs. This means that the majority of people aren't consuming enough whole plant foods, which is why we have a lot of work to do in encouraging everyone to EAT MORE VEG!

Our food environment

Although we believe eating more whole plant foods is the healthiest way to eat, adhering to our philosophy is not always straightforward. We are all shaped by the environment we inhabit. If you find yourself struggling with excess weight or feeling unwell, it's important to recognise that it's not solely your fault. We reside in a world where UPFs are pervasive. They're inexpensive to produce, have long shelf lives and are often marketed heavily. They exploit our natural instinct to seek out easily accessible calories. They are engineered to hit the perfect combination of fat, sugar and salt (often referred to as the 'bliss point') that our brains find irresistible. Resisting their allure can be challenging, and making healthy choices in this environment is far from easy. It is precisely these reasons that strengthen our resolve and commitment to support you in the face of this tide of UPFs. Choosing healthier plant-based options requires deliberate effort, strong motivation and the development of new habits. What makes eating more veg sustainable lies in the remarkable feeling of vitality that emerges once you incorporate more whole plant foods into your diet. As you start to experience the benefits, such as increased energy, improved sleep, enhanced mood and greater body confidence, you will naturally be compelled to continue. Feeling good is sustainable! We have witnessed this transformation thousands and thousands of times among the individuals we have supported through our app and courses.

Dave (with abundant hair lost in the taste of tomatoes

Progress over perfection

Progress over perfection is a key principle when it comes to our food choices. There is no such thing as a perfect diet. However, experts unanimously agree that incorporating more veg (whole plant foods) into our meals is a sensible approach to improve our short-, medium-, and long-term health. Many individuals hesitate to get started or focus on perfection, feeling that a slip-up will derail their efforts. But the key is to simply begin by eating more veg today!

If you are looking for support and a plan, then check out our recipe club and whole health tribe on our app, where we run monthly challenges with medical experts to really hold your hand in eating more veg.

We started one of Ireland's first juice bars

It's not just about being vegan

Our message extends beyond veganism alone. While veganism certainly has benefits for animals and the environment, it does not automatically guarantee a healthier diet compared to a standard Western diet. Merely substituting animal-based products with processed vegan alternatives, such as fake meats, vegan cheese and sugary vegan treats, can still result in a diet high in UPFs (ultra-processed foods), refined carbohydrates and refined fats.

That's why our emphasis lies on a wholefood plant-based diet, which prioritises the consumption of fruits, vegetables, legumes, whole grains, nuts and seeds, ensuring a more wholesome and nutritious approach to food choices.

The potential of plants

We started our little veg shop as the first step of our food revolution. In 2007, we were ready for the second step. We wanted our community and beyond to experience the benefits of the wholefood plant-based diet we were experiencing. Heart disease was and still is the biggest killer in the Western world. In 1992, the Lifestyle Heart Trial, run by Dr Dean Ornish, published its results, showing that in 82 per cent of cases heart disease could be reversed in a year by being put on a wholefood plant-based diet. We decided to put plant-based eating to the test in our local community and see how it would fare at helping reduce the indicators of heart disease in just four weeks.

We designed a four-week course with recipes and meal plans. We found a local nurse called Angela who was up for helping us by measuring participants' cholesterol, weight and blood pressure, the main metrics for heart disease, before and after. It was 2007, before social media had really caught on, so to promote our challenge and find 20 participants, we put up posters on lamp posts in Greystones and took an ad in the local parish

Steve juggling our new range of 'shepherd-less' pies

bulletin! We decided to run it for free, and 20 people signed up. On the first night, Angela took the participants' starting measurements. We taught them how to cook delicious plant-based meals such as red lentil dhal, Mexican chilli, Thai curry and other delights. We gave them a meal plan – porridge or chia puddings for breakfast, hearty veg soups and delicious plant-based meals for dinner and snacks too. We ran a class each of the four weeks where we cooked lots of dishes and everyone tasted them, and we talked through label reading, how to manage snacking, travelling and family life and the basic principles of eating a wholefood plant-based diet. At the end of the four weeks, Angela took everyone's finishing measurements. We were nervous, as we really didn't know if it would work. Amazingly, there was an average drop in cholesterol of 20 per cent, the average weight loss was 3kg and many of the participants' blood pressure had regulated – in just four weeks. It was an astounding success. We were over the moon!

Taking it online

A journalist joined a subsequent course and wrote about their very successful experience in *The Irish Times*. This brought a huge surge in interest, and we were overwhelmed with bookings. We decided to build an online course so we could help people all over the world. At that time, we happened to have a 16-year-old boy on work experience in the shop who was a programming prodigy, and we paid him to custom build us a course platform in 2008! It turned out we were ahead of the curve – at that time people didn't like to put their credit cards on the internet, as they were nervous about security issues, so the course didn't take off. We shelved it for a few years until the market was ready for it.

Now, more than 100,000 people from over 120 countries have been through the courses on our app! We have partnered with leading medical professionals – cardiologists, gastroenterologists, gynaecologists, neurologists, dieticians, skin experts, GPs and more – to create a suite of courses all based around the core principle of adopting a wholefood plant-based diet.

The benefits of a wholefood plant-based diet

Adopting a wholefood plant-based diet offers numerous benefits for your gut health, heart health, skin, weight and mental well-being. Additionally, it tends to be more cost-effective than a standard diet. Many of us eat without much thought, following the habits of our parents and those around us, simply eating what tastes good. However, making the transition to a wholefood plant-based diet, or even moving in that direction, can significantly improve your health.

In addition to the personal health benefits, embracing a plant-based diet also has a significant positive impact on the environment. The production of animal-based foods contributes to deforestation, water pollution, and the emission of greenhouse gases. By shifting towards a plant-based lifestyle, we reduce our carbon footprint, conserve water resources and help protect fragile ecosystems. It's a small change in our eating habits that can collectively make a big difference in preserving our planet for future generations.

At our annual apple-pie festival in 2018

The story of our journey and the success we witnessed in our community highlights the transformative power of a wholefood plant-based diet. It has the potential to improve our health, reverse chronic diseases and promote well-being. By embracing a plant-based lifestyle, you not only prioritise your own health but also contribute to the well-being of animals and the planet. It's a compassionate and sustainable way of eating that allows you to make a positive impact on your environment and combat climate change. So, let's come together, prioritise our health and join the global movement to EAT MORE VEG, knowing that every bite we take has the power to create a better future for ourselves and generations to come.

Steve sporting a top-knot and enjoying a tasty treat

SO

UPS

EASY MISO SOUP

Serves 4

- 1 litre warm water
- 2 cloves of garlic
- thumb-sized piece of fresh ginger
- 3 tbsp tamari or soy sauce
- 2 tsp (about 8g) dried seaweed (kelp, kombu, nori, arame)
- 1 tbsp dried mushrooms (optional)
- 150g fresh veg of choice (e.g. carrot, radish, red pepper, scallions, sugar snap peas, baby spinach, shiitake mushrooms) or firm tofu
- 2 tbsp fresh miso paste of choice (white is lighter and sweeter; dark is stronger)

This is our quick and easy take on a traditional miso soup. If you want to make it more filling, you can boil some wholemeal noodles in the broth, and add the veg and miso after. You can use whatever veg you like – we normally use carrot, red pepper and some scallions.

Blend the base stock: Place 1 litre of warm water, the garlic, ginger and tamari or soy sauce in a blender, and blend until nice and smooth.

Boil: Transfer into a medium-sized pot and put on a high heat. Roughly chop the seaweed (if it's not fine-cut) and add along with the dried mushrooms (if using). Bring to the boil and reduce to a simmer for 5 minutes.

Prep the veg: While the stock is simmering, prepare your veg – for example, grate or julienne carrots, cut pepper into thin strips, chop radishes into rounds, cut the sugar snaps into small pieces – or chop the tofu into small cubes.

Add the veg and miso: Turn the heat off, add your veg and stir the miso paste through with a fork.

Serve: Ladle into small bowls, and enjoy this wonderfully comforting elixir!

CRISPY TOFU THAI NOODLE SOUP

15 MINS PREP | 30 MINS COOK | 45 MINS TOTAL

Serves 2–3

Crispy tofu

200g firm tofu
2 tbsp tamari or soy sauce
1 tbsp cornstarch
1 tsp garlic powder
1½ tbsp oil

Soup

200g rice noodles

Veg

1 red bell pepper
1 carrot
3 scallions or green onions
1 handful of fresh coriander

Yellow curry paste sauce

1 clove of garlic, minced
1-inch piece of ginger, peeled and grated
1 red chilli
1 stalk lemongrass
juice of 1 lime
1 tbsp maple syrup
15g fresh coriander (just the stalks)
1 tsp ground turmeric
2 tbsp tamari
1 × 400ml can coconut milk
400ml veg stock
salt and ground black pepper

Garnishes

red chilli
peanuts or peanut rayu (see page 273)
sliced radishes
fresh lime wedges, for squeezing

Our kids love this! It's a super-tasty soup, straightforward to make and packed full of flavour. It makes a great dinner as well as lunch, and it's also good eaten cold for a meal on the go. Serving it with peanut rayu takes it to the next level!

Prep the tofu: You can bake in the oven or air fryer. If using an oven, preheat to 200°C fan/425°F/gas 7. Cut the tofu into cubes, about 2cm × 2cm. In a bowl, toss the tofu with tamari or soy sauce, cornstarch and garlic powder until evenly coated. Place the tofu cubes in an air fryer basket or baking tray, making sure they are not touching each other for better airflow. Toss the tofu lightly in 1½ tablespoons of oil. Bake in the oven for 20 minutes or air fry at 200°C (390°F) for about 12 minutes. Shake the basket or tray halfway through. The tofu should be golden and crispy. Set aside.

Prep the noodles: Cook the rice noodles according to the package instructions. Drain and rinse under cold water to stop the cooking process, then set aside.

Prep the veg: Finely slice the red pepper and the carrot, slice the green onions into rounds and finely chop the coriander including the stalk. Keep some of the green onions and coriander back to garnish.

Make the soup: Place all the ingredients for the yellow curry paste sauce into a blender and blend until smooth. Add to a pot and bring to a gentle boil, then reduce the heat and simmer for about 10 minutes to allow the flavours to meld together. Season with salt and pepper to taste.

Assemble: Divide the cooked noodles between the serving bowls. Ladle the hot soup over the noodles, making sure to distribute the vegetables equally. Top each bowl with a portion of the crispy air-fried tofu.

Garnish and serve: Garnish with the peanut rayu, reserved sliced green onions and chopped coriander, sliced red chilli and sliced radishes. Serve immediately, encouraging everyone to squeeze some lime juice over their soup to enhance the flavours.

IRISH ROOT VEGETABLE SOUP

Serves 6

1 onion
3 cloves of garlic
2 leeks
2 carrots
1 parsnip (about 250g)
6 tbsp water, for sweating
2 sprigs of thyme
2 bay leaves
4 tbsp white wine (optional but recommended!)
2 litres vegetable stock or water
juice of ½ a lemon
salt and ground black pepper

This cosy, comforting soup is rich in sweet flavours, with hints of white wine, thyme and parsnip. It's a hearty choice that's easy to make in bulk, perfect for freezing or savouring throughout the week. We cook this with no oil to make it lower in calories. Serve it with a slice of homemade sourdough bread (page 246) for the ultimate experience!

Prep the veg: Peel and finely chop the onion and garlic. Clean and finely chop the leeks, carrots and parsnip.

Sauté the veg: Heat a large pot over high heat. Add the prepped vegetables and 2 teaspoons of salt, cooking for 3–4 minutes while stirring.

Sweat the veg: Lower the heat to medium, add 6 tablespoons of water, cover with a lid, and sweat for 10 minutes. Stir occasionally and add more water if needed to prevent sticking.

Add the herbs and wine: Strip the thyme leaves and add them to the pot with the bay leaves and white wine, if using, cooking for 4 minutes while stirring.

Boil then simmer: Pour in the vegetable stock or water and bring to a boil. Once boiling, lower the heat and simmer for 5 minutes.

Blend: Turn off the heat, remove the bay leaves, and blend the soup with a stick blender until smooth, adjusting the thickness with hot water as needed.

Season and serve: Season with ¼ teaspoon of black pepper and additional salt, if you think it needs it, stir in the lemon juice, and serve warm.

LEEK AND POTATO SOUP

Serves 5

1 medium onion
3 cloves of garlic
4 medium potatoes
2 large leeks
1 tbsp oil
2 litres vegetable stock
juice of ½ a lemon (optional)
salt and ground black pepper

To serve

a few slices of sourdough (page 246)
5 tbsp plant-based yoghurt

This classic soup is always a great crowd-pleaser. If you'd like to bump up its nutritional profile, you can add a few handfuls of nettle leaves (wear gloves when picking them!), which is how we used to serve it in the café all the time. Best done in spring, this really increases the mineral content.

Prep the veg: Peel and finely slice the onion and garlic. Chop the potatoes and leeks into small bite-sized pieces, cleaning the leeks carefully first. Make sure to use the full length of the leek, including the green tops, as they taste fab and will give the soup that lovely light-green colour.

Sauté and sweat the veg: Put a large saucepan on a high heat and add 1 tablespoon of oil. Once it heats up, add the onion and leek and cook for 4 minutes, stirring occasionally. Next, add the potato and the garlic along with 2 teaspoons of salt, and cook, stirring regularly, for 5 minutes.

Boil then simmer: Now, add the vegetable stock and ½ teaspoon of black pepper. Bring to the boil, then reduce the heat to a gentle simmer and cook till the potato is nice and soft, about 10 minutes.

Blend and season: Remove the soup from the heat and blend with a stick blender till smooth. Divide between bowls and, if using, give a little squeeze of lemon over each portion. Serve with a slice of sourdough on the side and drizzle some plant-based yoghurt on top for a contrast of colour.

TIP: If you'd like to enrich your traditional leek and potato soup, you can add 100g of cashew nuts when adding the vegetable stock. They'll give it a richer, creamier taste.

CREAM OF BROCCOLI, CELERIAC AND ROASTED HAZELNUT SOUP

Serves 6

500g broccoli
2 onions
3 cloves of garlic
500g celeriac
1 tbsp oil
1½ litres vegetable stock
1 litre oat milk
150g hazelnuts
4 spoonfuls of coconut yoghurt (to garnish)
salt and ground black pepper

This smooth and silky soup, garnished with chunks of toasted hazelnuts, has always been popular in our café. The creaminess comes from an oat-milk base and adds a lovely indulgent quality. This is a great recipe for using up leftover broccoli stalks. You can use all broccoli stalks for this recipe or a mixture of florets and stalks.

Prep the veg: Roughly chop the broccoli. Peel and chop the onions and garlic. Peel and chop the celeriac into small similar-sized pieces.

Cook the base flavours: Put a large pot over a high heat. Add 1 tablespoon of oil and allow to heat up for a minute. Once hot, add the onion and cook for 3–4 minutes, stirring occasionally so that it doesn't stick. Add the garlic and cook for a further minute, stirring regularly.

Cook the veg: Add the celeriac, broccoli and 1 teaspoon of salt and cook for 3 minutes. Reduce the heat to medium, put the lid on and leave the veg to cook for 8–10 minutes, stirring occasionally. If the veg are sticking to the bottom of the pot, add a few tablespoons of the vegetable stock.

Boil and simmer: Add the vegetable stock and oat milk, then turn the heat up high and bring to the boil. Reduce the heat to low-medium and cook for a further couple of minutes.

Toast hazelnuts: While the veg are cooking, put a dry pan on a medium heat and add the hazelnuts. Toast them for about 5–7 minutes, until they start to turn golden and the room begins to smell of roasting hazelnuts. Transfer to a tea-towel, cover them with it and rub to remove as much of the skins as possible, which can be quite bitter. Discard the hazelnut skins. Add three-quarters of the hazelnuts to the soup. Using the bottom of a mug, crush the remaining quarter.

Blend and season: Remove the soup from the heat, add 1 teaspoon of salt and ½ teaspoon black pepper, and blend until smooth using a stick blender. Taste and season with more salt and black pepper if you think it needs it.

Serve: Divide between bowls and garnish with a splash of coconut yoghurt on top and some of the crushed toasted hazelnuts or some chopped herbs of choice and fresh black pepper.

TIP: This recipe also works really well with an equal quantity of parsnips instead of celeriac.

EASY TOMATO AND BASIL SOUP

Serves 4

2 small onions
3 cloves of garlic
2 carrots
2 medium potatoes
1 tbsp oil
2 × 400g tins of chopped tomatoes or 800g fresh
1 litre vegetable stock
1 tbsp maple syrup
small bunch of fresh basil
salt and ground black pepper

Optional

1 × 500g jar of roasted red peppers
a few hunks of sourdough bread (see page 246)

Garnish suggestions

chilli flakes
flaked almonds

This soup costs very little for the ingredients, takes half an hour to make and tastes fab. It's exactly what it says in the title!

Prep the veg: Peel and finely slice the onions and garlic. Cut the carrots and potatoes into similar-sized pieces so they cook evenly (wash but no need to peel).

Cook the veg: Put a large saucepan on a high heat and add 1 tablespoon of oil. Once hot, add the onions and cook for 3 minutes, stirring regularly. Add the garlic, carrots, potatoes, 2 teaspoons of salt and ½ teaspoon of black pepper, and cook for a further 3 minutes, stirring well. (The salt helps break down the vegetables' cell walls.)

Add sauce and simmer: Add the tomatoes, vegetable stock and maple syrup (and the jar of drained and rinsed roasted red peppers, if using) and bring to the boil, then reduce to a simmer for 10 minutes or until the potatoes are nice and soft.

Prep basil and blend soup: Pluck the basil leaves from the stalks and leave half aside for garnishing. Roughly chop the other half of the basil leaves and finely chop the stalks, then add both to the soup. Remove from the heat and blend till smooth using an immersion or stick blender.

Season: Taste then season to your liking. If you find it a little acidic, add another tablespoon of maple syrup.

Serve and garnish: Divide between bowls, scatter over the reserved basil leaves and some chilli flakes and flaked almonds, if using, or simply finish with a twist of black pepper– then serve with a couple of hunks of decent bread, such as our sourdough.

CREAM OF MUSHROOM AND LENTIL SOUP

Serves 6

3 cloves of garlic
1 onion
200g carrot
250g celeriac
350g button mushrooms
1 tbsp oil
180ml white wine
2 × 400g tins of green or brown lentils
2 litres vegetable stock
leaves from a small bunch of fresh thyme
salt and ground black pepper

Garnish

small bunch of chives

There's something really hearty and substantial about a mushroom soup, particularly one with lentils. This is a delicious belly-hug of a soup – like a fire on a damp day or an understanding smile from a stranger when you're feeling down, it warms you up from the inside out!

Prep the veg: Peel and finely dice the garlic and the onion. Finely slice the carrot into rounds, peel and finely chop the celeriac, and chop the button mushrooms into quarters.

Cook the onions: Put a large pot on a high heat, and add 1 tablespoon of oil. Once hot, add the onion and cook for about 4 minutes, stirring regularly.

Fry the remaining veg and add the wine: Add the garlic, carrot, celeriac, mushrooms and 2 teaspoons of salt to the pan, and cook, stirring regularly, for a further 5 minutes. Next, add the white wine and cook until it is all absorbed and evaporated, about 3–4 minutes.

Add the lentils and stock, then boil and simmer: Drain the lentils into a colander, give them a good rinse, then add them to the pot with the vegetable stock and fresh thyme leaves. Give it a good stir. Bring to the boil, then reduce heat and simmer for 5 minutes.

Blend: Remove from the heat and blend using an immersion/stick blender until smooth.

Season and garnish: Season according to taste. Divide between bowls, then, using a scissors, finely chop the chives and use them to garnish.

CHUNKY SPANISH LENTIL AND VEG ST-OUP

Serves 6

1 onion
3 cloves of garlic
2 medium leeks
2 carrots
2 medium potatoes
1 medium parsnip
1 tbsp oil
1 × 400g tin of chopped tomatoes
150g dried puy or green or brown lentils
3 tbsp tamari or soy sauce
2 bay leaves
½ tsp smoked paprika
2.2 litres vegetable stock or water
100g baby spinach
salt and ground black pepper

To serve

chilli flakes to garnish
good-quality sourdough bread (see page 246)

We love this soup – it's deeply nourishing and *so* wholesome. It sits somewhere between a soup and a stew – hence the name 'st-oup' – and will have you looking for seconds, and maybe even thirds ...

Prep the veg: Peel and finely slice the onion and garlic. Clean and chop the leeks (use all of the leek, including the green part) and carrots into small rounds. Chop the potato and parsnip into small bite-sized pieces, leaving the skins on.

Sauté and sweat the veg: Add 1 tablespoon of oil to a large pot (about 4 litres) and put it on a high heat. Add the onion, garlic, leek, carrots, potatoes and parsnip, along with 2 teaspoons of salt and ½ teaspoon of black pepper, and cook for 4 minutes, stirring regularly. Reduce the heat to low-medium, cover the pot, and let the vegetables sweat for 10 minutes – they will steam in their own liquid and soften – stirring occasionally. If anything starts to stick to the pot, add a few tablespoons of vegetable stock or water to deglaze the pan, scraping up any caramelised bits and stirring well.

Add the remaining ingredients (less the spinach): Add the rest of ingredients, except the spinach. Turn the heat up high, stir well and bring to the boil.

Simmer until the lentils are soft, then add the spinach: Once boiling, reduce the heat and simmer for 25 minutes or until the lentils are cooked – they must be fully cooked before serving, so make sure to test them. Season with additional salt and pepper to taste. Stir in the spinach and leave to wilt for 2 minutes.

Serve: To serve, garnish with chilli flakes for a bit of spice and accompany with a slice of good-quality sourdough bread.

SOUL-NOURISHING LENTIL SOUP

Serves 4–6

1 medium onion
2 cloves of garlic
3cm cubed piece of fresh ginger
2 medium carrots
200g celeriac (about ¼), parsnips or potatoes
1 tbsp oil
1 × 400g tin of chopped tomatoes
200g split red lentils
2 litres vegetable stock or water
2 tbsp curry powder
100g baby spinach or similar green
salt and ground black pepper

We find nothing nourishes quite like a cooked red lentil! This is one of those soups that always pleases, so it's well worth doubling the recipe and storing some in the freezer for rainy days when your soul needs some nourishing. We sometimes serve this with cooked brown rice for dinner.

Prep the veg: Peel and finely chop the onion, garlic and ginger. Cut the carrots and peeled celeriac or parsnip or potato into small bite-sized pieces so they will cook quickly.

Fry the veg: Add 1 tablespoon of oil to a large pot and allow it to heat up for 1 minute. Then add the onions, ginger and carrot, along with 1 teaspoon of salt, and cook on a high heat for 3 minutes or until the onions are starting to brown. Add the garlic, celeriac or parsnip or potato and another teaspoon of salt and cook for a further minute, stirring occasionally.

Sweat the veg: Add 5 tablespoons of water, put the lid on the pot, turn the heat down to medium and leave to cook for 5 minutes, stirring occasionally. If any of the veg start to stick, add another few tablespoons of water to deglaze the pan.

Add remaining ingredients, then boil and simmer: Add the chopped tomatoes, red lentils, vegetable stock or water, curry powder and ½ teaspoon of black pepper, and stir well. Turn the heat up high and bring to the boil with the lid on. Stir regularly, as you don't want any of the red lentils sticking to the bottom of the pot and burning. Once boiling, reduce to a simmer and leave to cook for 20 minutes (or until the red lentils are soft, broken down and cooked through), stirring regularly.

Add spinach: Remove the soup from the heat, add the washed fresh baby spinach (or similar green) and stir well.

Taste and season: Check the seasoning, and add more salt and pepper if necessary. We love this soup chunky, but if you prefer it smooth then blend using an immersion blender before serving.

20 THINGS we've LEARNED after 20 YEARS

1 No amount of drinking green juice or eating kale can improve a toxic self-image. If you are very self-critical and see yourself in a negative light, you probably need to do deeper work than just eating kale.

2 Be conscious of all that you are consuming. We are a product of more than just the food that we eat. This encompasses the people you spend time with, the media or social media you engage with, your social connections and what you do with your time.

3 Joy and laughter are two of the real unsung superfoods. We were once obsessed with finding the next superfood, believing that consuming more of it would make us superhuman. But, surprise, surprise, it didn't quite work out that way! At the World Organic Fair in 2014, Dave discovered cacao nibs, hailed as the ultimate health trend. He couldn't resist them, as there were free samples everywhere, and ate what felt like half his body weight in them, hoping for an instant upgrade. Instead, the theobromine – a natural stimulant – in cacao nibs had him wired for days, sleep becoming a distant memory. Lesson learned: true superpowers lie in the genuine moments of joy and laughter, not in a single food.

4 How you eat your food can be just as important as the food itself. Sometimes, it's not about obsessing over perfect healthy meals but savouring the experience of dining with friends, laughing and eating with gratitude. This joyful and relaxed approach to eating, even with less-than-healthy food, can be just as nourishing as hastily consuming a super-healthy meal on your own, feeling rushed and stressed.

5 'Use it or lose it' is the name of the game when it comes to our bodies. Movement is a precious gift that most of us are born with, and failing to embrace it results in reduced activity and mobility over time, which is exacerbated by our society's sedentary lifestyle. In the blue zones, where the longest-living populations reside, many people have vegetable gardens, rely on walking for transportation, dance at older ages, live in multi-generational homes that involve caring for grandchildren and often lack time-saving modern devices like dishwashers and cars, which naturally encourages more physical movement.

6 Diversity is crucial. Just as diverse ecosystems in nature are more resilient, our bodies benefit from diverse movement and diet. To enhance physical resilience, especially as we age, it's important to engage in a variety of movement activities. When we first started The Happy Pear, we got really into Ashtanga yoga – we got up and did the full primary series at 6 a.m. most days. We were really flexible in certain ways, but also quite stiff and rigid in others. So after about 10 years of this we started broadening our training to incorporate running, swimming, callisthenics, flexibility, animal movement – anything that would make us move differently. This has resulted in us being more physically flexible, stronger and resilient.

7 We are all connected, despite the illusion of separation. At the core, we are part of the same interconnected web of life. Our choices and actions have a ripple effect on the world around us. We are not separate from nature, but an integral part of it. Within our bodies, particularly in our large intestines, we harbour diverse ecosystems, called the microbiome, consisting of trillions of microorganisms. The genetic diversity of these microbes surpasses that of our own human cells. This realisation deepens our connection to nature and highlights the importance of nurturing and respecting both our internal and external ecosystems.

8 Health is far more than yoga, meditation, gratitude journals or the next trending superfood. We can often oversimplify what a healthy life is. However, most people know someone who lived a long, happy life, never ate kale or did yoga, smoked cigarettes and loved gambling – but they probably laughed a lot, had a lot of love and purpose in their life and likely weren't very stressed.

9 We are all a product of our environment. Dan Buettner, founder of Blue Zones, says that if you want to be happier or healthier, move somewhere there are happier and healthier people. Health is contagious! This may seem simplistic, but think of when someone in a room yawns: it's difficult not to yawn too. So one of the keys to becoming healthier is to have a healthier network of friends. That's not to say to stop being friends with anyone who is not healthy, but more to consciously cultivate friends who will support the habits that you want to incorporate into your life.

10 Sleep is the foundation of your health. If you sleep poorly, it affects every aspect of your life. (See page 257 for more.)

11 Cultivate your relationship with yourself. Make time for yourself – this could be enjoying a nice bath or shower, doing a puzzle or reading a novel. Or maybe it's making time for more esoteric practices such as breathwork or meditation, therapy, stress management and self-care to nurture a healthy mind and emotional balance.

12 Embrace lifelong learning and personal growth for better mental and brain health. There are so many things to be curious about and fascinated with in this life, and it doesn't need to be things to better your career: it can be history, typography or piano, or a new language. Explore new interests with curiosity and openness. Each new piece of knowledge and skill acquired becomes a foundation for better resilience and adaptability.

13 Find a movement practice that you love and can do by yourself. We started with Ashtanga yoga, but our individual yoga practices have evolved over the years, and it is one of the cornerstones of our physical health. When we travel or feel crap, yoga is one of the tools we turn to to feel better.

14 Our breath is an incredible tool that we often overlook. It has the power to dictate whether we feel relaxed or stressed, influencing our nervous system's response. By paying attention to our breath, we can help to manage stress, stay present and let go of worries about the past or future.

15 Look after yourself. This sounds so simple but it isn't. Look beyond society's beauty standards and others' expectations and embrace self-care practices that focus on self-compassion, self-acceptance and nourishing rituals. Try journalling or meditation, take up hiking – try to find new activities that bring you joy. Prioritise your own happiness and inner nourishment.

16 Gratitude is a habit worth cultivating. We all have a negativity bias – it's hardwired into our DNA for survival purposes. However, most of the time it does not serve us, as there is no sabre-tooth tiger looming around the next corner. Cultivating a more grateful way of being and shifting your focus towards the positive aspects of life will transform your life for the better. Gratitude really is a practice – you have to do it consistently to improve. Dave and his family say a 'grace' before dinner each night, and Steve's family say five things they are grateful for before bed. You could try journalling five things you are grateful for each day.

17 Understand the power of community. Surround yourself with a supportive community that encourages healthy habits. Having friends and loved ones who share your values can make a big difference to your well-being. Cultivate meaningful connections and lean on each other.

18 Define success on your terms. Society often defines success in very narrow, materialistic terms – wealth, status, appearance, etc. Redefine success for yourself in terms of what is important to you and your relationship with yourself and your loved ones.

19 Learn to slow down. In our fast-paced world, it's crucial to learn to prioritise downtime and rest to cultivate creativity and well-being. Learn your body's signs that it needs rest and time to recharge, and listen to them! Rest and renewal can be just as important as work. When we slow down and recharge, we access greater clarity, energy and presence. We reconnect with our deeper self, unlocking insights and allowing our creativity to flourish. Resisting the pressure to constantly be productive, and instead embracing rest benefits our overall well-being.

20 Cultivate contentment. In our always-wanting world, learning what is actually enough is important. Cultivating an intrinsic self-worth that is not based on society's standards is the key to contentment. Rather than always chasing the next big thing, we can find satisfaction in what we already have. This takes focus and practice, but when we slow down and appreciate the abundance around us, instead of focusing on lack, that inner contentment becomes a powerful counterweight to the constant messages telling us that we need more.

SAL

ADS

ASIAN-STYLE RAINBOW CRUNCH SALAD

Serves 6

1 medium carrot
250g red cabbage (about ¼ medium cabbage)
1 red pepper
handful of sugar snap peas
30g sesame seeds (white and black if possible)
30g sunflower seeds
100g sprouted beans (e.g. mung beans or aduki beans) or bean sprouts (the tails of sprouted mung beans)
100g baby spinach

Dressing

thumb-sized piece of fresh ginger, peeled
1 clove of garlic, peeled
1½ tbsp tamari or soy sauce
juice of 1 lemon
¼ medium red chilli
2 tbsp maple syrup
60ml sesame oil or oil of choice

Steve came up with this recipe about 15 years ago and we're still making it in the café today as it's so popular and is really packed with nutrition. With a rich variety of raw vegetables, sprouted beans and a super-flavourful dressing, it's a refreshing addition to any meal. To reduce the calories, you can simply replace the oil with apple juice.

Prep the veg: Grate the carrot and red cabbage – or if your knife skills are good, finely slice the cabbage into long thin strips and julienne the carrot. Finely slice the red pepper (removing the seeds and stalk), and slice the sugar snap peas lengthwise into long thin strips.

Toast the seeds: Put the sesame and sunflower seeds in a dry pan over a high heat for about 5 minutes, until they turn slightly brown and start to pop.

Assemble the salad: Combine the cabbage, carrot, pepper, sugar snap peas, sprouted beans and baby spinach in a large salad bowl.

Blend the dressing: Place all the ingredients for the dressing in a blender or food processor, and blend until nice and smooth.

Dress, mix and serve: Add the dressing to the salad and mix until well coated. Sprinkle the toasted seeds on top and serve!

TIP: Only dress the salad that you plan to consume immediately for the best freshness and crunch. An undressed salad can last for 3–4 days, while a dressed salad will keep for less than 1 day.

BLACK BEAN, ROASTED SWEET POTATO AND AVOCADO SALAD

Serves 4

1 large sweet potato
1 × 400g tin of black beans
2 avocados
100g cherry tomatoes
1 bunch of spring onions
1 red chilli
small bunch of fresh coriander
250g cooked brown rice
50g rocket

Dressing
50ml olive oil
juice of 2 limes
1 tbsp maple syrup
2 tbsp tamari or soy sauce

salt and ground black pepper

This brightly coloured salad really delivers on flavour. It takes a little time, as you have to roast the sweet potato, but it's so worth it. It's an excellent option for a warm salad as a dinner or a refreshing salad at any time of day.

Roast the sweet potato: Preheat the oven to 200°C fan/425°F/gas 7. Cut the sweet potato into bite-sized pieces, season with a pinch of salt, spread out on a baking tray, and roast in the oven until soft – about 25–30 minutes.

Prep the beans, veg and herbs: While the sweet potato is roasting, prepare the other ingredients. First, drain and rinse the black beans. Cut the avocado in half, remove the stone and, using a spoon, scoop the flesh out and dice into small pieces. Next, halve the cherry tomatoes, finely slice the spring onions and finely chop the red chilli (remove the seeds for less heat) and coriander, including the stalks.

Make the dressing: Whisk together all the ingredients for the dressing along with ½ teaspoon of salt. Adjust the taste to your liking by adding more salt, ground black pepper or lime juice as needed.

Combine the rice and beans and dress: In a large bowl, combine the cooked rice and black beans. Pour over the dressing and gently toss until everything is well coated.

Top with remaining ingredients and mix: Add the rocket, coriander, chilli, spring onions, roasted sweet potato, avocado and cherry tomatoes to the bowl. Gently mix to combine, then serve.

BEETROOT, SPINACH AND APPLE SALAD WITH TOASTED SEEDS

Serves 4 as a main and 10 as a side

500g raw beetroot (about 5 medium-large beets)
1 large apple
50g pumpkin seeds
50g sunflower seeds
50g baby spinach

Dressing
50ml olive oil
25ml balsamic vinegar
2 tbsp maple syrup
1 tsp salt

We have been making this salad for years in our café, and it is always very quick to sell out. It has just the right amount of crunch and crispness. Beetroot's vibrant red colour is reflective of how good beetroot is for blood flow and cardiovascular function.

Prep the beetroot: Remove all the dirt from the beetroot, top and tail them, then scrub the skin, but don't peel. Grate using a box grater or the grater function on a food processor. Add to your serving bowl.

Prep the apple: Core and finely slice the apple, then add to the bowl with the beetroot.

Toast the seeds: Put a dry pan on a high heat. Once hot, reduce to medium. Add the seeds and toast them for about 5–6 minutes, until they start to pop and colour and smell lovely – but be careful that they do not burn. Add half of the toasted seeds to the serving bowl along with the baby spinach.

Make the dressing and dress the salad: Whisk the dressing ingredients together and pour over the salad.

Garnish and serve: Sprinkle the remaining seeds on top and serve.

TIPS: Dress only what you are going to eat immediately, as the salad doesn't keep well once dressed. Also, if you are making this in advance, only add the seeds just before serving, as they will lose their crispness if sitting in the dressed salad for a while.

HAPPY PEAR FARMHOUSE SALAD WITH ROASTED-PUMPKIN-SEED PESTO

Serves 6 as a side, 2 as a main

1 head of radicchio or 200g red cabbage
1 × 180g packet of sprouted beans (such as sprouted lentils or mung beans)
100g rocket or baby mixed leaves of choice
100g baby spinach
1 firm ripe pear

Roasted pumpkin-seed-pesto dressing
50g pumpkin seeds
100ml olive oil or sunflower oil
20g fresh coriander or flat-leaf parsley
1 tbsp maple syrup
1 tbsp apple cider vinegar or balsamic vinegar

salt and ground black pepper

We grow most of the ingredients for this tasty, refreshing salad on our farm. It combines the sweetness of ripe pear and the unique roasted-pumpkin-seed-pesto dressing with the slight bitterness of radicchio and the pepperiness of rocket – a delightful balance of flavours.

Toast the seeds: Preheat the oven to 160°C fan/350°F/gas 4, then toast the pumpkin seeds on a baking tray for about 10 minutes. Alternatively, place them in a dry frying pan over a medium heat until they start to turn slightly brown – this should take about 6–8 minutes.

Blend the dressing: Put the pumpkin seeds into a food processor or blender, add the rest of the dressing ingredients along with a teaspoon of salt, and blend until it achieves a smooth consistency. Taste and adjust the seasoning to your liking.

Prep the veg for the salad: Halve the radicchio, remove the stem, slice it into thin strips and add to a large mixing bowl. If using red cabbage, finely slice it into thin strips, add to the bowl with a pinch of salt and mix. Rinse the sprouted beans, rocket or mixed leaves and baby spinach, and add to the mixing bowl. Core the pear, cut it into small bite-sized pieces, and add to the mixing bowl and mix well.

Dress the salad: Toss the salad with the dressing just before serving. Only dress the amount you plan on eating immediately because it doesn't store well once dressed.

KALE CAESAR SALAD

Serves 4

150g tempeh
3 baby gem lettuces
100g kale
50g capers

Tempeh dressing
4 tbsp tamari or soy sauce
2 tbsp apple cider vinegar
2 tsp maple syrup
2 tsp smoked paprika
1 tsp garlic powder

Sourdough croutons
2 tbsp oil
1 tbsp tamari or soy sauce
1 tbsp mixed herbs
4 slices of sourdough bread (see page 246)

Salad dressing
100ml vegan mayo (see page 275)
15ml caper brine

salt and ground black pepper

We've made a few tweaks to transform the traditional Caesar into a plant-based delight in our popular rendition of this classic. We've incorporated tempeh to create our own version of 'facon' (a tasty vegan stand-in for bacon) and added toasted sourdough croutons for an extra layer of crunch. The salad is dressed with vegan mayo for a truly indulgent, delicious Caesar experience.

Preheat: Preheat the oven to 200°C fan/425°F/gas 7.

Prep and bake the tempeh 'facon': Slice the tempeh into long thin strips, about 3mm thick. Mix the ingredients for the tempeh dressing in a bowl with a pinch of salt, add in the sliced tempeh and mix well. Place the dressed tempeh on a baking tray, ensuring each piece is well covered and spread out. Bake for 10 minutes, turn the tempeh over then bake for a further 15 minutes.

Make the sourdough croutons: In a bowl, mix together the oil, tamari or soy sauce, mixed herbs and a pinch of salt. Slice the sourdough bread into small cubes, about 1cm × 1cm, add to the bowl and mix well. Place on a baking tray and bake for 5 minutes, turn over then bake for a further 10 minutes.

Cool the tempeh and croutons: When the tempeh and sourdough croutons are cooked, remove from the oven and leave to cool.

Prep the veg: Cut the bases off the baby gem lettuce to free the leaves, wash and drain, then slice the leaves into thin pieces and add into a large bowl. (If you want the baby gem lettuce to last longer, cut them using a plastic knife, as it reduces oxidation or browning.) Rip the kale from its stalk, roughly tear and add to the bowl. Drain the capers (but keep the brine), add to the bowl and mix well.

Slice the tempeh: Once the tempeh has cooled, use scissors to slice it into thin pieces, about 2cm × 2cm.

Dress the salad: Mix the vegan mayo, caper brine and a pinch of black pepper together. In a large bowl, add the baby gem and kale leaves, the drained capers and the dressing and mix well.

Top with the 'facon' and croutons: Place the tempeh 'facon' and sourdough croutons on top, like little flavour bombs waiting to be enjoyed!

RED-PEPPER PESTO AND BEAN SALAD

Serves 4

1 × 400g tin of butter beans
1 × 400g tin of black beans
2 medium leeks
200g cherry tomatoes
1½ tbsp oil
pinch of salt
100g mixed baby leaves

Roasted-red-pepper pesto

100g almonds
150ml oil
30g basil
1 tsp salt
15ml balsamic vinegar
100g roasted red peppers (easiest to use jarred ones!)
2 cloves of garlic, peeled

This salad is always a hit with hungry people and anyone doing lots of exercise, as it is packed with flavour, protein and fibre. What makes it truly shine is the homemade roasted-red-pepper pesto, which transforms it from a simple bean salad into a gourmet delight. Whether you want a light lunch, a side dish or a healthy option for your next picnic, this salad is a versatile choice.

Preheat: Preheat the oven to 200°C fan/425°F/gas 7.

Prep the pulses and veg: Drain and rinse the butter beans and black beans. Slice the leek into bite-sized pieces (give it a good rinse, as sediment often hides in the green parts). Quarter the cherry tomatoes.

Roast the leeks: Toss the leek pieces in 1½ tablespoons of oil and a pinch of salt. Spread them out on a baking tray and roast for about 15 minutes, or until they are tender and lightly browned.

Assemble the salad: In a large bowl, combine the roasted leek, drained beans, quartered cherry tomatoes and mixed baby leaves.

Make the pesto: In a food processor or blender, add all the ingredients for the pesto and pulse until it comes together – we love when it's a little chunky and you can see all the different colours rather than when it's blended until it's just one colour. Taste and adjust the seasoning to your liking.

Add the pesto and season: Add the pesto to the salad, then toss to ensure everything is well coated. Taste and adjust the seasoning with additional salt if needed. Serve and enjoy!

QUINOA TABBOULEH SALAD

15 MINS PREP | 30 MINS COOK | 45 MINS TOTAL

Serves 4–6

250g quinoa
1 aubergine
2 tbsp oil
1 × 400g tin of black beans
2 scallions
100g roasted red peppers (easiest to use jarred ones!)
50g cucumber
small bunch of flat-leaf parsley
small bunch of fresh mint
100g rocket

Dressing

50ml olive oil
juice of 1 lemon
1 tbsp maple syrup
1 tbsp tamari or soy sauce

salt and ground black pepper

To serve

flatbreads (page 253) and hummus (page 262)

This take on traditional tabbouleh uses quinoa and adds hearty black beans, roasted red peppers and some creamy roasted aubergines, with a splash of tamari or soy sauce to bring an unexpected umami twist. Perfect as a summer main course, a family-dinner side or a vibrant potluck contribution, this salad is a light summer favourite of ours.

Preheat: Preheat the oven to 200°C fan/425°F/gas 7.

Cook the quinoa: Add the quinoa to a medium saucepan with 400ml of water and a good pinch of salt and put the lid on. Turn the heat on high and bring to a boil, then reduce the heat to medium, set the lid ajar and leave to simmer for 6–8 minutes, until there is roughly ½ cm of water left in the bottom of the pot. Turn off the heat and put the lid back on fully to trap the remaining steam. This will give you lovely fluffy quinoa. Leave to cool in the pot with the lid on.

Roast the aubergine: Chop the aubergine into bite-sized pieces, toss with 2 tablespoons of oil and a pinch of salt, spread out well on a baking tray and bake till soft – about 20–25 minutes. You want to make sure you cook them till they reach a melt-in-your-mouth texture.

Prep the veg: Drain and rinse the black beans. Finely dice the scallions and roasted red pepper. Dice the cucumber into bite-sized pieces. Remove the mint leaves from their stalks, then finely chop the mint leaves and flat-leaf parsley.

Make the dressing: Whisk together the olive oil, lemon juice, maple syrup and tamari or soy sauce, and season to taste with salt and ground black pepper.

Bring the salad together: In a large bowl, start by adding the cooked quinoa, then the black beans along with the cucumber, roasted pepper and scallions. Add the dressing and, lastly, the herbs, rocket and roasted aubergine, and gently mix through. Taste and season with more salt and ground black pepper or freshly squeezed lemon juice to your liking. We often serve this with flatbreads and some hummus.

THE FARM and WHAT it MEANS

When we were growing up, farming seemed like a backwards occupation to us – muddy fields, tractors, battling the elements – lacking the glamour of tech and an office job in the city. But no amount of fancy tech or fame matters if we don't have food to eat.

Our brother Darragh was the driving force behind our farm. He's the purest of us four brothers (Steve, Mark, Dave and Darragh) – the one most likely to have been a priest! He grew tired of us needing to import most of the organic produce for our shop from Holland. While the quality was great, it didn't build local resilience or local knowledge of growing healthy veg and fruit. And in an ever-changing economy and climate, knowing how to grow food has become increasingly important. These feelings, among others, sparked our dream of starting a local organic farm.

Trusting our instincts

In early 2022, the business had become more financially stable, and we had some funds available. We decided to buy four acres of local land, and taking food production into our own hands became our mission. Although some people felt we were better off spending our money elsewhere, we trusted our instincts, and we all feel this is one of the most important things we have done in our 20 years of business.

Our four-acre farm follows a regenerative organic approach. This means we are committed to prioritising and regenerating the soil. The core idea is that if we feed the soil through good natural practices, the soil then nourishes the fruit and veg growing in it, which stands in stark contrast to modern chemical farming. Our dream is to reconnect ourselves and our community with the land, ensuring access to local food, and share our blueprint with others interested in starting small-scale organic farms.

On our farm, we adhere to 'no dig' principles, inspired by Charles Dowding, a pioneer of 'no dig' horticulture. It's exactly as it sounds – no digging, turning or rotavating the soil in order to preserve the mycelium network and mycorrhizae, the tiny white roots on the plants and in the soil that act as nature's data cables, transferring nutrients and water while enabling plant communication. Charles has conducted experiments comparing 'no dig' with traditional growing methods, and he consistently achieves higher yields with fewer weeds and less work using the 'no dig' approach.

WEEKENDER

Chris and Margot

Alessia aka Queen of the Farm

Darragh, always proud of our veg!

The people who make it work

Sustaining a dream relies on people. Darragh enlisted the incredible Chris Somerville as the leader of our farm, along with our dear friends Alessia and Ruadhan. Much of the farm's infrastructure has been built on community energy. Every Saturday morning, friends, family and newcomers come together to lend a hand, get their hands in the soil and experience nature. We're blessed to have such a supportive group who contribute their sweat and energy to our dream of providing quality local organic produce to the community.

Our farm is now in its second year. It has required a significant financial investment of approximately €250,000. Breaking even is getting a lot closer, and while our focus is to be fully financially sustainable, we can't guarantee it will ever fully recoup the investment capital. Yet, deep within us, we know it's the right thing to do. Our first milestone is to reach 100 weekly organic veg boxes, which we are selling directly to local people and families in our community. We are also providing our organic produce to a number of local shops and restaurants.

We're committed to being as open-source as possible about our farm, sharing financial performance, growing methods, successes and challenges to support others interested in similar initiatives. Our plan is to eventually provide training courses and empower others with the knowledge we've gained so they can start their own farming adventures providing local food for local people. If you'd like to learn more, please reach out to us. We would be thrilled to have you visit the farm and join us on a Saturday morning!

Harmony with nature and community

Our farm has highlighted the crucial importance of reconnecting with nature and fostering local biodiversity, both for the environment and for future generations. It serves as a powerful lesson for our kids to witness first-hand that food is not simply created in factories or found on supermarket shelves but grown in harmony with nature's rhythms. It's essential for them to understand the origins of their meals and develop a deep appreciation for the natural world.

Our farm has taught us invaluable lessons about the significance of immersing ourselves in nature and actively participating in our food production. It has shown us that it's about so much more than just the food itself. Our entire nervous systems relax while we're working there, and leaving becomes a challenge because of the deep sense of connection we experience. The farm has become a sanctuary where we find solace, joy and belonging – a place where nature's embrace and the shared purpose of nurturing the land intertwine to create truly transformative experiences.

Jess and Justyna

YOU CAN DO IT TOO

Living in a city or urban environment shouldn't deter you from getting involved in your own food production. Here are some additional actionable ideas if you feel inspired to take steps towards a closer connection with your food:

Try growing your own vegetables:
Even with limited space, you can grow veg – in containers on balconies, rooftops or even window sills. Start with easy-to-grow plants like tomatoes, lettuce or herbs. It's a rewarding experience to nurture and harvest your own food and great to do if you have kids.

Join a local veg box scheme or community-supported agriculture (CSA) programme:
This is what we do at our farm! Local veg box schemes or CSAs allow urban dwellers to support local farmers by subscribing to a weekly or monthly box of fresh, local, usually organic produce. By subscribing or becoming a member, you not only access organic, locally grown food but also contribute to the sustainability of local farms.

Participate in a community garden:
Darragh, our brother, was one of the founding members of Greystones Kilcoole Community Garden, a group that grows veg on a community plot in Greystones. Many towns and cities have community gardens where individuals can rent or share plots of land to grow their own food. Joining a community garden not only provides an opportunity to grow your own produce but also fosters a sense of community and knowledge-sharing with fellow gardeners.

Volunteer at an urban farm or any farm:
Urban farms are sprouting up in cities worldwide, providing opportunities for people to get involved in food production. Consider volunteering your time and skills at one, where you can learn about sustainable growing practices and contribute to the local food system. Just as importantly, you will likely meet really good people and foster new relationships!

Support local farmers' markets:
Visit your local farmers' market to purchase fresh, locally grown produce directly from farmers. This supports local agriculture and allows you to connect with the people who grow your food, fostering a deeper appreciation for the farming community.

Learn and share:
Educate yourself about sustainable and regenerative farming practices. We have a number of podcast episodes on these topics that you can find online. You could attend workshops, take online courses or read books on organic gardening and permaculture. Share your new-found knowledge with friends, family and your community to inspire others to get involved in their food production.

By taking these small steps, even in an urban environment, we can actively participate in our food production and nurture a deeper understanding of where our food comes from. This empowers us to make a positive impact on our own lives, the environment and the future of our children.

Mary Miles helping to tie some cucumbers

SANDW
& BUR

ICHES
GERS

PLANT-BASED PHILLY CHEESESTEAK

Serves 2

1 onion
1 red pepper
200g oyster mushrooms
¾ of a large baguette
2 tbsp oil
2½ tbsp tamari or soy sauce
1 tbsp maple syrup
pinch of salt
4 slices vegan cheese
1 tbsp mustard
2 tbsp vegan mayo (page 275)
handful of rocket (optional)

In 1999, we lived in Philadelphia for a few months, teaching golf at a camp. We ate lots of Philly cheesesteak that summer on South Street (we ate everything back then!). This is our vegan version of the classic, without any of the animal fats or cholesterol. We cooked this on the TV show *John Torode's Ireland*, and John was blown away by how simple and tasty it is.

Prep the vegetables and bread: Peel and slice the onion. Deseed and slice the red pepper. Slice the mushrooms. Cut the baguette into 2 equal parts for the sandwiches and split each part in half.

Char the mushrooms: Heat a large pan over a high heat with 1 tablespoon of oil. When hot, add the sliced mushrooms and cook for 3–4 minutes to develop a char. Press the mushrooms down, using a clean, heavy pot, to increase charring for another 2–3 minutes. Stir and press down again for 2–3 more minutes before removing the pan from the heat.

Flavour the mushrooms: Add the tamari or soy sauce and maple syrup to the mushrooms, stirring quickly for about a minute to coat them evenly. Remove the mushrooms from the pan and set aside.

Cook peppers and onions: In the same pan, add another tablespoon of oil. Add the sliced peppers and onions with a pinch of salt. Reduce the heat to medium and cook for 5–8 minutes until they're soft and beginning to brown. Remove from the pan.

Melt the cheese with mushrooms: Return the mushrooms to the pan and place the slices of vegan cheese on top. Cook on a low heat until the cheese starts to melt.

Assemble the sandwich: Mix the mustard and vegan mayo, then spread on the cut sides of the baguette halves. Split the cheesy mushroom mixture between the two baguettes, spreading it out evenly. Add the cooked onion-and-pepper mixture on top, and if using, add a handful of rocket leaves. Close the sandwiches with the top halves of the baguette and enjoy your vegan Philly cheesesteak experience!

Dave and Fia
smiling in the sun!

KING OYSTER MUSHROOM 'BLT' SANDWICH

Serves 2

5 king oyster mushrooms
1 tsp oil
2 large beef tomatoes
1 head of baby gem lettuce
4 slices of sourdough bread
60g vegan mayo (see page 275)

Dressing

4 tbsp tamari or soy sauce
2 tbsp maple syrup
½ tsp dried garlic
¼ tsp ground chilli powder
1 tsp smoked paprika

salt and ground black pepper

Our mom used to make BLT (bacon, lettuce and tomato) sandwiches growing up, which we would devour. This twist on the classic uses king oyster mushrooms coated in a maple smoked umami sauce to mimic the savoury flavour of bacon.

Preheat: Preheat your oven to 180°C fan/400°F/gas 6, or air fryer 180°C/350°F using the bake function.

Prepare the mushrooms: Cut the king oyster mushrooms lengthwise into strips approximately ½cm thick.

Bake the mushrooms: Place the mushrooms on a baking tray or in the air fryer basket, with about 1 teaspoon of oil, and mix to ensure they're well coated. Then bake for 10 minutes, mixing occasionally for even searing.

Make the dressing: While the mushrooms bake, combine all the dressing ingredients in a mixing bowl, with a pinch of salt and pepper.

Dress the mushrooms: When the mushrooms are done, add them to the bowl with the dressing and toss until well coated. Place them back on the baking tray or in the basket and return them to the oven or air fryer for an additional 5–10 minutes, shaking once to ensure even caramelisation. Season with salt and pepper to taste after cooking.

Prepare the remaining ingredients: While the mushrooms finish, slice the beef tomatoes, cut the bases off to free the baby gem lettuce leaves and wash and drain, and toast the sourdough bread if desired.

Assemble the sandwich: Spread vegan mayo on one side of each bread slice. On two slices, layer the tomato, lettuce and dressed mushrooms. Top with the remaining slices of bread, mayo-side down.

SHAWARMA SKEWERS WITH OYSTER MUSHROOMS AND BEETROOT

Serves 4

Shawarma

1 medium beetroot
250g oyster mushrooms
1 tbsp sumac (optional)
1½ tbsp smoked paprika
1 tsp ground black pepper
½ tsp salt
3 tbsp tamari or soy sauce
2 tbsp maple syrup
2 tbsp oil

Coriander salad

½ cucumber
10g fresh coriander leaves
1 pomegranate
10 cherry tomatoes
pinch of salt

Tahini cream

300g natural soy yoghurt
6 tbsp light tahini
pinch of garlic powder
juice of ½ a lemon
pinch of salt

To serve

4 flatbreads (see page 253)
pickled chillies

The first time we made these, we were tired after a long day and were craving something that was indulgent, yet based around real good-quality food. Lucy, who worked with us doing social media, grew up in the Middle East and shawarma was always her favourite – she adored these! You'll need two large metal skewers for this, but if you don't have any, you can just fry the beetroot and mushrooms in a pan.

Prepare the vegetables: Cut the beetroot in half lengthwise. Using a vegetable peeler, peel long strips the width of the beetroot. Tear the oyster mushrooms in half lengthwise.

Marinate: In a large bowl, combine the beetroot strips and mushrooms with the sumac (if using), smoked paprika, ground black pepper, salt, tamari or soy sauce and maple syrup. Mix well and leave to marinate.

Make the coriander salad: Finely dice the cucumber and coriander. Remove the pomegranate seeds (ensuring you remove all the white pithy bits) and quarter the cherry tomatoes. Combine these in a bowl with a pinch of salt, mix and adjust seasoning as desired.

Prep the tahini cream: Mix the soy yoghurt, tahini, garlic powder, lemon juice and a pinch of salt in a bowl until smooth. Adjust the taste with additional salt or lemon juice if needed.

Cook the shawarma: Thread the marinated mushrooms and beetroot onto two metal skewers, alternating two layers of mushrooms with one layer of beetroot until the skewers are full. Heat a large frying pan with 2 tablespoons of oil over high heat. Cook the skewers on each side for 2–3 minutes until they are lightly charred and the beetroot has started to caramelise. Remove and, using a sharp knife, carve the mushrooms and beetroot off the skewers into bite-sized pieces.

Assemble and serve: Spread a dollop of tahini cream on each flatbread, add a portion of the coriander salad, some mushroom and beet mixture, and finish with pickled chillies. Repeat with the remaining flatbreads.

REAL FALAFEL WITH TAHINI CREAM AND CHILLI SAUCE

*PLUS OVERNIGHT SOAKING

Makes 6–8 wraps

Falafel

250g dried chickpeas
1 tsp baking soda
3 cloves of garlic
1 small onion
25g flat parsley
50g fresh coriander
1 tbsp ground cumin
1 tbsp ground coriander
½ tsp cayenne powder
½ tsp baking powder
3 tbsp sesame seeds
sunflower or vegetable oil for frying (about 400ml)

Tahini cream

8 tbsp light tahini
500g natural soy yoghurt
juice of 1 lemon
1 tsp garlic powder

Salad

½ red onion
½ cucumber
2 ripe tomatoes

salt and ground black pepper

To serve

6–8 flatbreads (see page 253)
100g pickled chillies
100g pickled red cabbage or sauerkraut (see page 296)
100g chilli sauce

We call these real falafel because we have so many recipes for no-fry or high-protein baked falafel, but none are properly deep fried like a traditional falafel. So we decided to go authentic and make proper epic falafels, served with lots of pickles and an amazing tahini cream and chilli sauce.

Soak the chickpeas overnight: Place the dried chickpeas in large bowl with the baking soda, cover with twice the volume of water, and leave overnight.

Make the falafel mix: Peel the garlic and onion, then drain and rinse the soaked chickpeas. Place them in a food processor along with the garlic, onion, parsley, fresh coriander, ground cumin, ground coriander, cayenne powder, baking powder, ¾ teaspoon salt, ½ teaspoon black pepper and sesame seeds. Pulse for 2–3 minutes until it comes together while leaving some texture remaining.

Heat the oil: Heat about 400ml sunflower or veg oil in a deep fryer or a saucepan to approximately 170°C/325°F, or until bubbles rise from the bottom of the pan.

Shape the falafels: Form the falafel mixture into small 3–4cm diameter balls or thick coin shapes, and set them aside on a lined baking tray.

Fry the falafels: Carefully deep-fry the falafels in batches for about 4 minutes each, until golden and crispy. Place them onto kitchen paper to drain off excess oil.

Make the tahini cream: Combine the tahini, soy yoghurt, lemon juice, garlic powder and a pinch of salt in a bowl. Mix until creamy.

Prep the salad: Peel and finely dice the onion, and finely dice the cucumber and tomatoes. Combine them in a bowl with a pinch of salt.

Assemble the wraps: Spread a generous amount of tahini cream on each flatbread. Add about 3 tablespoons of the salad mixture, followed by 3–4 falafels. Top with some pickled chillies, pickled cabbage and chilli sauce.

STICKY SESAME TOFU BURGERS WITH CHARRED PINEAPPLE AND KIMCHI MAYO SLAW

Serves 2

Kimchi mayo slaw

¼ white cabbage
¼ red cabbage
½ carrot
handful of fresh coriander
3 tbsp vegan mayo (see page 275)
1 tsp chilli powder (Korean gochugaru works best)
1 tbsp kimchi juice (from a jar of kimchi or sauerkraut)

Pineapple

½ a fresh pineapple

Teriyaki sauce

1 clove of garlic
½ thumb-sized piece of ginger
¼ red chilli
5 tbsp tamari or soy sauce
3 tbsp maple syrup
1 tbsp vinegar of choice or mirin

Burgers

200g firm tofu
2 tbsp oil
40g white flour or cornflour
45g sesame seeds (both white and black if you have them)

To serve

spicy pesto or tomato ketchup (we used The Happy Pear Spicy Red Pepper Pesto)
2 burger buns

These burgers are a taste sensation. They are an absolute fusion of flavours – the combination of sweet, tangy and spicy elements makes them next level!

Prepare the kimchi slaw: Thinly slice the white and red cabbages. Grate the carrot. Dice the fresh coriander, stalks and leaves. Mix the vegan mayo with the chilli powder and kimchi juice. Combine the mayo mixture with the cabbage, carrot and coriander, then set aside.

Char the pineapple: Remove the skin and core from the pineapple, then cut into 2 × 1cm slices. Heat a dry pan and cook the pineapple slices for 1–2 minutes on each side, until gently charred.

Make the teriyaki sauce: Peel and finely dice the garlic and ginger. Finely dice the red chilli. Mix the tamari or soy sauce, maple syrup, vinegar, garlic, ginger and chilli together in a bowl.

Prep and cook the tofu: Cut the tofu into 1cm-thick slices, slightly larger than the burger buns. Heat a non-stick pan with 1 tablespoon of oil. Fry the tofu slices for 2 minutes on each side, until golden. Add 2 tablespoons of the teriyaki sauce to the tofu in the pan, coating both sides of the tofu.

Coat and fry the tofu: Place the flour or cornflour in a bowl. Place the sesame seeds in another bowl. Add the seared tofu to the flour and coat evenly. Dip the coated tofu in the teriyaki sauce, then into the sesame seeds. Heat the pan again with 1 tablespoon of oil and fry the tofu for 1 minute on each side until sesame seeds are golden. Remove the tofu from the pan. Add the remaining teriyaki sauce to the pan and cook until bubbling and reduced. Return the tofu to the pan, spooning the sauce over to coat evenly.

Assemble the burgers: Toast the burger buns. Spread a generous dollop of spicy pesto or tomato ketchup on the bottom buns. Add a generous amount of the kimchi slaw. Place the sticky sesame tofu on the top, and drizzle any remaining teriyaki sauce over it. Add some charred pineapple, then cap with the top parts of the buns and serve immediately.

BEETROOT, WALNUT AND FETA BURGERS

Serves 4

60g cashew nuts
140g walnuts
400g raw beetroot
10 scallions
80g vegan Cheddar-style cheese
4 tbsp fresh mint (about 20g unpicked)
3 tbsp oil
1 lemon
100g breadcrumbs
150g hummus (see page 262)
salt and ground black pepper

When we wrote our first book this was one of the standout recipes. Here is an even better version that is quicker to make and packed full of flavour.

Preheat: Preheat the oven to 180°C fan/400°F/gas 6.

Soak the cashews: Place the cashews in a bowl and cover with boiling water. Let them soak for 10 minutes.

Toast the walnuts: Roughly chop the walnuts, spread them on a baking tray, and toast in the oven for 6–7 minutes until starting to turn golden. Remove and set aside.

Prepare the vegetables and cheese: Peel the beetroot and grate it. Finely chop the scallions. Grate the vegan Cheddar-style cheese. Pick and finely chop the mint leaves.

Cook the beetroot and scallions: Heat a frying pan over a medium heat, add 1 tablespoon of oil, then the grated beetroot, chopped scallions and 1 teaspoon of salt. Cook for 4–5 minutes, stirring regularly. Transfer to a large bowl to cool.

Process the cashew mixture: Drain the soaked cashews. In a blender (an immersion blender can be used for this) or food processor, combine the cashews with 2 tablespoons of oil, the juice of ½ the lemon, ¼ teaspoon of salt and a pinch of black pepper. Blend until smooth.

Make the burgers: To the large bowl with the cooked beetroot and scallions, add the processed cashew mixture, grated vegan cheese, toasted walnuts, breadcrumbs, juice of the remaining ½ lemon, the chopped mint, and another ½ teaspoon of salt and ¼ teaspoon of black pepper. Mix well and adjust the seasoning to taste.

Shape the burgers: Divide the mixture into four equal portions, about 170g each. Shape into burger patties and place on a baking tray lined with baking parchment.

Bake the burgers: Bake the patties in the preheated oven for 25 minutes, or until they are firm and golden.

Serve: Remove the burgers from the oven. Top each one with a generous dollop of hummus, some microgreens or chopped herbs of choice and serve immediately.

Savour the JOY
STEVE 24
DAVE 24
PLANT-BASED YOGHURT
CHOCOLUV BROWNIE
SLOW DOWN
Z Z Z
The Happy Pear
Natural Food Market

The
NOURISHING
power of
PLANT-BASED
food
The Happy Pear
Did you Know
organic
is
own
lcoole.
come and
it out!!

QU
MIDW
DINN

ICK
VEEK
IERS

CREAMY MUSHROOM LINGUINE

Serves 2–3

Creamy cashew sauce
100g cashew nuts
500ml non-dairy milk of choice
juice of ½ lemon
1 tsp garlic powder
2 tbsp nutritional yeast

Pasta
250g linguine pasta
1 large red onion
2 cloves of garlic
250g mushrooms of choice (e.g. oyster, shiitake, chestnut)
1 tbsp oil
2 tbsp tamari or soy sauce

salt and ground black pepper

Garnish (optional)
1 fresh chilli, seeds removed and sliced finely
3 sprigs of fresh oregano or thyme, leaves removed from the stalks

This has consistently been one of our family-favourite dinners and one of the most popular recipes in our recipe club on our app. The flavours of this deliciously creamy pasta dish meld together beautifully to create a delightful meal in just 20 minutes. Use wholemeal pasta to make it higher in fibre and healthier.

Prepare the cashews: Place the cashew nuts in a small pot and cover with boiling water. Simmer gently for 5–10 minutes, then drain and rinse to wash away any residue.

Cook the pasta: Fill a large saucepan with boiling water and add 1 tablespoon of salt. Add your pasta and cook according to package instructions.

Prepare the vegetables: Peel and finely slice the onion and garlic. Finely chop the mushrooms.

Cook the vegetables: Heat a large wide-bottomed pan over a high heat. Add 1 tablespoon of oil, followed by the onion and ½ teaspoon of salt. Reduce the heat to medium and cook for 4–5 minutes, stirring occasionally, until the onions brown slightly. Add the chopped mushrooms and garlic and cook for another 4–5 minutes. Stir in the tamari or soy sauce, cook for an additional minute, then turn off the heat.

Prepare the cashew sauce: While the mushrooms are cooking, make the cashew sauce. Add the drained and rinsed cashew nuts and the rest of the sauce ingredients to a blender or food processor. Blend at high speed until smooth.

Combine the pasta, sauce and mushrooms: Drain the cooked pasta, reserving some pasta water, and return to the pan. Add the creamy cashew sauce and mix, making sure the pasta is well coated. Turn the heat to medium and cook for 1–2 minutes, stirring continuously, to allow the sauce to thicken. If the sauce is too thick, add a little reserved pasta water until you reach your desired creamy texture. If it is too watery, cook for a few minutes more, stirring constantly to avoid sticking. Taste and adjust the seasoning with salt and black pepper as needed. Add the mushrooms and mix through, keeping a few aside to garnish.

Garnish and serve: Sprinkle with the reserved mushrooms – and, if you like, finely sliced fresh red chilli and/or fresh oregano or thyme. Serve hot!

ULTIMATE MAC AND CHEESE

Serves 3

300g macaroni

Sauce

100g cashew nuts
350ml oat milk
squeeze of lemon juice
2 tbsp nutritional yeast
½ tsp garlic powder
½ tsp ground turmeric
1 tbsp mustard

Breadcrumb topping

40g breadcrumbs
3 tbsp oil
2 sprigs of fresh thyme or ½ tbsp dried thyme
2 tbsp nutritional yeast

salt and ground black pepper

Mac and cheese is Dave's wife Sabrina's childhood comfort food. He has been cooking this recipe for her for years and tweaking it and finally consistently gets an 8/10 from her for it. Sabrina is a tough marker, so he's pretty pleased about this! This recipe delivers the perfect balance of really tasty and straightforward to make. We normally finish it off in the air fryer, as it is quicker and easier, but it works just as well in the oven.

Preheat: If using an oven instead of an air fryer, preheat it to 190°C fan/410°F/gas 7.

Cook the pasta: Bring a pan of salted water to the boil, cook the macaroni according to the package instructions, then drain and rinse it under cold water to cool it down and stop it cooking.

Boil the cashews: Put the cashew nuts in a small pot and cover with boiling water. Put them over a medium heat and gently simmer for 5 minutes. Drain and rinse well to remove any residue.

Prepare the cheese sauce: Put all the ingredients for the sauce in a blender, along with a teaspoon of salt and a pinch of black pepper. Blend until smooth, adjusting with a little water if it is too thick.

Prepare the breadcrumb topping: Combine the breadcrumbs with the oil, chopped fresh thyme leaves (remove the leaves from the stalk first) or dried thyme, nutritional yeast and a pinch of salt.

Combine the pasta and the sauce: In the saucepan you cooked the pasta in, mix the pasta with the cheese sauce and cook over a medium heat for a couple of minutes until it reaches your desired level of creaminess.

Assemble: Transfer the pasta mixture to a casserole dish, level it out, and evenly scatter the breadcrumb topping over it.

Bake: Bake for 10–15 minutes in the oven, or 3–5 minutes in the air fryer at 190°C/375°F, until the breadcrumbs are golden brown.

Serve: Remove from the oven or air fryer and serve your delicious mac and cheese hot and bubbling. Enjoy the rich flavours and satisfying crunch!

CREAMY SPICED BLACK BEAN QUESADILLAS

Makes 5

Cashew cheese sauce

100g cashew nuts
220ml oat milk
½ tsp garlic powder
1 tsp lemon juice

Quesadillas

½ red onion
2 scallions
1 × 400g tin of black beans
10 cherry tomatoes
small bunch of fresh coriander
1 red chilli
1 avocado
1 tbsp oil
1 tsp cumin seeds
1 tsp ground cumin
¼ tsp smoked paprika
1 tbsp tamari or soy sauce
juice of ½ a lemon or 1 lime
5 wholemeal or corn tortillas

salt and ground black pepper

Packed with a flavourful combination of black beans, a delicious cashew 'cheese' and spices, these quesadillas are a family favourite that always go down well.

Soak the cashews: Place the cashews in a bowl and cover with just-boiled water. Let soak for 5 minutes.

Prepare the vegetables and beans: Peel and thinly slice the red onion. Thinly slice the scallions at an angle. Drain and rinse the black beans. Quarter the cherry tomatoes. Finely chop the coriander and red chilli (deseed for less heat). Thinly slice the avocado.

Cook the black bean salsa: In a hot pan, add 1 tablespoon of oil and fry the onions, scallions and chilli for 2 minutes, stirring continuously. Add the cumin seeds, ground cumin, smoked paprika, tamari or soy sauce, citrus juice and a pinch of salt and pepper. Cook for 30 seconds, then add the beans and tomatoes. Cook for 2 more minutes, mashing lightly.

Make the cashew cheese sauce: Drain and rinse the soaked cashews. Place in a blender with the oat milk, garlic powder, lemon juice, and a pinch of salt and pepper, and blend until smooth.

Assemble: Heat a dry pan and warm a tortilla for 30 seconds. Spread about 3 tablespoons of cashew cheese on the tortilla, add a portion of the bean mixture on one side of the tortilla, and top with avocado slices, chopped coriander and chilli. Fold the tortilla over, cook until browned, then remove and slice. Repeat with the remaining tortillas.

Serve: Enjoy the quesadillas hot! Any remaining cashew cheese can be stored in the fridge for up to 5 days.

EASY 10-MINUTE INDIAN DHAL

Serves 2 on its own, or 4 with an accompanying grain

3 cloves of garlic
thumb-sized piece of ginger
bunch of scallions
1 × 400g tin of chickpeas
1 × 400g tin of lentils
10 cherry tomatoes
3 wholemeal pitta breads
1 tbsp oil
1 handful of baby spinach
1 × 400g tin of coconut milk
1 × 400g tin of chopped tomatoes
2 tbsp curry powder
1 tbsp tamari or soy sauce
1 tsp salt
½ tsp black pepper

To serve

1 lime
1 fresh red chilli (optional)
small bunch of fresh coriander or other fresh herb of choice

We have cooked this dish hundreds of times, and it is always well received. It's richly flavoured and deeply nourishing – and ready in just 10 minutes. Here, we serve it with toasted wholemeal pitta bread, but it's also perfect with wholemeal couscous or a pack of pre-cooked brown rice.

Preparation: Peel and finely chop the garlic and ginger. Finely chop the scallions, removing any limp outer leaves. Drain and rinse the chickpeas and lentils. Cut the cherry tomatoes in half.

Toast the pittas: Put the pitta breads in the toaster at max heat.

Cook the dhal: Heat 1 tablespoon of oil for 1 minute in a large saucepan over a high heat. Add the garlic, ginger and scallions and cook for 1 minute. Add the cherry tomatoes and cook for an additional 2 minutes.

Add the remaining ingredients: Add the chickpeas, lentils, baby spinach, coconut milk, chopped tomatoes, curry powder, tamari or soy sauce and salt and black pepper. Stir well and bring to a boil. Once boiling, reduce the heat and simmer for 2 minutes, stirring occasionally to prevent it from sticking to the bottom of the pan. Remove from the heat.

Garnish and serve: Finely chop the fresh coriander (including the stalks). Squeeze the juice of the lime over the dhal and add the coriander. Stir to combine. If desired, finely slice the chilli and sprinkle on top for added heat. Cut the toasted pitta breads into soldiers (strips) and serve them on the side of your easy dhal. Enjoy!

CAULIFLOWER CURRY BAKE

Serves 4

Sauce

3 cloves of garlic
2cm piece of fresh ginger
1 × 400g tin of coconut milk
400ml vegetable stock
1½ tbsp medium curry powder
1 tsp ground turmeric
3 tbsp tamari or soy sauce
1 tbsp maple syrup
juice of 1 lime

Veg

500g sweet potato
1 × 400g tin of black beans
6 vegan sausages, defrosted if from frozen
1 medium leek
1 head of cauliflower
2 tbsp oil
1 tbsp tamari or soy sauce
pinch of salt
10g fresh coriander, basil, flat parsley or chives

This is a really handy one-pan dish – simply prep all the veg, put them in a pan with the sauce, bake in the oven and that's it: delicious dinner ready! It's great served with rice or toast for a family dinner. You can substitute the veg here for pretty much any other veg that you have to hand.

Preheat: Preheat your oven to 200°C fan/425°F/gas 7.

Prep the sauce: Peel the garlic and ginger. Roughly chop them, place in a blender with the coconut milk, vegetable stock, curry powder, turmeric, tamari or soy, maple syrup and lime juice and blend until smooth.

Prep the veg: Cut the sweet potato into bite-sized pieces (leaving the skin on). Drain and rinse the black beans. Slice the sausages into bite-sized pieces. Slice the leek into 1–2cm rounds, washing thoroughly first to remove any hidden sediment.

Combine the veg and sauce: Place the chopped sweet potato, black beans, sliced sausages and leek into a large, deep oven dish. Pour the blended sauce over the vegetables and mix well.

Prep the cauliflower: Cut the cauliflower head into four equal-sized steaks from top to bottom. Place the steaks and any smaller pieces, including the leaves (thinly sliced), on a separate baking tray. Coat with 2 tablespoons of oil, drizzle with 1 tablespoon of tamari or soy sauce, and sprinkle with salt.

Bake: Place the casserole dish and the tray of cauliflower in the oven. Bake for 30–40 minutes, or until the sweet potato and cauliflower are tender and cooked through.

Chop the herbs: While the bake is in the oven, roughly chop your chosen fresh herb.

Garnish and serve: Once baked, remove both the dish and tray from the oven. Carefully place the roasted cauliflower steaks on top of the curry bake in the casserole dish. Garnish with the chopped herbs and serve hot.

10-MINUTE LOWER-FAT BASIL PESTO PASTA

Serves 2–4

200g of your preferred pasta
180g cherry tomatoes (optional)

Basil pesto (makes 350g)
50g fresh basil leaves
3 cloves of garlic
75ml water
75ml neutral-tasting olive oil (or sunflower oil)
juice of ½ a lime
100g roasted cashew nuts

salt and ground black pepper

Garnish
chilli flakes
pink peppercorns

We make tons of pesto (literally!) and absolutely love it. Here we use half oil, half water to make the pesto lower in fat while still tasting great. This dinner can be made in 10 minutes from scratch and is still super-satisfying and delicious.

Boil the pasta: Fill a medium-sized pot with boiling water, add a generous pinch of salt, and cook the pasta according to the package instructions.

Prep the tomatoes: While the pasta is cooking, quarter the cherry tomatoes.

Make the pesto: Pluck the basil leaves from their stalks. Peel the garlic cloves. In a blender or food processor, add the basil leaves, peeled garlic, water, oil, lime juice, roasted cashew nuts and 1 teaspoon of salt. Blend until smooth. If your blender or food processor is strong enough, you can include the basil stalks; otherwise, reserve them for another use.

Combine: Once the pasta is cooked, drain it and transfer to a frying pan or large pot. Pour the pesto over the pasta and toss until the pasta is evenly coated.

Add tomatoes and heat: Stir in the quartered cherry tomatoes, if using, and heat the mixture, making sure everything is warmed through. Taste and adjust the seasoning with additional salt, pepper or lime juice if needed.

Garnish and serve: Serve the pesto pasta hot, garnished with a sprinkle of chilli flakes and pink peppercorns for a burst of colour and flavour.

ONE-POT CREAMY TOMATO PASTA

Serves 5

1 onion
3 cloves of garlic
1 aubergine
150g mushrooms of choice
1½ tbsp oil
3 tbsp tamari or soy sauce
100ml water
2 × 400g tins of chopped tomatoes
100g tomato purée
1 tablespoon maple syrup
500ml veg stock
500ml non-dairy milk (we use oat milk)
500g wholemeal pasta (use gluten-free if you prefer)
2 tbsp nutritional yeast (optional)
small bunch of fresh basil leaves
2 tsp chilli flakes to garnish (optional)
salt and ground black pepper

This is an easy, tasty midweek dinner that also works well as a cold salad the next day if you make extra. If you are Italian, apologies upfront for cooking the pasta in the sauce in one pot, which is a big no-no in traditional Italian cooking, but it works fab here and saves on washing up! We love to serve this with a slice of delicious crusty bread which works perfectly to mop up any juices left on the plate!

Prep the veg: Peel and finely chop the onion and garlic. Slice the aubergine into small bite-sized pieces and finely chop the mushrooms.

Sauté the onion and garlic: Heat 1½ tablespoons of oil in a large saucepan over a high heat. Once the pan is warm, add the chopped onion. Cook for 3 minutes, stirring regularly, until it starts to brown.

Cook the vegetables: Add the mushrooms, garlic and aubergines to the pan. Sauté for 3–4 minutes, then add the tamari or soy sauce. Continue to cook until the tamari or soy sauce is absorbed or evaporated (about 2 minutes). Add the water and simmer for an additional 5 minutes, until the aubergine and mushrooms are soft.

Add the tomatoes and seasonings: Stir in the tinned tomatoes, tomato purée, maple syrup and ½ teaspoon of black pepper until well combined.

Add the pasta and liquids: Pour in the vegetable stock and non-dairy milk, and add the pasta. Stir well to combine.

Cook the pasta: Bring the mixture to a boil, then reduce the heat to a simmer. Leave the lid off so some of the liquid can evaporate. Stir occasionally with a wooden spoon to prevent the pasta from sticking together.

Check the pasta: Once the sauce has reduced and the pasta is cooked but still al dente (has a slight bite to it), stir in the nutritional yeast if using. Taste and add salt if needed.

Garnish and serve: Roughly tear the basil leaves and sprinkle over the pasta. If you like some heat, sprinkle some chilli flakes on top as well. Serve immediately!

SUPER-GREENS PESTO PASTA

Serves 4

150g kale (or cabbage)
100ml water
300g dried pasta of choice
100g cashew nuts
1 large or 2 small cloves of garlic
75ml sunflower oil
75ml water
juice of 1 lime or 1 lemon
salt

To serve (optional)
chilli flakes
nutritional yeast

Feast your senses on this vibrant kale-pesto pasta recipe. As the number-one most nutrient-dense food on the planet, kale infuses this dish with a powerhouse of vitamins and minerals. This is a favourite dinner in Steve's home – they all think it's still a simple basil pesto!

Prepare the kale: Remove the tough centre stalks of the kale using a knife or your hands. Roughly chop the leaves.

Steam the kale: Add about 100ml of water and a pinch of salt to a large saucepan with a lid. Add the chopped kale or cabbage, cover, and bring to a boil. Once boiling, reduce the heat to a simmer, and let the leaves steam until they are tender and slightly wilted (3–5 minutes).

Cook the pasta: Bring a large pan of salted water to a boil. Add the pasta and cook according to the package instructions. Before draining, reserve a cup of the starchy pasta water. Drain the pasta, return to the pan and set aside.

Toast the cashews: Return the pan that was used to steam the kale to a medium heat (ensure there's no water left in it first). Add the cashew nuts and toast for 5–7 minutes, stirring occasionally, until they start to turn golden and smell fragrant. Remove from the heat and set aside.

Make the pesto: Peel the garlic, then add to a food processor with the toasted cashew nuts, sunflower oil, 75ml of water, ¾ teaspoon of salt, juice of the lime or lemon and all of the steamed kale or cabbage. Blend until smooth. Taste and adjust the seasoning with additional salt or citrus juice if needed.

Combine the pasta and pesto: Add the pesto to the pan with the cooked pasta. Mix it through, adding a few tablespoons of the reserved pasta water if needed to loosen the sauce. Heat over a low heat until warmed through.

Serve: Top with chilli flakes and/or nutritional yeast if desired.

TIP: This recipe also works beautifully with other green leafy vegetables like York cabbage, savoy cabbage, cavolo nero or even chard.

CARAMELISED RED ONION AND MUSHROOM TART TATIN

15 MINS PREP · 30 MINS COOK · 45 MINS TOTAL

Serves 2–4

- 4 red onions
- 2 cloves of garlic
- 150g mushrooms (oyster mushrooms are ideal)
- 1 tbsp oil
- 3 tbsp maple syrup
- 1 tbsp balsamic vinegar
- 2 tbsp tamari or soy sauce
- 15g fresh thyme
- 200g vegan cream cheese
- 1 sheet vegan puff pastry (320g), thawed if frozen

This is super-easy to make and serves as a beautiful light meal – the caramelised onions elevate the earthy mushrooms, and the flaky puff pastry gives it an indulgent quality.

Preheat: Preheat your oven to 180°C fan/400°F/gas 6.

Prepare the vegetables: Peel the onions and cut them into fine half-moons. Peel and finely dice the garlic. Roughly chop the mushrooms into slices.

Caramelise the vegetables: Heat a large wide-bottomed frying pan over medium heat. Once hot, add 1 tablespoon of oil, followed by the onions, garlic and mushrooms. Cook for 10–15 minutes, stirring regularly, until they begin to char. To prevent sticking and to deglaze the pan, add 2–3 tablespoons of water as needed.

Create the glaze: In a mug, combine the maple syrup, balsamic vinegar and tamari or soy sauce. Stir with a fork and add to the vegetables in the pan. Allow the mixture to reduce for 1–2 minutes, stirring frequently. Remove from the heat and allow to cool slightly.

Add the thyme: Strip half the thyme leaves from the sprigs and stir them into the vegetable mixture.

Assemble the base: Line a baking tray the same size as your puff pastry sheet with baking parchment. Spread the cooked vegetable mixture evenly across the tray. Dot the vegan cream cheese in small blobs over the vegetable mixture, distributing it as evenly as possible.

Top with the pastry: If necessary, trim the puff pastry to fit the size of your baking tray. Place it over the vegetables and cream cheese, tucking in the edges.

Bake the tart: Bake in the preheated oven for 20–30 minutes, or until the pastry turns golden.

Serve: Remove the tart from the oven, and place a board larger than the pan over the top. Carefully invert the tart so the pastry is on the bottom. Garnish with the remaining thyme leaves, slice and serve warm.

WHAT we've LEARNED about FAILURE

We consider ourselves experts at failure. Our biggest failures have been tough to swallow in the moment. Our egos have taken a bruising, and tears have been shed. However, in retrospect, each failure has allowed something better to emerge: something more authentic, more fulfilling, and more closely aligned with who we are and what we stand for. Here's what we've learned about failing and trying again.

There is always a silver lining

In 2008, we had a sprout farm that grew wheatgrass and sprouts, like alfalfa. At the time in Germany there was a highly publicised E. coli outbreak linked to sprouts (which later turned out to be unfounded). As a result, the entire sprout business collapsed virtually overnight. We were devastated and unsure of what to do next.

However, during that difficult period, Steve's great sundried tomato pesto recipe, which our mom used to make in small batches for our shop, proved to be a lifeline. With the sprout business stagnating, our brother Darragh decided to try selling the pesto to local shops instead. The rest, as they say, is history.

This failure ultimately led to the birth of our thriving food products business, which has since sold over 15 million products. This experience taught us the invaluable lesson that failure, while painful in the moment, can sometimes be the catalyst for unexpected success and growth.

You can't go it alone

The expression 'If you want to go fast, go alone; if you want to go far, go together' has certainly rung true in our experience. We are brilliant at starting new projects. We are both highly creative individuals and would happily start a new business every week. This is simply how we are wired. But our team balances and tempers our blind spots. Our brother Darragh, who runs The Happy Pear, is much more structured and methodical in his approach. Paul, our finance director, as well as our dad, Donal, who helps with strategy, and Gemma, all bring a similar level of process-orientation and attention to detail.

In our experience, it takes a team with a varied and complementary skill set to truly succeed. Learning to recognise both our weaknesses and our strengths and surrounding ourselves with people who excel in the areas we struggle in has been vital on our journey.

Failure has been our greatest teacher

In 2020, we had four cafés and a central production kitchen to serve them. We had set up the central kitchen with the plan to open more cafes, because we knew it would ensure the quality of our food and enable us to scale while maintaining high standards. We had a great foundation in place to expand The Happy Pear and spread our message further.

We had a particularly successful café located in Dublin Airport that operated 4 a.m. to 9 p.m. and was

12 December 2020: our 40th birthday party on the beach

Exhausted after an all-nighter before opening our sourdough bakery

the first fully plant-based and compostable food outlet of its kind in any airport in the world. We had big dreams of opening similar cafés in other airports internationally. However, life had other plans. As we all know, 2020 brought the Covid-19 pandemic.

The pandemic forced us to close three of our cafés. We also had to shut down our central production kitchen. This brought us full circle, back to our original café and shop on Church Road in Greystones – where we had started in 2004. The hardest part was having to lay off our wonderful staff. It was a devastating blow, but one we've learned valuable lessons from.

Now, we have a leaner team of about 80 people, and we work hard to keep our businesses efficient and nimble. We've learned valuable lessons about sustainable growth and the importance of aligning our ambitions with our capabilities. True failure only occurs when you stop trying and cease learning from your experiences. Reframing failure as feedback and an opportunity to learn and grow, rather than a dead end, is a mindset that has been instrumental to our success.

You never know what life has in store

We have found time and time again that life will test you. We remember a particularly difficult day in 2013, nine years into our Happy Pear journey. We were sitting out the front of our veg shop, sharing a bowl of porridge.

At that time, we were weathering the perfect storm of financial challenges: Fridges and ovens were breaking, rents were being increased, insurance was being hiked. We were chatting over that bowl of porridge, dismayed at the prospect that this could be the end for our venture.

However, despite the setbacks, we kept going. Just a couple of months later, our first book came out. It stayed at number one in the bestseller charts for months and went on to sell over 120,000 copies.

On the rising tide of social media, our business was catapulted to an entirely new level.

The trials we faced in that difficult period proved to be the very catalyst that led to our next breakthrough. It is only by weathering life's tests and challenges that the true treasures can be unlocked. Each obstacle we've overcome has forged our resilience, tempered our resolve, and helped us to continue to take the next step.

Sometimes you just have to laugh

Of course, not every failure is as difficult as what we've mentioned here. Every day, life presents us with opportunities to see the lighter side of being human, and sometimes these 'failures' aren't opportunities for growth and introspection – they're just a chance to giggle at ourselves. In 2018, we were invited to meet Prince Charles at one of his Scottish castles. It was a private gathering, and we and some other guests were to meet him in the afternoon at an event to celebrate his work supporting organic farming and products, and then we were to attend a fancy black-tie dinner in the evening. Needless to say, we were absolutely thrilled, and dusted off our tuxedos, ready for the evening do. However, when we arrived at Edinburgh Airport in our usual casual attire of shorts, we were informed that we could not meet a prince and future king dressed so informally! We were quickly whisked off to the nearest clothing shop to buy some proper trousers before the event. Although we were slightly red-faced after committing such a faux-pas, people saw the funny side of it. (One of the memorable moments was when we showed Prince Charles our signature handstand moves while wearing our tuxedos. He good-naturedly declined to show us his handstand, explaining that in his kilt, it would not be appropriate for him to attempt!)

SHAKE BAR
The Happy Pear
The Happy Pear
open

The Happy Pear
The Happy Pear

DIN
OUR
ACTU
E

ERS
KIDS
ALLY
AT

EASY BURRITOS WITH GUACAMOLE

Serves 4

1 × 200g block of firm tofu
3 tbsp tamari or soy sauce, divided
2 tbsp nutritional yeast
1 × 400g tin of kidney beans
70ml water
3 ripe avocados
2 limes
4 large wholemeal wraps
150g cherry tomatoes
salt and ground black pepper

To serve (optional)
kimchi
spicy barbecue sauce
alfalfa sprouts
chopped fresh coriander

This has been on Dave's weekly family menu for a few years. It's easy to make, fun to eat and full of nutrient-packed ingredients – the perfect sharing food for a family dinner or a casual get-together.

Preheat: Preheat your oven to 180°C fan/400°F/gas 6 or air fryer to 180°C/360°F.

Prepare the tofu: Chop the tofu into small cubes, place in a bowl, add 2 tablespoons of tamari or soy sauce and 2 tablespoons of nutritional yeast and mix until the tofu cubes are coated. Transfer to a lined baking tray and place in the preheated oven or air fryer and bake for 10 minutes.

Prepare the kidney beans: While the tofu is baking, drain and rinse the kidney beans. Heat a wide-bottomed pan over a high heat, add the beans, a pinch of salt, and ½ teaspoon of black pepper. Cook for 2 minutes, stirring occasionally. Add 70ml of water and the remaining tablespoon of tamari or soy sauce and cook for a further minute. Mash the beans using a potato masher until they have a smooth, paste-like texture (you may need to add a little more water). Continue cooking until most of the water has been absorbed or evaporated (approximately 1 minute) and the beans are a spreadable paste-like consistency.

Make the guacamole: Halve the avocados and remove the stones. Scoop out the flesh, chop it into small pieces and transfer to a bowl. Add a pinch of salt and black pepper and the juice of the 2 limes. Mash to your desired texture using a potato masher or fork. Taste and adjust the seasoning as needed.

Toast the wraps: Place a wide-bottomed pan over a high heat. Once hot, reduce to medium. Toast each wrap on the pan for 1–2 minutes on each side, or until it starts to turn golden.

Serve: Chop the cherry tomatoes in half. Place a toasted wrap on each plate. Serve the beans, guacamole, tofu and cherry tomatoes in separate bowls in the middle of the table, allowing everyone to assemble their own burritos. Enjoy with optional kimchi, spicy barbecue sauce, alfalfa sprouts and chopped coriander.

CREAMY ROASTED-VEG PASTA BAKE

20 MINS PREP · 30 MINS COOK · 50 MINS TOTAL

Serves 6

2 red peppers
1 yellow pepper
1 aubergine
3 red onions
5 cloves of garlic
6 tbsp oil, divided
½ red chilli
2 × 400g tins of chopped tomatoes
1 tbsp maple syrup
400g wholemeal penne pasta
3 tbsp white flour
300ml oat milk
salt and ground black pepper

An easy-to-make, delicious pasta bake that really hits the spot! Steve first made this in Poland for his Polish family and they adored it. We use wholemeal penne, as it's higher in fibre, but you can use whatever pasta you have – brown rice pasta is our favourite gluten-free pasta.

Preheat the oven: Set your oven to 200°C fan/425°F/gas 7.

Prepare the veg for roasting: Deseed the the red and yellow peppers and cut them and the aubergine into bite-sized pieces. Peel and slice 2 red onions into half-moons. Peel 3 cloves of garlic. Spread the veg on two baking trays. Drizzle with 1 tablespoon of oil per tray and a pinch of salt and mix well.

Roast the vegetables: Place the trays in the oven and roast for 30 minutes, stirring once or twice, until the veggies are slightly charred at the edges.

Prepare the additional veg: Peel and finely dice the remaining red onion and 2 cloves of garlic. Deseed and finely chop the red chilli.

Start the tomato sauce: In a large pot over a medium heat, warm 1 tablespoon of oil. Add the diced onion, garlic and chilli. Cook for 4–5 minutes, until the edges of the onions char slightly and the garlic turns golden. Stir in the chopped tomatoes, 1 teaspoon of salt and the maple syrup. Bring to a boil, then simmer for 5–10 minutes, stirring regularly. Adjust the seasoning as needed and remove from the heat.

Cook the pasta: Fill a large pot with boiling water, add 1 tablespoon of salt, and cook the pasta according to the package instructions. Once cooked, drain the pasta.

Make the béchamel sauce: In a separate pot over a medium heat, add 3 tablespoons of oil. Sift in the flour and whisk continuously to make a roux. Cook for 1 minute. Gradually add the oat milk, whisking constantly. Bring to a boil and let thicken for about 3 minutes. Season with salt and pepper, and remove from the heat.

Combine pasta, tomato sauce and roasted veg: Mix the roasted vegetables with the tomato sauce and cooked pasta. Transfer to a large casserole dish (32cm × 22cm × 6cm).

Add béchamel and bake: Pour the béchamel sauce over the top of the pasta mixture and spread, leaving a little space around the edges, then bake for 10 minutes.

Serve: Enjoy this with fresh bread and a hearty salad on the side.

SPANISH CHICKPEA, POTATO AND PESTO BAKE

Serves 4

2 onions
2 large cloves of garlic
2 carrots
1 × 400g tin of chickpeas
700g potatoes, similar in size for even cooking
1 tbsp oil
2 × 400g tins of chopped tomatoes
1½ tsp smoked paprika
1 tbsp maple syrup or liquid sweetener of choice
200g pesto of choice (we prefer a spiced red pesto, but all work well!)
salt and ground black pepper

Inspired by the vibrant Jose Lopez who worked with us in the very early days, this dish features a hearty chickpea stew topped with sliced potatoes and rich pesto. It's a savoury treat that will feed your soul!

Prep the veg and chickpeas: Peel and finely chop the onions and the garlic. Thinly slice the carrots. Drain and rinse the chickpeas.

Prep the oven and potatoes: Preheat your oven to 180°C fan/400°F/gas 6. Boil a kettle of water. Cut the potatoes in half lengthwise, and place them in a medium-sized saucepan. Cover with the boiled water and add 1 tablespoon of salt. Bring to a boil, then simmer for 15 minutes until just tender but not overcooked!

Cook the veg: While the potatoes are simmering, heat a large saucepan or frying pan over high heat. Add 1 tablespoon of oil. Once the oil is hot, add the diced onions and carrots, along with a pinch of salt. Sauté for 4–5 minutes, stirring regularly, until the onions are slightly browned at the edges. Add the garlic and continue to cook for another minute, stirring constantly.

Make the chickpea stew: To the saucepan with sautéed vegetables, add the chopped tomatoes, drained chickpeas, smoked paprika, maple syrup, 2 tablespoons of the pesto, 1 teaspoon of salt and ½ teaspoon of black pepper. Bring to a boil, then cover and simmer for 10 minutes, stirring occasionally. Season with more salt or black pepper to taste if needed.

Assemble the bake: When the potatoes are done, drain them and let them cool slightly. Then slice them lengthwise into approximately 1 cm-thick slices. In a casserole dish (around 20cm × 30cm × 5cm), pour in the chickpea stew and spread out evenly. Arrange the potato slices in an even layer on top of the stew. Dollop the remaining pesto over the potatoes, and gently spread to cover.

Bake: Place the casserole dish in the preheated oven and bake for 15–20 minutes, or until the pesto and potatoes are golden and aromatic.

Serve: Serve hot, accompanied by a fresh green salad. Enjoy this colourful and savoury dish as a tribute to the joy and zest for life Jose Lopez brought into the kitchen!

ROASTED VEG LASAGNA

Serves 6

1 sweet potato
1 tbsp oil

Cashew cream sauce
150g raw cashew nuts
300ml oat milk
3 tbsp nutritional yeast (optional)
1 tsp lemon juice
½ tsp garlic powder (optional)

Tomato sauce
1 onion
3 cloves of garlic
150g mushrooms
½ red chilli
1 medium carrot
1 tbsp oil
2 tbsp tamari or soy sauce
2 × 400g tins of chopped tomatoes
100g tomato purée
1 tbsp maple syrup

salt and ground black pepper

To assemble
250g lasagna sheets

We grew up eating lasagna every week – it was one of our favourite meals. This roasted veg lasagna swaps traditional béchamel with a creamy cashew sauce and features a rich tomato sauce filled with vegetables. It's a flavourful and healthier take on the classic, perfect for satisfying your lasagna cravings.

Preheat and prep the sweet potato: Preheat the oven to 180°C fan/400°F/gas 6 or the air fryer to 180°C/350°F. Chop the sweet potato into bite-sized pieces. Season with some salt and a tablespoon of oil and toss, then place on a baking tray and roast for 20 minutes. Set aside once done.

Soften the cashews: Place the raw cashew nuts in a small pot, cover with water, and boil for 10 minutes to soften the nuts for a smooth sauce.

Prep the tomato sauce: Peel and finely chop the onion and garlic. Finely dice the mushrooms and chilli, removing the seeds if less spice is desired. Grate the carrot.

Sauté the veg for the sauce: Heat a frying pan with a tablespoon of oil over high heat. Sauté the onion and mushrooms with a pinch of salt for 6–8 minutes. Add the tamari or soy sauce and cook for another minute.

Add additional sauce ingredients: Add the carrot, garlic and chilli to the pan. Cook for 3 minutes, stirring regularly. If it starts to stick, deglaze with 2 tablespoons of water.

Combine the sauce components: Stir in the chopped tomatoes, tomato purée, maple syrup, 1 teaspoon of salt, ½ teaspoon black pepper and the roasted sweet potato. Bring to a boil, then simmer for 10 minutes. Adjust seasoning to taste.

Blend the cashew cream sauce: Drain the softened cashews and place in a blender with the oat milk, nutritional yeast, lemon juice, garlic powder, ½ teaspoon of salt and ½ teaspoon of black pepper. Blend until smooth and season to taste.

Assemble the lasagna: In a 20cm × 20cm × 5cm baking dish, layer as follows: ¼ of the cashew cream, lasagna sheets to cover (no overlap), ½ tomato and veg sauce, another layer of lasagna sheets, another ¼ of the cashew cream, then the remaining tomato and veg sauce. Finish with a final layer of lasagna sheets topped with the remaining cashew cream.

Bake and serve: Bake in the oven for 25 minutes or in the air fryer for 20 mins or until the lasagna sheets are tender. Let it rest for 5 minutes to maintain its shape, then using a scissors (this is the best way to cut lasagna, trust us!), cut into squares and serve hot.

GRANNY'S IRISH STEW

MINS PREP · MINS COOK · MINS TOTAL

Serves 6

Stew

1 large onion
3 cloves of garlic
3 carrots
4 stalks of celery
1 leek
1 parsnip
1 large tomato
1 tbsp oil
2 bay leaves
2 litres water, plus 100ml for sweating vegetables
2 tbsp tamari or soy sauce
1 tbsp dried thyme

Mushrooms

250g oyster mushrooms or other mushrooms
1 tbsp oil
3 tbsp tamari or soy sauce
1 tbsp maple syrup
Juice of ¼ lemon

Mashed potatoes

1½ kg potatoes of choice
50ml oat milk
2 tbsp oil

salt and ground black pepper

When we were little, every Sunday we went to our grandparents Granny and Jack's house, and stew was always our favourite dish. It just felt like a warm hug. This is our plant-based take on it, using compressed oyster mushrooms in place of the traditional lamb. It is the most perfect dish for a rainy day or day that you want something comforting!

Prep the vegetables: Peel and finely dice the onion and garlic. Finely dice one carrot and the celery (including the leaves). Slice the two remaining carrots into 1cm-thick rounds. Cut the leek in half lengthwise, wash thoroughly and slice into 1cm rounds. Dice the parsnip into 1cm cubes. Dice the tomato.

Cook the potatoes: Wash the potatoes and cut into even pieces, leaving the skins on. Boil a large saucepan of water, add a pinch of salt and cook the potatoes until tender, about 20 minutes. Drain, add the oat milk and oil, mash until smooth and season with salt and pepper.

Sauté the vegetables: Heat a large saucepan with 1 tablespoon of oil over a high heat. Add the onions, finely diced carrot, celery, leek, bay leaves and ½ teaspoon of salt. Cook for 4–5 minutes until the onions begin to brown. Add 100ml water, 2 tablespoons of tamari or soy sauce, garlic and thyme. Put the lid on, reduce the heat to medium and sweat for 6–7 minutes.

Add the remaining vegetables: Add the carrot rounds, parsnip, tomato, 2 litres of water, ½ teaspoon of salt and a pinch of black pepper. Bring to a boil, then simmer for 20 minutes without the lid.

Prep the mushrooms: Tear the mushrooms into chunks. Put a pan on a high heat and add 1 tablespoon of oil. Add half the mushrooms to the pan (you will need to cook them in two batches), and make sure they are evenly spread out. Place a clean saucepan on top of the mushrooms to compress them and to enhance the charring. Cook for 2–3 minutes on each side. Mix the tamari or soy sauce, maple syrup and lemon juice to make a dressing, coat the mushrooms in half the dressing and set aside. Repeat the same process with the second batch of mushrooms. Deglaze the pan with 3 tablespoons of water and add to the stew.

Combine: Add half the mushrooms to the stew, taste and check the seasoning, adjust with tamari or soy sauce if needed, then simmer for a few minutes until it reaches the desired thickness.

Serve: Add a scoop of mashed potatoes to each plate, then a ladle of stew, and top with the remaining mushrooms.

EASY HEART-WARMING RED LENTIL DHAL

Serves 4–6

300g brown rice (we prefer short grain)
2 red onions
3 cloves of garlic
½ thumb-sized piece of ginger
1 courgette
1–2 tbsp oil
400g dried red lentils
1 × 400g tin of chopped tomatoes
1 × 400g tin of coconut milk
2 litres vegetable stock
2 tsp ground cumin
pinch of chilli powder
2 tbsp mild curry powder
2 tbsp tamari or soy sauce
100g baby spinach
1 lime
small bunch of fresh coriander
salt and ground black pepper

One of our all-time favourites and go-to meals – a smooth red lentil curry (served here with brown rice) offering comfort and warmth with every spoonful! It's also low in calories yet high in vitamins, minerals and fibre. You can soak the red lentils for an hour or two beforehand to reduce the cooking time and enhance the flavour.

Cook the rice: Put the rice on to cook as per the instructions on the back of the packet.

Prep the vegetables: Peel and slice the onions. Peel and finely chop the garlic. Peel and finely chop or grate the ginger. Wash and chop the courgette.

Sauté the base flavours: In a large pot, sauté the onions, garlic, and ginger with 1–2 tablespoons of oil on a high heat, stirring regularly. Add more water as needed to prevent sticking.

Sweat the vegetables: Add the courgette to the pot with 1 teaspoon of salt and cook for 3–4 minutes, stirring occasionally.

Cook the lentils and spices: Add the lentils to the pot, along with the tin of chopped tomatoes, the coconut milk and the 2 litres of vegetable stock. Stir in the ground cumin, chilli powder, curry powder, 1 teaspoon of salt, ½ teaspoon of black pepper and tamari or soy sauce.

Simmer: Bring the mixture to a boil, then reduce the heat and simmer for 25 minutes, or until the lentils are tender and the dhal is your preferred consistency. Stir often to prevent sticking.

Add spinach and taste: Add the baby spinach and stir through – it will wilt and become creamy in a matter of minutes. Add the juice of the lime. Taste and season the dhal with more salt, pepper, chilli or lime.

Serve: Chop the fresh coriander. Serve the dhal hot with the rice, a sprinkle of the coriander on top, a few slices of toasted sourdough bread and some pickled red onion (see page 308) for a delicious meal.

Spot Ned the minion!

IKARIAN LONGEVITY STEW

Serves 6

2 onions
3 cloves of garlic
2 carrots
2 leeks
200g broccoli
100g kale
1 × 400g tin of black beans
1 × 400g tin of chickpeas
1 × 400g tin of lentils
2½ litres vegetable stock
150g dry wholemeal pasta, such as fusilli
1 × 680g jar of tomato passata or 2 × 400g tins of chopped tomatoes
100g tomato purée
2 tbsp tamari or soy sauce
chilli flakes to taste (optional)
salt and ground black pepper

This recipe is based on a stew that one of the longest-living families in the world seemingly ate every day for lunch. It's oil-free and full of beans, lentils and lots of cruciferous veg (broccoli and kale) – a great dish to nurture your immune system. We love to serve this with some delicious sourdough bread (see page 246).

Prepare the vegetables: Peel and finely dice the onions and garlic. Slice the carrots and cut the leeks into thin rounds. Cut the broccoli into small florets and finely chop the stalk, making sure to use it as well. Separate the kale leaves from the stalks, and finely chop both leaves and stalks. Drain and rinse the black beans, chickpeas and lentils.

Fry the onions: In a large pot over a high heat, add the diced onions. Cook for 3-4 minutes, stirring regularly. If they begin to stick, add 2 tablespoons of water or vegetable stock to deglaze the pot.

Cook and sweat the vegetables: Add the leeks, garlic, carrots, broccoli stalks and florets, kale stalks and a generous pinch of salt to the pot. Cook for 2 minutes, stirring regularly. Add 50ml of vegetable stock, cover with a lid, reduce the heat to low-medium and let the vegetables sweat for about 10 minutes, stirring occasionally.

Add the remaining ingredients: To the pot, add the black beans, chickpeas, lentils, pasta, tomato passata, tomato purée, tamari or soy sauce, the rest of the vegetable stock and the kale leaves. Stir to combine. With the lid on, bring the stew to a boil. Then reduce the heat to low and let it simmer for 10 minutes. Stir occasionally.

Taste and season: After simmering, taste the stew and adjust the seasoning with salt and black pepper. If you prefer a spicier stew, add some chilli flakes to your liking.

Serve: Serve the stew warm with fresh bread on the side for a hearty and nourishing meal.

TIP: This stew can also be cooked in a slow cooker. Combine all the ingredients and cook on low for 6–8 hours or on high for about 3–4 hours, until the flavours are well combined and the vegetables are tender.

EASY SPANAKOPITA – SPINACH AND FILO PASTRY PIE

Serves 4–6

60g cashew nuts
3 large leeks
2 cloves of garlic
8 tbsp olive oil, divided
450g frozen spinach
20g fresh mint leaves
2 lemons
300g firm tofu
1 tsp garlic powder
2 tbsp nutritional yeast
7 sheets of filo pastry (270g), thawed if frozen
salt and ground black pepper

This is a real hit in Steve's family. Crisp, creamy and filled with spinach and homemade feta, it's surprisingly easy to make. We make one large pie here but you could also make samosa-style individually wrapped versions.

Preheat and prep the cashews: Preheat the oven to 180°C fan/400°F/gas 6. Place the cashew nuts in a bowl, cover with boiling water, and leave to soak for 10 minutes to soften.

Prep the leeks and garlic: Chop the leeks into approximately 1 cm rounds and clean thoroughly. Peel and finely dice the garlic cloves.

Cook the leeks: Heat a wide-bottomed pan with 1 tablespoon of oil over a high heat. Once hot, add the leeks and a pinch of salt, cooking for 4–5 minutes while stirring regularly. Add the diced garlic and cook for an additional 2 minutes.

Add the spinach and steam: Reduce the heat to medium and add the frozen spinach. Cover with a lid and let it steam in its own liquid for 6–8 minutes. Remove the lid and continue to cook for another 2–3 minutes, until most of the liquid has evaporated.

Season the filling: Finely chop the mint leaves. Turn off the heat, add the mint leaves, juice of 1 lemon and ¼ teaspoon of black pepper to the leek-and-spinach mixture. Mix well, then leave to cool with the lid off to allow excess moisture to evaporate.

Make the vegan feta: Drain and rinse the soaked cashew nuts. Add them to a food processor along with the tofu, garlic powder, nutritional yeast, juice of the second lemon, 4 tablespoons of olive oil and 1 teaspoon of salt. Blend until smooth.

Combine the filling: Mix the vegan feta with the leek-and-spinach mixture until well combined. Taste and adjust the seasoning with more salt, pepper, lemon juice or mint if needed.

Assemble the pie: Spread the mixture out evenly in an ovenproof dish approximately 32cm × 22cm × 5cm. Lay the first sheet of filo pastry on top, trimming it to fit the dish. Using a pastry brush, brush the filo with some of the remaining 3 tablespoons of olive oil. Repeat this with the remaining filo sheets, layering and oiling them.

Bake the pie: Place the pie in the preheated oven, and bake for 25–30 minutes, until the filo is golden brown.

Serve: Cut the pie with scissors or a sharp knife, serve, and enjoy!

CREAMIEST VEGAN BUTTER 'CHICKEN'

Serves 4

500g oyster, shiitake or chestnut mushrooms
1 tbsp oil

Marinade

4 tbsp vegan roasted-red-pepper pesto or harissa paste
2 tsp garam masala
½ tsp ground turmeric

Sauce

50g cashew nuts
20g vegan butter
1 tbsp oil
½ tsp cumin seeds
2 whole cardamom pods
½ tsp ground turmeric
1 onion
½ thumb-sized piece of fresh ginger
2 large cloves of garlic
½ tsp garam masala
½ tsp ground cumin
½ tsp ground coriander
1 × 400g tin of chopped tomatoes
1 × 400g tin of coconut milk, cream from the top only
½ lemon

salt

To serve

15g fresh coriander
4 tbsp yoghurt

Butter chicken, also known as murgh makhani, is thought to have originated in a restaurant trying to use up leftover chicken tandoori cooked in a super-buttery creamy sauce. We do the same here, using marinated mushrooms grilled and then finished in a creamy, rich sauce – delicious served with brown rice.

Soak the cashews: Place the cashews in a bowl and cover them with just-boiled water. Let them sit for at least 10 minutes to soften.

Prep and marinate the mushrooms: Cut the mushrooms into strips. Combine the marinade ingredients in a bowl with a pinch of salt. Toss the mushroom strips in the marinade until well coated.

Fry the mushrooms: Heat 1 tablespoon of oil in a large frying pan over high heat. Once hot, add the marinated mushrooms and cook for 10 minutes, stirring regularly, until they start to char and turn golden. Remove from the pan and set aside. If your pan is small you may have to cook them in two batches to ensure they are properly cooked.

Start the butter sauce: In the same pan where you cooked the mushrooms, melt the vegan butter with 1 tablespoon of oil over a medium heat. Scrape up any leftover bits from the mushrooms to flavour the sauce. Add the cumin seeds, cardamom pods and turmeric. Cook for 1 minute, until fragrant.

Prep and sauté the onion and spices: Peel and dice the onion. Peel and finely chop the garlic. Peel and grate or finely dice the ginger. Add the onion to the pan along with ¾ teaspoon of salt and cook for 4–5 minutes until softened. Add the ginger and garlic and cook for another minute, stirring constantly. Add the remaining spices and cook for 1 minute.

Simmer the sauce: Add the chopped tomatoes and the top layer of cream from the coconut milk tin. Stir until combined then bring to a boil and simmer for 1 minute.

Blend the sauce: Drain and rinse the soaked cashews and add them to the sauce. Blend using an immersion blender or carefully transfer the mixture to a blender or food processor and blend until smooth.

Finish the sauce: Return the blended sauce to the pan. Add the mushrooms and heat through. Taste and adjust the seasoning with more salt, if needed, and the juice of ½ a lemon.

Serve: Accompany this with your favourite rice or naan. Garnish with fresh coriander and a tablespoon of yoghurt to serve.

ROASTED CARROT FALAFEL WITH TAHINI DRIZZLE

Serves 4

Falafel
400g carrots
1 × 400g tin of chickpeas
2–3 medium cloves of garlic
20g fresh coriander
3 tbsp light tahini
2 tsp ground cumin
pinch of chilli powder (optional)
2 lemons

Tahini drizzle
8 tbsp tahini
3 tbsp lemon juice
1 small clove of garlic
2 tbsp olive oil
2–6 tbsp water, as needed

salt and ground black pepper

To serve
4 wholemeal pitta breads

Suggested accompaniments
hummus (see page 262)
avocado slices
kimchi (see page 300)
spiced pesto or chilli sauce

Enjoy these delicious air-fryer or oven-baked falafels, with homemade tahini drizzle, perfect for stuffing into pitta breads or folding up in wraps for a family dinner. Double the batch and freeze some for an effortless future meal.

Preheat: Preheat your oven to 200°C fan/425°F/gas 7 or air fryer to 200°C/400°F.

Prepare the carrots: Slice the carrots into 1cm rounds and spread them out on a lined baking tray. Season with 1 teaspoon of salt and toss to coat. Bake for 20 minutes in the air fryer or 25 minutes in the oven, until the edges begin to char and they are fully cooked.

Make the falafel mix: Drain and rinse the chickpeas. Peel the garlic cloves and chop them finely. Chop the coriander, including the stalks, as finely as possible. In a food processor, combine the tahini, prepared garlic, coriander, chickpeas, ground cumin, 1 teaspoon of black pepper, chilli powder if using and the juice of the 2 lemons. Add the roasted carrots once they're ready, and process everything until the mixture is well combined, adding a bit of water if needed to get the right consistency.

Shape and cook the falafels: Shape the mixture into small patties, about the size of half a lime – you should get 10–15. Place the falafels on a lined tray and bake in the oven or air fryer for 10–15 minutes until they are nicely browned and crispy.

Make the tahini drizzle: Whisk together the tahini and lemon juice in a bowl. The mixture will thicken initially. Finely mince the clove of garlic and stir in with the olive oil, then season with ¼ teaspoon of salt. Gradually add water until the desired consistency is reached, adjusting the seasoning to taste with more salt or lemon juice if desired.

Serve: Toast the pitta breads and stuff with the falafel and some tahini drizzle, as well as your choice of additional accompaniments.

CREAMY MUSHROOM PUFF PASTRY PIE

Serves 4

400g mushrooms
1 medium leek
1 small sweet potato
1 medium potato
3 cloves of garlic
1 tbsp oil
150ml white wine
1 × 320g roll of vegan puff pastry, thawed if frozen
50ml non-dairy milk (for brushing pastry)

Béchamel sauce

8 tbsp oil (120ml)
8 tbsp flour (65g)
1 tsp garlic powder
1½ tbsp Dijon or wholegrain mustard
2 tbsp nutritional yeast (optional)
800ml oat milk (or non-dairy milk of choice)

salt and ground black pepper

This pie is the epitome of comfort food, featuring savoury mushrooms, root vegetables and leeks enveloped in a creamy mustard sauce, all topped with a flaky puff pastry crust. An ideal hearty meal for the whole family, this dish pairs wonderfully with peas and mashed potatoes.

Preheat: Set your oven to 200°C fan/425°F/gas 7.

Prepare the veg: Finely chop the mushrooms. Clean the leek and slice into 1 cm-thick rounds. Chop the sweet potato and potato into bite-sized pieces, leaving the skin on. Peel the garlic and finely chop.

Cook the veg: Heat 1 tablespoon of oil in a wide-bottomed pan on a high heat. Once hot, add the leek, mushrooms and garlic with ½ teaspoon of salt. Cook for 4–5 minutes, stirring regularly. Add half the white wine to deglaze the pan. Add the potatoes and remaining wine along with another ½ teaspoon of salt, and cover. Reduce heat to low-medium and steam for about 8–10 minutes, stirring occasionally or until the potatoes are tender. Remove from the heat.

Make the béchamel sauce: In a separate saucepan on a high heat, add the oil. Sift in the flour then cook, whisking constantly, for 1 minute. Add 1 teaspoon salt, ¼ teaspoon black pepper, garlic powder and mustard (and nutritional yeast if using). Gradually whisk in the oat milk. Bring to a boil, then simmer for 3–4 minutes, whisking regularly, till it reaches a creamy consistency. Season to taste with more salt and black pepper.

Combine the sauce and veg: Mix the béchamel sauce into the cooked vegetables. Transfer this mixture into a casserole or pie dish.

Prepare the pastry: Lay the puff pastry over the dish. Crimp the edges with a fork to seal. Score a criss-cross pattern on top with a knife, without cutting through. Pierce a small hole in the centre, then brush with non-dairy milk.

Bake the pie: Place the pie in the oven, and bake for 25 minutes until golden and crisp.

Serve: Let the pie cool slightly before serving with peas and mashed potatoes.

‘STEAK’ AND KIDNEY PIE

Serves 6

2 × 320g sheets of vegan puff pastry, defrosted if frozen
800ml vegetable stock
1 tsp garlic powder
400g mixed mushrooms (oyster, shiitake, chestnut)
2 medium onions
4 cloves of garlic
1 small carrot
4 sprigs of fresh thyme
1 × 400g tin of kidney beans
8 tbsp olive oil (120ml – 30ml for veg & 90ml for béchamel)
3 tbsp tamari or soy sauce
½ tsp smoked paprika
2 bay leaves
6 tbsp white flour (50g)
50ml non-dairy milk
salt and ground black pepper

This is our take on the classic English pie, where we use mushroom ‘steak’ and kidney beans in a rich, creamy umami sauce with a crispy puff pastry casing. Steak and kidney pie is often served with a pint of beer and a football match, but this is best with kombucha and some yoga on the side!

Preheat: Set the oven to 200°C fan/425°F/gas 7.

Blind bake the bottom crust: Line a pie dish with pastry, cover with baking parchment, weigh down with dried beans, and bake for 15 minutes. Remove the beans and parchment, bake for an additional 5 minutes, then cool.

Prepare the vegetable stock: Combine the vegetable stock and garlic powder.

Prepare the vegetables and beans: Slice the mushrooms thinly. Peel and finely chop the onions and garlic. Chop the carrot into small pieces. Pick the thyme leaves from the stems. Drain and rinse the kidney beans.

Sauté the mushroom mixture: Heat 1½ tablespoons of olive oil in a large pan over high heat. Add the sliced mushrooms, chopped onions, carrots and garlic with a pinch of salt and pepper. Flatten with another pan and cook for 3–4 minutes, then reduce the heat to medium and cook for 6–10 minutes, until the liquid evaporates. Add 1 tablespoon of tamari or soy sauce, smoked paprika, bay leaves and the kidney beans, cook for another 2 minutes, then remove from the heat.

Make the sauce: In a separate saucepan over a medium heat, whisk 6 tablespoons of olive oil and flour to make a paste. Gradually add in the seasoned vegetable stock and let it thicken, stirring continuously. Bring to a boil and simmer for 2–3 minutes, then stir in 2 tablespoons of tamari or soy sauce. Season with salt and pepper to taste.

Combine the sauce and mushroom mixture: Pour the sauce into the pan with the mushrooms and kidney beans, stirring well to combine.

Fill the pie: Fill the blind-baked pastry base with the mixture, leaving some space at the top. Cover with the other sheet of pastry, seal the edges, crimping together with a fork, and poke some fork holes in the top.

Brush with non-dairy milk and bake: Brush non-dairy milk over the top crust with a pastry brush. Place the pie in the oven and bake for 25–30 minutes, or until the pastry is golden brown.

Serve: Serve this savoury pie hot, paired with your favourite salad for a complete meal.

SHEPHERDLESS PIE

Serves 4–6

Lentil and vegetable filling

2 onions
3 cloves of garlic
1 carrot
1 parsnip
10 fine beans
2 × 400g tins of lentils
1 tbsp oil
2 × 400g tins of chopped tomatoes
1 tsp smoked paprika
2 bay leaves
1 tbsp maple syrup
2 tbsp tamari or soy sauce

Mashed potato topping

1½ kg potatoes
100ml oat milk
3 tbsp olive oil

salt and ground black pepper

Garnish

few sprigs of fresh thyme

Growing up, shepherd's pie was one of our favourite dishes on a cold winter's evening. This is our 'shepherdless' version, and it's the most popular main course in our range of food products. It's super easy to make, and if you want to make it a little richer, add some grated cheese to the top before baking.

Prep the veg: Preheat the oven to 200°C fan/425°F/gas 7. Peel the onions and garlic and finely dice. Chop the carrot, parsnip and fine beans into bite-sized pieces. Drain and rinse the lentils. Cut the potatoes into even, bite-sized pieces for even boiling, leaving the skins on.

Cook the potatoes: Fill a large saucepan with boiling water. Add the chopped potatoes and 1 tablespoon of salt. Bring to a boil, then reduce to a simmer, and cook for 20 minutes or until soft. Drain and set aside.

Sauté the aromatics and veg: Heat a large saucepan over a medium heat, add 1 tablespoon of oil, and sauté the onions for 5–6 minutes, until lightly browned. Add the garlic, chopped vegetables and lentils with a pinch of salt. Cover and sweat for 5 minutes, stirring occasionally. If necessary, add 2 tablespoons of water to prevent sticking.

Make the lentil-vegetable filling: Stir in the chopped tomatoes, 1 teaspoon of salt, ½ teaspoon of black pepper, the smoked paprika, bay leaves, maple syrup and tamari or soy sauce. Mix well, bring to a boil, then reduce the heat to medium, and simmer for 5–6 minutes. Remove from the heat and adjust the seasoning to taste.

Mash the potatoes: To the boiled and drained potatoes, add the oat milk, 3 tablespoons of olive oil, 1 teaspoon of salt, and ½ teaspoon of black pepper. Mash until smooth and adjust the seasoning to taste.

Assemble the pie: In a casserole dish, add all the lentil filling, ⅔ of the way up the dish, then top with the mashed potato, spreading evenly.

Texture the topping: Use a fork to create ridges on the mashed potato topping for a crispy finish.

Bake: Bake in the preheated oven for 15 minutes, or until the potato topping is golden.

Garnish and serve: Remove the thyme leaves from their stalks and sprinkle over the cooked pie. Serve hot with your favourite salads.

TIP: Top the potato with 100g of your favourite pesto before baking to take it to the next level!

CRISPY TOFU AND MUSHROOM RAMEN

Serves 4

Pickled radish

5 medium radishes
50ml vinegar

Broth

1 onion
2 cloves of garlic
½ thumb-sized piece of ginger
1 bunch of scallions
1 red chilli
1 tbsp sesame oil
1 tbsp finely chopped dried seaweed (for example, hijiki)
2 litres vegetable stock
15g fresh coriander, plus extra for serving
2 cinnamon quills
1 star anise pod
3 tbsp tamari or soy sauce
1 tbsp miso paste
8g dried mushrooms – for example, porcini or shiitake
300g noodles

Crispy tofu and mushrooms

200g fresh mushrooms – for example, oyster mushrooms
200g firm tofu
1 tbsp oil
2 tbsp tamari or soy sauce
1 tbsp coconut sugar or brown sugar
1 tsp mirin or vinegar of choice

salt and ground black pepper

To serve

2 tbsp sesame seeds

It was a long way from ramen that we grew up, but this is a dish that Steve's family all love – there's something fun and comforting about slurping noodles together! This makes a beautiful light meal, packed with flavour and nutrition. We crisp some firm tofu and mushrooms, add them to an aromatic umami broth with noodles and serve with some pickled radish – it's a great dish!

Pickle the radish: Thinly slice the radishes and place in a jar. Cover with 50ml of vinegar, add a pinch of salt, and top up with water to ensure the radishes are covered. Set aside to pickle while you prepare the rest of the dish.

Preheat: Preheat your oven to 180°C fan/400°F/gas 6.

Prepare the vegetables: Peel and finely dice the onion and garlic. Peel and grate the ginger. Finely chop the white part of the scallions and half of the red chilli. Set aside the green parts of the scallions and the other half of the chilli for garnish.

Make the broth: Heat a large pot over a high heat. Add the sesame oil, then the onion, garlic, ginger, white part of the scallions, chilli, dried seaweed and a pinch of salt, and sauté for 3–4 minutes. Add a bit of vegetable stock to deglaze the pan if anything starts to stick. Finely chop the coriander stalks and add them to the pot. Pour in the vegetable stock, and add the cinnamon quills, star anise pod, tamari or soy sauce, miso, and dried mushrooms. Stir well, bring to a boil, then simmer for 5 minutes. Adjust the seasoning with more tamari or soy sauce, salt or black pepper as needed.

Bake the tofu and mushrooms: Slice the mushrooms and cube the tofu. Toss with the oil, spread on a baking tray and bake for 10 minutes, shaking occasionally. Mix 2 tablespoons of tamari or soy sauce, the coconut or brown sugar and the mirin or vinegar in a bowl. Coat the baked tofu and mushrooms in this mixture, then bake for another 10 minutes until crispy. Set aside.

Cook the noodles: Cook the noodles according to the package instructions. Drain and rinse to prevent sticking.

Prepare the garnishes: Finely chop the green parts of the scallions, the remaining coriander leaves and the remaining half of the red chilli.

Assemble and serve: Divide the noodles among four bowls. Ladle the hot broth over the noodles. Top with the crispy tofu and mushrooms, then garnish with the chopped scallions, chilli, sesame seeds and pickled radish.

20 WAYS to eat MORE VEG (and to get your kids to eat MORE VEG!)

1 Start with fruit, as it is sweeter – seasonal fruit typically has more flavour than fruit out of season.

2 Try porridge in the morning instead of cereal, and be creative with the toppings – try berries, granola, caramelised banana, nut butter (see page 32 for ideas)!

3 For someone who struggles to eat veg, blend it into a smooth soup. See pages 50–67 for great soup recipes that we have been making for decades!

4 Make a smoothie. Dave makes a big smoothie for his teenage daughter every morning before school. He uses frozen berries, blueberries, banana, almond butter, seeds, Carrageen moss (for healthy skin) and a little apple juice and water. You can also add in something green, like spinach or avocado, to a fruit smoothie.

5 Add avocado or cherry tomatoes as part of a dinner. They will amp up the nutrients, colour and freshness.

6 Add tinned beans or chickpeas to a curry to up the fibre content. Beans are also high in protein, a great source of energy and one of the most consumed foods of the longest-living populations in the world – they make up about 50 per cent of their calories!

7 Have a spoonful or two of hummus alongside your dinner – it's packed with chickpeas and other goodness.

8 Think international cuisines such as Thai or Mexican – they lend themselves really well to veg-centred eating.

9 Bulk roast sweet potatoes in the oven or air fryer, store them in the fridge, and eat them for a couple of days as part of your dinner – they're easy to eat and tasty.

10 Eat dried fruit if you don't like fresh fruit – it's packed with nutrients. Just make sure to brush your teeth, as the fructose can stick to the enamel of your teeth and encourage tooth decay.

11 Use lentils – they are full of protein, fibre and other nutrients and are really inexpensive. Our favourites are red lentils – try the red lentil dhal on page 148 or the nourishing lentil soup on page 67.

12 Expand your definition of salad! Instead of just thinking of it as lettuce, tomato and cucumber, try some of the salads in this book, such as the black bean, roasted sweet potato and avocado salad on page 76.

13 Make a plant-based burger with blended cooked veg, beans and grated root veg (see page 107). No one will know what's in it with all the sauces and condiments, so it's a great way to sneak veg in.

14 Roast drained tinned chickpeas or beans in the air fryer with some tamari and nutritional yeast for 10 minutes and serve as a side for a crispy way of getting some nutrients in.

15 Add some frozen spinach to any soups, chillies, stews, curries or dhals to bump up the nutrient profile.

16 Eat sprouts such as broccoli or alfalfa – they're believed to be 10–30 times more nutritious than the healthiest veg by weight and are easy to add to any sandwich or alongside your dinner.

17 Choose whole grains instead of white grains – e.g. brown rice instead of white rice and wholemeal couscous instead of regular white couscous. Use wholemeal pasta instead of white pasta – it's higher in fibre, much better for your microbiome and a really easy switch. (We know it's not technically veg but it's a healthier choice nonetheless!)

18 Start by making one meal a week plant-based, and make it an easy one that you know you and your family will eat, such as creamy mushroom linguine (see page 112) or one-pot creamy tomato pasta (see page 124).

19 Try making some fermented foods – they are literally homemade probiotics that can build up your gut health and immune system and cost pennies to make. Sauerkraut and basic ferments are the easiest to start with (see pages 294–314).

20 Involve your kids in the cooking and preparation of food – that way they'll be more invested in it and more likely to be curious to try it. Encourage your kids to help grow some veg, herbs or even fruit, as they will be more likely to try it. Steve's son Ned helps grow strawberries and carrots and as a result is much more likely to eat these.

All the baby Pears:
our kids, May, Elsie,
Theo, Izzy, Ned, Fionn
and baby Fia.

DARE TO
DREAM BIG
FARM
FIRE CIDER
Menu
Mezze Platter
(Hummus, Baba Ganoush, Mohammara,
Zhoug, Shirazi (cucumber, + walnut salad)
Homemade Pitta Bread
Main
Fire-Roasted Aubergine, Tahini, Tabbouleh
Torshi Makhloot (pickled Vegetables)
Za'atar Spiced roasted Cauliflower
with Toum (lebanese garlic + lemon sauce)
Dessert
Baklava + Muhallebi
Tea + Coffee

We are PART of NATURE
The Happy Pear
Granola

STE
MEA
IMP

E’S
S TO
ESS

GOLDEN ROASTED CAULIFLOWER STEAKS WITH TAHINI CREAM

Serves 2–4

Cauliflower

1 cauliflower
1 tbsp ground turmeric
2 tbsp oil
2 tbsp cumin seeds

Tahini cream

500g natural soy yoghurt
8 tbsp light tahini
juice of 1 lemon

Glaze

2 tbsp tamari or soy sauce
1 tbsp maple syrup
3 tbsp oil
½ tbsp smoked paprika

salt

To serve

fresh coriander or flat parsley
1 pomegranate

Cauliflower can still be seen as a bland veg – we used to hate it growing up – but this dish will change all that. It makes a wonderful centrepiece dish that is packed with flavour and is surprisingly filling as well as beautiful. We served this as part of a fancy plant-based feast we cooked for 150 people in Zakynthos in Greece and it was adored!

Prep the cauliflower: Wash and cut the cauliflower into quarters, including the leaves.

Boil the cauliflower: Place the cauliflower and leaves in a pot of boiling water with a good pinch of salt and turmeric. Simmer until al dente, about 8–10 minutes, then drain.

Make the tahini cream: Stir the soy yoghurt, tahini, lemon juice and a pinch of salt together in a bowl to create the cream.

Sear the cauliflower: Heat a wide-bottomed pan on a high heat and add 2 tablespoons of oil. Once hot, add in the cumin seeds and carefully place the cooked cauliflower on top, cut side down, and cook on each cut side until golden brown in the centre, about 3–4 minutes on each side.

Make the glaze: Mix the tamari or soy sauce, maple syrup, oil and smoked paprika together in a small bowl for the glaze.

Prep the garnish: Chop the coriander or parsley and deseed the pomegranate.

Assemble and serve: Spread some tahini cream on each plate, place a quarter cauliflower on top, drizzle with the glaze, and garnish with some pomegranate seeds and coriander or parsley.

MUSHROOM AND PUMPKIN WELLINGTON WITH REDCURRANT JUS

Serves 6

Almonds
200g almonds
2 tbsp tamari or soy sauce
2 tbsp maple syrup

Wellington
1 leek
2 cloves of garlic
200g oyster mushrooms
10 medium sage leaves
10 sprigs of fresh thyme
200g pumpkin
200g cooked chestnuts
1 tbsp oil
3 tbsp tamari or soy sauce
pinch of salt
½ tsp black pepper
150g cooked couscous
2 × 320g sheets vegan puff pastry, defrosted if frozen
2 tbsp oat milk or non-dairy milk of choice

Redcurrant jus
100g fresh redcurrants
4 tbsp maple syrup
200ml red wine
1 tbsp balsamic vinegar
500ml vegetable stock

This Wellington is a stunning centrepiece, perfect for any festive occasion, such as Christmas dinner. The savoury filling encased in flaky puff pastry pairs beautifully with the tangy and sweet redcurrant jus, making it a hit for any gathering. Serve with roasted veggies for a complete meal. This recipe makes 2 Wellingtons.

Roast the almonds: Preheat the oven to 200°C fan/425°F/gas 7. Roughly chop or crush the almonds, then spread on a baking tray. Drizzle with 2 tablespoons of tamari or soy sauce and 2 tablespoons of maple syrup, and roast for 10 minutes.

Prepare the veg: Slice the leek and wash thoroughly. Peel and dice the garlic. Roughly chop the mushrooms. Remove the sage leaves and thyme leaves from their stalks, and finely chop the sage. Grate the flesh of the pumpkin, discarding the skin and the seeds. Roughly chop the cooked chestnuts.

Cook the filling: Heat a large pan, add 1 tablespoon of oil, and sauté the leek for 3–4 minutes, stirring occasionally. Add the garlic, mushrooms, grated pumpkin and a pinch of salt, and cook for a further 7–10 minutes. Stir in the chestnuts, tamari or soy sauce, thyme, sage, and black pepper, and cook for 3–4 minutes, stirring regularly. Remove from the heat and mix in the cooked couscous and roasted almonds. Adjust the seasoning to taste.

Assemble the Wellingtons: Lay out one sheet of puff pastry on a piece of baking parchment. Place half of the filling in the centre lengthwise, leaving space at the edges. Compact the filling to help it hold its shape. Fold the pastry over the filling, connecting in the centre. Brush with a little water or oat milk and press the join together, sealing it, and then trim any excess. Once the Wellington is sealed, carefully roll it over so that the seam is at the bottom. Tuck and seal both ends. Lift the baking parchment with the Wellington and place on a baking tray. Cut out decorations from any leftover pastry, if you like. Gently score the pastry in a criss-cross pattern (ensuring not to cut through the pastry) and place any pastry decorations on top. Brush with oat milk. Repeat this process with the second sheet of pastry to make the second Wellington.

Bake the Wellingtons until golden: Bake in the preheated oven for 30–45 minutes, until golden. →

Make the redcurrant jus: Combine the redcurrants, maple syrup, red wine, balsamic vinegar and vegetable stock in a saucepan. Put on a high heat and bring to a boil. Whisk to break down the currants. Once boiling, reduce to a simmer and cook until it reduces by about ⅔, which will likely take over 20 minutes.

Serve: Use a serrated knife to slice the Wellingtons. Serve with the redcurrant jus and your choice of roasted vegetables. Enjoy!

TIP: If fresh redcurrants are unavailable, you can use 2 tablespoons of redcurrant jelly instead of the currants and maple syrup. And if cooked chestnuts are unavailable, just use 200g of cashew nuts instead.

hey! Did you know
our organic farm
veg is grown on
our own farm in
Kilcoole.
we think it's
forking excellent.
come and try
it out!!

MUSHROOM BOURGUIGNON WITH PUMPKIN AND MASH

Serves 4–6

400g mixed mushrooms (we used portobello, chestnuts and oyster mushrooms)
2 tbsp tamari or soy sauce
1 tsp smoked paprika
4 tbsp oil, divided
1 small pumpkin, about 500g
4 large shallots
3 cloves of garlic
1 large carrot
3 sticks of celery
2 medium tomatoes or 1 × 400g tin of chopped tomatoes
750g potatoes
50ml oat milk or non-dairy milk of choice
3 sprigs of thyme, leaves picked
2 bay leaves
500ml red wine
2 tbsp maple syrup
30ml water
salt and ground black pepper

When we were kids this was one of our dad's big dishes – the whole house would smell of wine, which we thought was so strange! Originally a French beef stew, braised in red wine and garnished with shallots, here we use a selection of mushrooms instead, which give a wonderful texture and depth of flavour.

Preheat: Preheat the oven to 200°C fan/425°F/gas 7.

Prep and bake the mushrooms: Rip up the oyster mushrooms, slice the portobello mushrooms, and quarter the chestnut mushrooms – we want a variety of texture here. Add them to a bowl along with the tamari or soy sauce, smoked paprika, 1 tablespoon of oil, a pinch of salt and a pinch of black pepper, and mix well. Add to a baking tray and bake for 15 minutes. Remove and leave to cool.

Prep and bake the pumpkin: Carefully cut the pumpkin into bite-sized cubes, leaving the skin on and ensuring to remove the seeds and innards. Add to a baking tray along with a pinch of salt and a drizzle of oil. Bake for 20 minutes, until soft.

Prep the rest of the veg: While the mushrooms and pumpkin are in the oven, peel and slice the shallots into quarters lengthwise, and peel and finely dice the garlic. Dice the carrot and celery into 1cm cubes. Dice the tomatoes, if using fresh, into small pieces.

Boil and mash the potatoes: Cut the potatoes into small pieces. Add to a large saucepan, along with a generous pinch of salt. Cover with just-boiled water, bring to a boil, then simmer until the potatoes are soft and well cooked. Drain and mash them with 1 teaspoon of salt, a pinch of black pepper, 50ml of oat milk and 2 tablespoons of oil until smooth and creamy.

Fry the shallots and veg: When the potatoes are cooking, heat a large casserole dish or saucepan with a lid on high heat. Once hot, add 1 tablespoon of oil along with the shallots and fry for 3–4 minutes. Add the garlic, carrot and celery along with a pinch of salt and the thyme and bay leaves. Put the lid on and leave to cook for 3–4 minutes.

Deglaze: Remove the lid, add in the red wine and deglaze the pan, incorporating any of the stuck bits into the sauce, stirring well.

Add the veg and season: Add in the chopped tomatoes, mushrooms, baked pumpkin, maple syrup and 30ml of water. Bring to a boil and reduce to a simmer. Taste and adjust the seasoning to your liking.

Serve: Place a big dollop of mash on each plate and lots of luscious bourguignon on top.

MUSHROOM STEAK AND PEPPER SAUCE

Serves 2

Peppercorn sauce

5 green or assorted peppercorns
1 shallot
1 tsp oil
50ml red wine
100ml vegetable stock
1 tbsp miso
2 tbsp coconut cream
1 tsp maple syrup

Dressing

2 tbsp miso
1 tbsp maple syrup
1 tbsp red wine vinegar
1 tsp garlic powder

Mushrooms

1 tbsp oil
400g flush of oyster or maitake mushrooms

salt and ground black pepper

A friend who works with us, Steffan, recently started growing oyster mushrooms and came in with an amazing flush of them which inspired this dish. It is a gourmet take on the classic steak and pepper sauce, perfect for highlighting the taste of freshly harvested mushrooms, with their texture becoming tender and their flavour intensifying when cooked just right. These go wonderfully with some freshly cooked chips.

Prepare the peppercorn sauce: Heat a medium saucepan on a high heat. Toast the peppercorns for 3–4 minutes. Remove from the pan into a pestle and mortar and grind till smooth. Alternatively, use ⅓ teaspoon freshly ground pepper. Peel and finely dice the shallot. Put the same saucepan back on a high heat, add 1 teaspoon of oil and the shallot, and sauté for 3–4 minutes, stirring regularly. Deglaze the pan with red wine, then cook until the wine virtually evaporates. Add the vegetable stock and 1 tablespoon of miso, and bring to a boil. Stir in the coconut cream and a pinch of salt. Reduce the heat, cook for a further minute and season with the ground peppercorns and maple syrup. Blend until smooth and keep warm.

Make the dressing: Combine 2 tablespoons of miso, the maple syrup, red wine vinegar and garlic powder in a saucepan. Put on a high heat, bring to a boil and reduce for 1–2 minutes, then remove from the heat.

Cook the mushrooms: Put a griddle pan on a high heat, add 1 tablespoon of oil, and mix it around to coat the pan. Add in the mushrooms and, using another clean saucepan, press down on it to compress it and leave the pan there. This will encourage more evaporation of the liquid from the mushroom, which will concentrate the flavour and give it a more tender texture. It will also give more char. Cook until golden on both sides, about 3–4 minutes, seasoning with salt. Brush one side with the mushroom dressing, cook for a further 1 minute, then flip and repeat. The mushroom should look darker in colour, like a thin steak, and have lovely griddle lines.

Serve: Divide the mushroom steak between 2 plates with the peppercorn sauce on the side. Accompany with freshly cooked chips or French fries.

CREAMY HARISSA AUBERGINE WITH ZHOUG

Serves 2

2 aubergines, approximately 300g each
4 tbsp olive oil
2 tbsp tamari or soy sauce

Harissa paste
3 red chillies
8 sundried tomatoes (30g)
40g almonds
2 cloves of garlic
4 tbsp oil
2 tbsp water

Avocado salsa
1 avocado
100g cherry tomatoes
15g fresh coriander
¼ red onion
1 tbsp olive oil

Zhoug
2 cloves of garlic, peeled
20g fresh coriander
1 green chilli
½ tsp ground cardamom
1 tsp ground cumin
75ml oil
juice of ½ a lemon
½ tsp salt
pinch of black pepper
pinch of chilli flakes

Tahini cream
300ml soy yoghurt
4 tbsp tahini
juice of ½ a lemon

salt

We had a fancy dinner party recently and this went down a treat. With the creamy aubergine, spicy harissa, aromatic zhoug, refreshing avocado salsa and topped with lush tahini cream, this meal combines so many delicious textures and flavours. Perfect for a flavourful and satisfying dinner!

Prepare the aubergines: Preheat the oven to 220°C fan/475°F/gas 9. Cut the aubergines in half lengthwise, and cut into the flesh with a knife to create a checkerboard effect, but being careful not to cut through the skin. Line a baking tray with parchment, sprinkle with salt, and place the aubergine halves on it, flesh facing up – the salt on the parchment will help draw more moisture out of the aubergine. Mix 4 tablespoons of olive oil with 2 tablespoons of tamari or soy sauce. Using a pastry brush, brush the aubergine halves with the oil and tamari mixture, ensuring it seeps into the cuts. Bake in the preheated oven for 25 minutes.

Make the harissa: Chop the tops off the chillies, slice them lengthwise, and leave the seeds in. Place on a baking tray and roast for about 10–12 minutes, until the edges begin to char. Meanwhile, soak the sundried tomatoes and almonds in boiling water. Once the chillies are roasted, drain the tomatoes and almonds. Peel the garlic cloves. Add the chillies, drained tomatoes, almonds and peeled garlic to a food processor with 4 tablespoons of oil, 1½ teaspoons of salt and 2 tablespoons of water. Blend until fairly smooth, but leaving some texture – you don't want it too homogenous.

Finish the aubergines: After 25 minutes of baking, remove the aubergines from the oven. Smear the harissa paste evenly over each half. Return to the oven and bake for an additional 10 minutes.

Prepare the avocado salsa: Halve and pit the avocado, scoop out the flesh and dice. Quarter the cherry tomatoes. Finely chop the fresh coriander. Peel and finely dice the red onion. In a bowl, mix the avocado, tomatoes, coriander and red onion with 1 tablespoon of olive oil and a sprinkle of salt.

Make the zhoug: Blend all the zhoug ingredients until smooth. Taste and adjust the seasoning as needed.

Prepare the tahini cream: In a bowl, combine the soy yoghurt, tahini, lemon juice and a pinch of salt. Adjust the seasoning to taste.

Assemble and serve: Spread some of the tahini cream on each plate, then drizzle some zhoug over it. Place the baked aubergine on top, and serve with avocado salsa on the side or some pickled red onions for contrast (see page 308).

VEGAN HOISIN 'DUCK' PANCAKES

Serves 2 (makes 6 pancakes)

250g oyster mushrooms

Hoisin marinade

3 tbsp tahini
5 tbsp water
1 tbsp miso paste
3 tsp brown sugar
1 tsp Chinese 5 spice
½ tsp chilli powder
2 tbsp rice wine vinegar
2 tbsp tamari or soy sauce

Pancakes

150g plain flour
300ml water
2 tsp ground flaxseeds
6 tsp sunflower oil for frying

Garnish

½ medium cucumber
3 scallions
1 small red chilli
pickled cucumber (see page 309)
1 tbsp sesame seeds

One day when filming for YouTube, Steve wanted to try to recreate an old favourite of his growing up. We seldom ate out as kids, but Steve distinctly remembers eating a hoisin duck pancake as a kid and adoring it. Here we use oyster mushrooms as the carrier for the wonderful hoisin flavour. They crisp up lovely when baked or fried and contrast so well with the soft Chinese-style pancakes. They're pretty simple to make, and you'll return to them many a day as they're so tasty!

Preheat: Preheat the oven to 180°C fan/400°F/gas 6.

Prep and marinate the mushrooms: Slice the oyster mushrooms into long thin strips. In a medium bowl, whisk together all the ingredients for the hoisin marinade. Toss the mushrooms with ¾ of the marinade, ensuring they're well coated. Set aside to marinate.

Make the pancake batter: Add the flour, water and ground flaxseeds to a blender. Blend until smooth, about 30 seconds. Let the batter sit for 2–3 minutes to allow the flax to thicken.

Cook the mushrooms: Spread the marinated mushrooms on a lined baking tray in a single layer. Bake in the oven for 20 minutes, until the edges are crispy, or cook for 10–15 minutes in an air fryer. For a fried version, heat a pan over a high heat with 2–3 tablespoons of oil. Add the mushrooms and fry, stirring constantly, until browned (about 5 minutes).

Prepare the garnish: Cut the cucumber into 10cm-long thin strips. Thinly slice the scallions diagonally. Slice the red chilli, removing the seeds for less heat.

Cook the pancakes: Heat a pan over a high heat. Add 1 teaspoon of sunflower oil, pour a thin layer of batter on to form a 15cm pancake. Lower the heat to medium, cook for 1 minute, then, using a silicone spatula, flip and cook for another minute. Repeat with remaining batter. Keep cooked pancakes warm in foil while preparing the rest.

Assemble the pancakes: Spread a teaspoon of the remaining hoisin marinade on each pancake. Add 2–3 tablespoons of cooked mushrooms, 3–4 strips of cucumber and a sprinkle of scallions, chilli, pickled cucumber and sesame seeds. Serve and enjoy!

CHANA MASALA WITH EASY GRAM FLOUR DOSA

Serves 3–4

Chana masala

2 × 400g tins of chickpeas
1 large red onion
2 cloves of garlic
½ thumb-sized piece of ginger
small bunch of fresh coriander
1½ tbsp oil
1 tbsp garam masala
1 tsp chilli powder
1 tbsp ground cumin
1 tbsp ground coriander
1 tsp ground turmeric
½ tsp cinnamon
½ tsp black pepper
2 × 400g tins of chopped tomatoes
50g baby spinach

Dosa

100g gram (chickpea) flour
½ tsp ground cumin
½ tsp ground coriander
½ tsp garlic powder
200ml oat milk or water
sunflower oil, for frying

salt and ground black pepper

To serve

pickled red onion (see page 308)

Dave went to India with our friend Raj for his brother's Sikh wedding. They ate a chana masala with flatbreads that was to die for. We serve our version with a simple gram flour dosa, so it's quicker and easier to make, gluten-free and just as tasty!

Prepare the chana masala base: Drain and rinse the chickpeas. Peel and roughly chop the onion. Peel and finely chop the garlic and ginger. Finely chop the coriander stalks, setting the leaves aside.

Cook the onions: Heat 1½ tablespoons of oil in a large wide pan over high heat. Add the onions and cook for 4–5 minutes until they start to brown, stirring occasionally.

Add the aromatics and spices: Reduce the heat to medium. Add the ginger, garlic and coriander stalks, cooking for 2 minutes. Stir in all the spices and cook for another minute.

Make the sauce: Add the chopped tomatoes and 1 teaspoon of salt to the pan and mix. Cook for 3–4 minutes then blend until smooth using a stick blender or a food processor.

Combine and cook the chana masala: Return the sauce to the pan, add the chickpeas, and cook for 1–2 minutes. Stir in the spinach until wilted. Adjust the seasoning with additional salt or pepper if needed. Stir in the fresh chopped coriander leaves.

Prepare the dosa batter: Sift the chickpea flour into a large mixing bowl. Add the cumin, coriander, garlic powder and ½ teaspoon of salt. Create a well in the centre, pour in the oat milk or water, and whisk until smooth.

Cook the dosa: Lightly oil a pan with sunflower oil, and use kitchen paper to remove the excess. Heat the pan on high, then reduce to medium. Pour in a quarter of the batter, spreading it into a thin pancake. Cook for 2 minutes per side. Repeat for the remaining batter. Keep cooked pancakes warm in foil while preparing the rest.

Serve: Reheat the chana masala if necessary, and serve with the warm dosas. Garnish with fresh coriander leaves and some pickled red onion!

WHAT we have LEARNED from our COMMUNITY

The most liveable community in the world

In 2002, 22-year-old idealistic Dave embarked on a journey to an International Rainbow gathering in the picturesque hills of Costa Rica. This gathering attracted thousands of individuals seeking a utopian experience, where the emphasis was on camaraderie, sharing and a moneyless society built on bartering. On paper, it sounded like a dream come true. However, for Dave, who hailed from a close-knit village in Ireland, where genuine community support was deeply ingrained, the atmosphere at the gathering felt artificial and insincere. The stark contrast left him yearning for the authentic, organic sense of community he had grown up with.

Greystones has won the award for Most Liveable Community in the World under 20,000 People twice in the last 15 years (2008 and 2021). It is a special little town nestled between the Irish Sea on one side, the Wicklow Mountains to the west and Bray Head to the north, and it's only 25 kilometres south from Dublin City.

We have lived in Greystones for over 40 years. When we were growing up, it was a small fishing village with a quaint harbour that was falling apart. On our way to school every day, we used to walk across a goat field, which, unsurprisingly, is now a housing estate. As kids, we had an insufferable amount of energy, so our mom had us on every sports team you could join – we represented Greystones in tennis, rugby, golf, baseball, GAA, hurling: you name it and we were playing it! As a result, we were well integrated into the Greystones community.

Melting pots and soul massages

When we started The Happy Pear in 2004, we wanted it to be more than a business: from the start we envisioned it as a melting pot, a spot where a welcoming atmosphere and laughter were as important as the food on the plate. We dreamed of contributing to Greystones's vibrant spirit and community, and we like to think we've played a small part in the town's story.

Once, in the early days, Steve was on our daily trip into the fruit market in Dublin at 4 a.m., and he bumped into an old friend of ours, Alan Coleman, who was still out partying. Al was delighted to join Steve buying the veg, thought it was great craic and ended up coming back to 'play shop' for the day. He ended up working with us for about a year (and is now an investor!) and used to say that The Happy Pear was so much more than the food: it provided a soul massage, which is what people really needed!

Our first-ever staff meeting

Swim-rise in May 2019

Stephen and Kelly from NYC

Some of the crew that swam from Bray to Greystones in July 2023

We were late to gymnastics! This was our best effort at a pyramid as the queue for lunch watched!

At the beginning of The Happy Pear, we were veg missionaries, and we started going to local schools to do smoothie demos. We would set up in the hall with our 'smoothie roadshow', and three to four classes would come in at a time (usually over 100 kids!) and we would do our best to make fruit and veg and health as attractive as possible. We would divide them into boys and girls, Steve would take one group and Dave the other, and we would go head to head to try to make the best smoothie – the teachers would decide the winner. Invariably it was a draw, but by the end the kids would literally be fighting over apples and carrots! It was heartwarming to see. It's always funny when someone who starts to work with us says, 'I remember you came into my school' – which was likely 10 to 15 years ago. It's a visual reminder of how long we have been doing this for.

To this day, we continue to engage with local schools, hosting fundraising events for local schools and evenings for parents with practical tips and strategies for getting kids to eat healthier. We remain as committed as ever to supporting our local community and empowering families to eat more veg!

One of the many swim-rise beach parties!

The Greystones Blue Zone?

We are big fans of Blue Zones research and its message about the importance of community and relationships. We have always liked the idea of helping Greystones to become a blue zone of sorts – a place where we can grow old as part of a strong community and have helped to create a town that supports healthy choices.

To a degree, The Happy Pear is synonymous with Greystones. We are really proud to be part of this community and are as committed as ever to help make it even stronger. To us, Greystones represents a way of life – a place surrounded by natural beauty and a community that embodies the true meaning of togetherness.

A decade of swim-rise

We always thought winter sea swims were for 'crazy' people – certainly not for us. Yet following an impromptu dip one September morning in 2014, after a challenge from a swimmer named Niall, something started to unfold. We showed up a second day to meet Niall, and unbeknownst to us, Caroline, a friend, joined. The next day at sunrise, Hugo, a person who was just back from Thailand and couldn't sleep, joined. The fourth day we brought tea, which gave us a reason to stand around and get to know one another, the sea stripping away life's worries. We were aware that something was happening, and it just kept unfolding. The growing camaraderie and the thrill of the cold kept us returning. During that first winter, jokingly, we considered each swim at the start of a month as 'renewing our membership' for the month!

Our Instagram stories and photos captured these moments to share with others online, reminding them of the beauty and uplifting capacity of nature. They made even the coldest Irish mornings look tropical and beautiful! We received countless messages from followers who wanted to join. Fed up with replying individually, Steve threw open the invitation on social media for a mass swim at sunrise, which Siobhan named 'swim-rise'. Expecting a handful, we were gobsmacked when 150 people joined us, swimming and sharing in our free pot of porridge! The simple joy of that swim bonded us, and the event grew, sometimes drawing what could have been over a thousand people, and even featuring a hot tub on the beach that the local fire brigade very kindly filled with water for us to heat with a wood fire!

It has been nearly a decade of 'swim-rise', swimming at sunrise all year around in the cold Irish Sea. There is plenty of research validating how good sea swimming is for your health, but the real benefits, we find, are to our spirits: they soar, worries and fears are washed away and a child-like wonder emerges! And we are blessed to share our swim-rises with a glorious community of friends who we love dearly.

What we KNOW about CREATING a COMMUNITY

Be intentional about fostering community:
Recognise our innate need for social connection and consciously decide to foster community. This deliberate intention is the cornerstone of community building.

Greet and connect:
Begin with the basics – smile and say hello to those around you (you don't always need to do this – we don't always feel like it either). Community culture is a living thing and can be changed: even if you live in an 'unfriendly' area, you can be the change you want to see, and start that ripple of friendliness spreading. Positivity, friendliness and openness is contagious, just like the common cold! Simple acts of recognition can spark conversations and lay the groundwork for lasting relationships in your neighbourhood. Just asking someone's name is the start of getting to know them. It's often said that it takes 30 to 40 hours to create a trusted friend, and that all starts with a simple hello!

Engage actively:
Seek out groups or activities that resonate with you, whether it's volunteering, signing up for a local Parkrun, joining the local tennis club or participating in local events. These shared interests create natural opportunities for connection and community engagement.

Embrace authenticity:
Let your true self shine through. People gravitate towards authenticity, and showing your genuine self, including your vulnerabilities, can strengthen the bonds within your community. We connect much more over our vulnerabilities and our 'weaknesses' than we do through our achievements and successes.

The Happy Pear
The Happy Pear
NO PARKING

DESS
&CA

ERTS
KES

CARAMEL CHOCOLATE BANANA CAKE

Serves 12

Topping

2 ripe bananas, peeled
150g caster sugar
2 tbsp water

Cake

2 tbsp ground flaxseeds
6 tbsp water
50g walnuts
200g self-raising flour
1½ tsp ground cinnamon
3 ripe bananas
120ml sunflower oil
150g maple syrup
100g chocolate chips or chopped chocolate

This is such a pretty cake and a delicious way to turn what could become 'just banana bread' into a truly magnificent centrepiece! Our friend Lucy suggested we try this, and it worked out so well.

Preheat: Preheat the oven to 160°C fan/350°F/gas 4.

Prepare the tin and the bananas: Line a 20cm springform tin with baking parchment. Carefully slice the bananas for the topping lengthwise and place them cut-side down in the tin.

Make the caramel and pour over the bananas: Add the 150g caster sugar to a wide saucepan and heat on medium. Add the 2 tablespoons of water and mix once – after that, occasionally swirl the saucepan but don't stir the sugar. Wait until it breaks down and starts to become golden and turn to a smooth caramel (be patient – this will take about 4–6 minutes, depending on your hob). As it reaches the end, you can stir it to ensure a smooth texture. Remove when the caramel is lightly golden. Pour all the caramel over the bananas and leave to cool.

Make the flax egg: In a glass or cup, mix the ground flaxseeds and water and leave to sit for 5 minutes until it coagulates.

Mix the dry ingredients: Roughly chop the walnuts so they are bite sized, then add to a large bowl with the flour, and cinnamon.

Blend the wet ingredients, and mix with the dry ingredients: Peel the 3 bananas for the cake. Add them to a blender with the sunflower oil, maple syrup and soaked ground flaxseed, and blend till smooth. (If you don't have a blender, mash the bananas in a bowl then mix well with the wet ingredients.) Add the wet mixture to the bowl of dry ingredients, and mix into a lovely smooth batter. Add the chocolate chips and stir through.

Pour the batter over the bananas and bake: Pour the batter on top of the caramel bananas, then bake in the preheated oven for 35–45 minutes, until a skewer comes out clean.

Serve: Run a palette knife around the edges of the tin to loosen the cake from the sides. Place a flat plate or board on top of the cake and carefully flip the cake so the bananas will be on top. Open the catch and release the base of the tin. Carefully and slowly remove the baking parchment – if any caramel or banana sticks, just replace it. Leave to cool and set, then cut and enjoy!

CHOCOLATE HAZELNUT LOAF CAKE

Serves 10

2 tbsp ground flaxseeds
90ml water
150g hazelnuts
120g vegan butter
150g self-raising flour
150g caster sugar
pinch of salt
½ tsp almond extract (optional)
120g non-dairy milk

Chocolate coating

80g vegan butter
200g dark chocolate

This is such a stunning-looking cake and surprisingly easy to make – and chocolate and hazelnut are such a wonderful marriage. We've added almond extract – if you don't like that almond note you can leave it out, but it really accentuates the nuttiness of this beauty!

Preheat the oven, line the tin, and prepare the flax egg: Preheat the oven to 170° fan/375°F/gas 5. Line a 1lb loaf tin with baking parchment. Mix the ground flaxseeds with 90ml of water and leave to coagulate.

Toast and process the hazelnuts: Add the hazelnuts to a baking tray and toast them in the oven for 10–12 minutes, until golden. Rub the nuts in a tea-towel to remove the skins. In a food processor, blend ⅔ of the skin-less hazelnuts to a meal (it will look similar to ground almonds). Leave the remaining ⅓ of the hazelnuts aside for decoration.

Mix the dry ingredients: In a large bowl, mix the self-raising flour, ground hazelnuts, caster sugar and a pinch of salt.

Combine the wet and dry ingredients: Melt 120g of vegan butter in a pan over medium heat. Then add the melted butter to a bowl with the prepared flax egg, almond extract (if using) and non-dairy milk, and stir well. Pour the wet mixture into the dry ingredients and mix until well combined.

Bake: Pour the batter into the lined tin, smoothing the top. Bake for 45–50 minutes, or until a skewer comes out clean. Allow the cake to cool in the tin for approximately 1 hour. Then remove from the tin and parchment and leave to finish cooling for a further hour. You want it to be completely cool before coating in chocolate.

Make the chocolate coating: Cut the vegan butter for the chocolate coating into cubes and melt in a saucepan. Chop the dark chocolate into small pieces and add to the melted butter, heating and stirring until fully melted and mixed together.

Coat and decorate: Let the chocolate and butter mixture cool a little, so it's a bit thicker but still spreadable – this makes it stick to the sides more easily. Pour the chocolate and butter mixture over the cooled cake, and use a palette knife to spread it around till the sides, edges and top are fully coated. Cut the remaining hazelnuts in half and arrange them on the top and sides of the cake. Sprinkle over any leftover hazelnut dust, then place in the fridge to set for 10 minutes before slicing. Enjoy the rich and nutty flavours that make this dessert a true showstopper!

PORTUGUESE CHOCOLATE MOUSSE CAKE

*PLUS 2 HOURS TO SET IN THE FRIDGE

Serves 12

Sponge

1 tbsp ground flaxseeds
3 tbsp water
130g plain flour
150g coconut sugar or brown sugar
1 tsp baking powder
40g cacao powder
150ml non-dairy milk
180ml sunflower oil or other neutral-tasting oil
½ tsp pure vanilla extract

Chocolate mousse

250g chocolate chips (54% cocoa)
75ml sunflower oil
160ml aquafaba (chickpea water from a 400g tin)
1 tsp vinegar or lemon juice
20g caster sugar

To decorate

2 tbsp cocoa powder

There's a chocolate café in Lisbon that only sells one type of cake, which we thought was strange – but when we tasted the cake we understood why! This is our tribute to that very cake: it's easy and quick to make for something so elegant.

Preheat the oven, line the tin and make the flax egg: Preheat the oven to 180°C fan/400°F/gas 6. Line a 20cm springform tin with baking parchment on the bottom and sides. Mix 1 tablespoon of ground flaxseeds with 3 tablespoons of water and let it sit for 3 minutes.

Make the cake: In a large bowl, sieve in the flour, coconut sugar, baking powder and cacao powder and mix well. In another bowl, combine the non-dairy milk, 180ml oil, vanilla extract and flax egg until homogenous. Gradually mix the wet ingredients into the dry until well combined. Pour the mixture into the tin, level it, then bake for 20 minutes in the preheated oven, rotating halfway through. Remove from the oven and cool in the tin completely.

Make the mousse: Melt the chocolate chips in a bowl over a pan of simmering water (don't let the bottom of the bowl touch the water) or in a microwave. Remove from the heat and mix in the sunflower oil. Using an electric mixer, whip the aquafaba with the vinegar or lemon juice until stiff peaks form. Gradually add the sugar on slow speed, then increase to high and whip for 5–8 minutes. With the mixer running, slowly add the melted chocolate until fully incorporated. Continue mixing for another minute until you have a smooth, yet liquid, mousse-like texture.

Assemble: Spread the chocolate mousse evenly over the cooled sponge cake. Refrigerate for at least 2 hours to allow the mousse to set.

Serve: Carefully remove the cake from the tin. Using a sieve, dust the top of the cake with the cocoa powder. For clean slices, use a hot knife to cut through the mousse without squashing it.

CHOCOLATE COFFEE CARAMEL 3-TIERED CAKE

Makes 12 large slices

Chocolate sponge
300g self-raising flour
250g sugar
70g cacao powder
1 tsp baking powder
¼ tsp baking soda
300ml strong black coffee
100g coconut or soy yoghurt
100ml vegetable oil
1 tsp vanilla extract

Caramel sauce
200g sugar
3 tbsp water
50g vegan butter
100ml coconut cream (scooped from a tin of coconut milk)

Buttercream
300g vegan butter
580g icing sugar
4 tbsp cocoa powder
2 tbsp ground coffee powder
2 tbsp non-dairy milk

This is a big, magnificent cake with a really light chocolate sponge and a balanced buttercream, where both the cocoa and coffee offset the sweetness, and the coffee adds an amazing, subtle mocha-like flavour. A beautiful, impressive cake that slices perfectly!

Preheat the oven and prep the tins: Preheat the oven to 180°C fan/400°F/gas 6. Grease and line three 20cm springform cake tins with baking parchment.

Mix the dry ingredients: Sieve the flour, sugar, cacao powder, baking powder and baking soda into a large bowl; mix well. Make a well in the centre of the dry ingredients.

Mix the wet ingredients: In a jug, combine the coffee, coconut or soy yoghurt, vegetable oil and vanilla extract.

Make the batter: Pour the wet ingredients into the well of the dry ingredients. Mix until smooth using a spatula. Divide the batter evenly among the three cake tins, smoothing the tops.

Bake: Bake the cakes for 22–26 minutes, rotating halfway through. Check for doneness with a skewer – it should come out clean. Leave the cakes to cool completely in their tins.

Make the caramel sauce: In a saucepan, on a medium heat, mix the sugar with 3 tablespoons of water until the sugar dissolves and it resembles a syrup. Then cook without stirring for 5–6 minutes. Cut the 50g of vegan butter into 6 cubes. Once the sugar turns golden, add the cubed vegan butter and coconut cream and carefully mix through. Remove from the heat and whisk to a smooth caramel.

Prepare the buttercream: Add the 300g vegan butter to a large bowl, and cream using an electric whisk or fork. Sift in the icing sugar, cocoa powder and coffee powder. Add 2 tablespoons of non-dairy milk and combine until smooth.

Assemble: Level the cakes, if necessary, with a serrated knife until they are flat. Place a little buttercream on the serving plate, and put the first cake on top to secure. Carefully spread ⅓ of the buttercream to the edges using a spatula, and drizzle some caramel on the first layer. Repeat with the second layer, ensuring to be gentle so the buttercream only comes to the edge. Top with the final layer and the remaining buttercream. Drizzle with caramel, saving some for serving. Cut into big door-stopper slices and enjoy!

SUPER-CHEWY CHOCOLATE CHIP COOKIES

Makes 12 cookies

1 tbsp ground flaxseeds
3 tbsp water
80g vegan block butter
125g self-raising flour
115g caster sugar
35g brown sugar or coconut sugar
3 tbsp oat milk or non-dairy milk of choice
100g dark chocolate chips
sea salt

These are our favourite cookies! We make a version of these every day in the bakery, with a little coarse sea salt sprinkled on top, and they are just delicious. This is an easy-to-make-at-home version, and the reason why we drop the baking tray on the counter is because it increases the chewiness and gives them a beautiful look!

Preheat the oven and line the trays: Preheat the oven to 170°C fan/375°F/gas 5. Line two baking trays with baking parchment.

Make the flax egg: Mix the ground flaxseeds with the water, and set aside to thicken.

Melt the vegan butter: Place the vegan butter in a pan on a low heat. Once melted, remove from the heat and set aside.

Mix the dry ingredients: Using a sieve, sift the flour and both sugars into a large bowl.

Mix the wet ingredients: In another bowl, mix the melted butter, oat milk and flax egg together.

Combine: Add the wet ingredients to the dry ingredients and stir together. Ensure not to mix too much, as you don't want to develop the gluten. Add 80g of the chocolate chips, and mix through the cookie dough, leaving 20g to decorate before baking. Cover the bowl and put it in the fridge to cool for 30 minutes or the freezer for 10 minutes.

Shape the cookies: Remove the cookie dough from the fridge or freezer and scoop out a generous heaped tablespoon for each cookie (about 45g). Roll into a ball and place on the lined trays (we fit 6 cookies on a 40cm × 28 cm tray). Ensure to leave space for them to spread as they bake. Pat the cookies flat with the palm of your hand. Add a few of the remaining 20g of chocolate chips to the top of each cookie.

Bake: Bake for 6 minutes, then remove the trays from the oven and drop them on the counter – being careful not to spill the cookies! – to make a single bang that will flatten the cookies. Return the tray to the oven for a further 6–8 minutes, until golden. Remove from the oven and sprinkle with a little sea salt. Leave to cool before eating, if you can!

TIRAMISU

Serves 6–8

Sponge
200g self-raising flour (standard or gluten-free)
180g sugar
250g oat milk
20ml oil

Cream
500ml plant-based cream
6 tbsp icing sugar
1 vanilla pod
250ml vegan cream cheese

Coffee soak
2 tbsp icing sugar
200ml strong black coffee
50ml Marsala or coffee liqueur (optional)

To serve
50g cacao powder
chocolate (optional)

This is our best version to date of the classic. Translated to English, it means 'pick me up', and it is such a magnificent pick-me-up. One of our all-time favourite desserts, a good tiramisu like this is difficult to stop eating! The flour can be replaced with GF flour to make it gluten-free.

Preheat the oven and line the tray: Preheat the oven to 160°C fan/350°F/gas 4. Line a baking tray, about 23cm × 35cm × 5cm, with baking parchment.

Make and bake the sponge: Sieve the flour and sugar into a large bowl and mix well. Add in the oat milk and oil and fold the batter together until well combined but not over-mixed. Pour the batter into the lined tray and level it out. Bake for 15–18 minutes, until it starts to go lightly golden. (If using gluten-free flour, bake for about 15 minutes, – when you insert a wooden skewer it should come out dry.) Set aside and leave to cool.

Whip the cream: Add the plant-based cream to a large bowl along with the icing sugar. Split and scrape out the seeds from the vanilla pod and add. Using an electric whisk, whip the cream until you reach stiff peaks – this should take 3–4 minutes. Add in the vegan cream cheese and whip again until it's well combined and smooth with stiff peaks. You want to ensure it's thick enough to hold its shape.

Make the coffee soak: Sieve the 2 tablespoon of icing sugar into the coffee, add in the Marsala or coffee liqueur if using and mix well.

Plate up and decorate: Get the plate you want to serve the tiramisu on, and cut the sponge in half. Put a sheet of baking parchment on top of the sponge, flip it over and remove the bottom baking paper. Carefully transfer half of the sponge to the plate, with the bottom of the sponge now facing up (so the coffee will soak in better).

Gently pour half the coffee mixture onto the sponge, and use a pastry brush to spread the mixture evenly. Add half of the cream on top, and spread it out so that the sponge is well covered. Sieve some cacao powder over it.

Next, carefully place the remaining half of the sponge on top, again bottom side up – try to line it up so it's exactly on top of the base layer. Pour over the remaining coffee mixture and spread evenly with the pastry brush. Add the remaining cream, spread and finish with a coating of cacao powder, and if you have any chocolate, shave it and sprinkle over the top!

RASPBERRY CARAMEL APPLE PIE

30 MINS PREP · 60 MINS COOK · 90 MINS TOTAL

Serves 10–12

2 × 320g sheets of vegan shortcrust pastry, thawed if frozen
plain flour, for rolling
50ml water
200g light brown sugar
1 tsp sea salt
4 tbsp unsalted vegan butter
100g vegan cream or coconut cream
6 Bramley cooking apples
340g frozen raspberries
non-dairy milk, for brushing

Brian, winner of our 2023 apple-pie contest!

We have been running our annual apple-pie festival for 18 years now! It's a fun celebration of the apple season and is centred around our apple-pie contest. We run it every October, and four judges of different generations taste apple pies and collectively decide the winner. This raspberry caramel apple pie, with its unique twist on a classic dessert, comes from Brian, the winner of our 2023 contest. This recipe, a family favourite from his native South Africa, has been slightly changed to make it easier, and is now shared for you to enjoy.

Preheat: Preheat the oven to 180°C fan/400°F/gas 6.

Roll out the pastry: Dust the counter and rolling pin with a little flour. Take one sheet of pastry and roll it to approximately 5mm thick, rotating for evenness.

Line the dish: Transfer the pastry to a 30cm × 20cm × 6cm greased baking dish, press it in, then trim most of the excess, leaving a little hanging over the edge of the dish. Reserve the rest of the pastry for later.

Make the caramel sauce: In a small pan, add 50ml of water and the sugar and mix. Put over medium heat, don't stir, and wait until the sugar turns into a golden syrup, about 8 minutes. Stir in the sea salt and butter. Slowly mix in the vegan cream, and cook for a few minutes, stirring regularly, until it thickens enough to coat the back of a spoon.

Prepare the filling: Peel the apples and cut each into 6 equal segments. Toss the apples in the caramel sauce along with the frozen raspberries, ensuring they're all evenly coated.

Assemble the pie: Pour the caramel-coated apples and raspberries into the pastry-lined dish. Dust the counter and rolling pin with flour, then roll out the second sheet of dough. Cut into 2cm strips, and arrange in a lattice on top of the fruit mixture. Using a pastry brush, brush with a little non-dairy milk for a golden finish.

Bake: Place the pie in the preheated oven and bake for about 60 minutes, or until the pastry is golden and the filling is bubbling. Ideally, let the pie rest for 20 minutes before serving. (We know how hard this step can be!)

APPLE AND BERRY CRUMBLE

Serves 7

8–10 apples (approx. 1.5kg)
200g blackberries or berries of choice (blueberries are recommended for colour)
120ml water
2 tbsp maple syrup or brown sugar
2 tsp cinnamon

Crumble topping

150g oats (gluten-free if necessary)
100g ground almonds
3 tbsp pumpkin seeds
3 tbsp sunflower seeds
30g desiccated coconut
100g vegan butter or coconut oil
90g brown sugar or coconut sugar

To serve

Vegan double cream or vegan vanilla ice cream

Dave's kids' favourite book when they were little was *The Gruffalo*, so they all got into the habit of calling this crumble a gruffalo grumble! This is a dessert that delivers such joy – it's simple to make and so comforting, and it actually came third place in our annual apple-pie contest one year.

Preheat: Set your oven to 170°C fan/375°F/gas 5.

Prepare the fruit: Wash the apples, core and chop into bite-sized pieces. If using strawberries, remove the tops.

Stew the fruit: Place the apples, berries, water, maple syrup or brown sugar and cinnamon in a medium pot. Bring to a boil, then cover with a lid, reduce the heat, and simmer for 20 minutes or until the fruit is tender but still holds its shape, stirring occasionally.

Prepare the crumble topping: In a separate bowl, mix together the oats, ground almonds, pumpkin seeds, sunflower seeds and desiccated coconut. Melt the vegan butter or coconut oil and allow it to cool slightly, then add it to the dry mixture along with the brown sugar or coconut sugar. Mix well.

Assemble: Transfer the stewed fruit into a 20cm × 28cm × 5cm ovenproof dish, spreading it out. Evenly sprinkle the crumble topping over the fruit.

Bake: Place the dish in the preheated oven and bake for 20 minutes or until the topping is golden and the fruit is bubbling.

Serve: Best enjoyed warm with a pour of vegan double cream or vegan vanilla ice cream.

EASY BAKEWELL TART

Makes 12–18 bars

1 × 320g sheet vegan shortcrust pastry, thawed if frozen
125g self-raising flour
175g icing sugar
200g ground almonds
pinch of salt
150g vegan butter, softened
1 tsp almond extract
120ml water
200g raspberry jam or jam of choice
75g fresh raspberries
25g flaked almonds

Bakewell tart is one of our favourite summer treats! Mom used to buy almond fingers when we were kids, and they were always devoured – these are like a fancier version. It can be served as a tart, but we often cut it into finger slices that remind us of our childhood. You can take any seasonal fruit that you like or have, make a jam out of it and use it as the basis for this recipe.

Preheat the oven and line the dish: Preheat the oven to 180°C fan/400°F/gas 6. Line a 25cm × 18cm × 3.5cm tin with baking parchment.

Roll out and blind bake the pastry: Unroll the pastry, and transfer it to the lined baking tin. Trim it to roughly fit the base of the tray (no need to bring it up the sides). Place another sheet of baking parchment on top of the pastry and fill with cooking beans or dried beans to weigh it down. Bake for 10 minutes. Remove the beans and the top baking parchment, then pop back in the oven for 5 minutes so the base cooks. Remove and allow to cool.

Make the frangipane: While pastry is blind baking, sieve the flour and sugar into a large bowl and mix in the ground almonds with a pinch of salt. Whisk to combine, making sure there are no lumps. In a saucepan over a low heat, melt the butter, and then add in the almond extract and 120ml of water, and add into the dry ingredients. Mix until combined into a smooth batter.

Add the jam layer on top of the pastry: Spoon the jam on top of the cooked, cooled pastry and spread over it in an even layer.

Add the frangipane: Carefully spoon the almond mixture on top of the raspberry layer. It will be quite thick, so gently spread it over the jam till it's fully covered. Dot the raspberries over the almond mixture and scatter flaked almonds on top.

Bake: Bake for 30–35 minutes, until a skewer comes out dry or almost dry. Remove from the oven and allow to cool fully in the tray before cutting. Slice into squares or fingers of whatever size you prefer.

THE LATE LATE SHOW
The WORLD of the HAPPY PEAR
The Happy Health
THAI TASTIC
WAHOO! I'M A COMPOSTABLE POUCH
The Happy Pear
Seedie Cookie Bites
The Happy Pear
Tiffin Bites
We are ALL connected

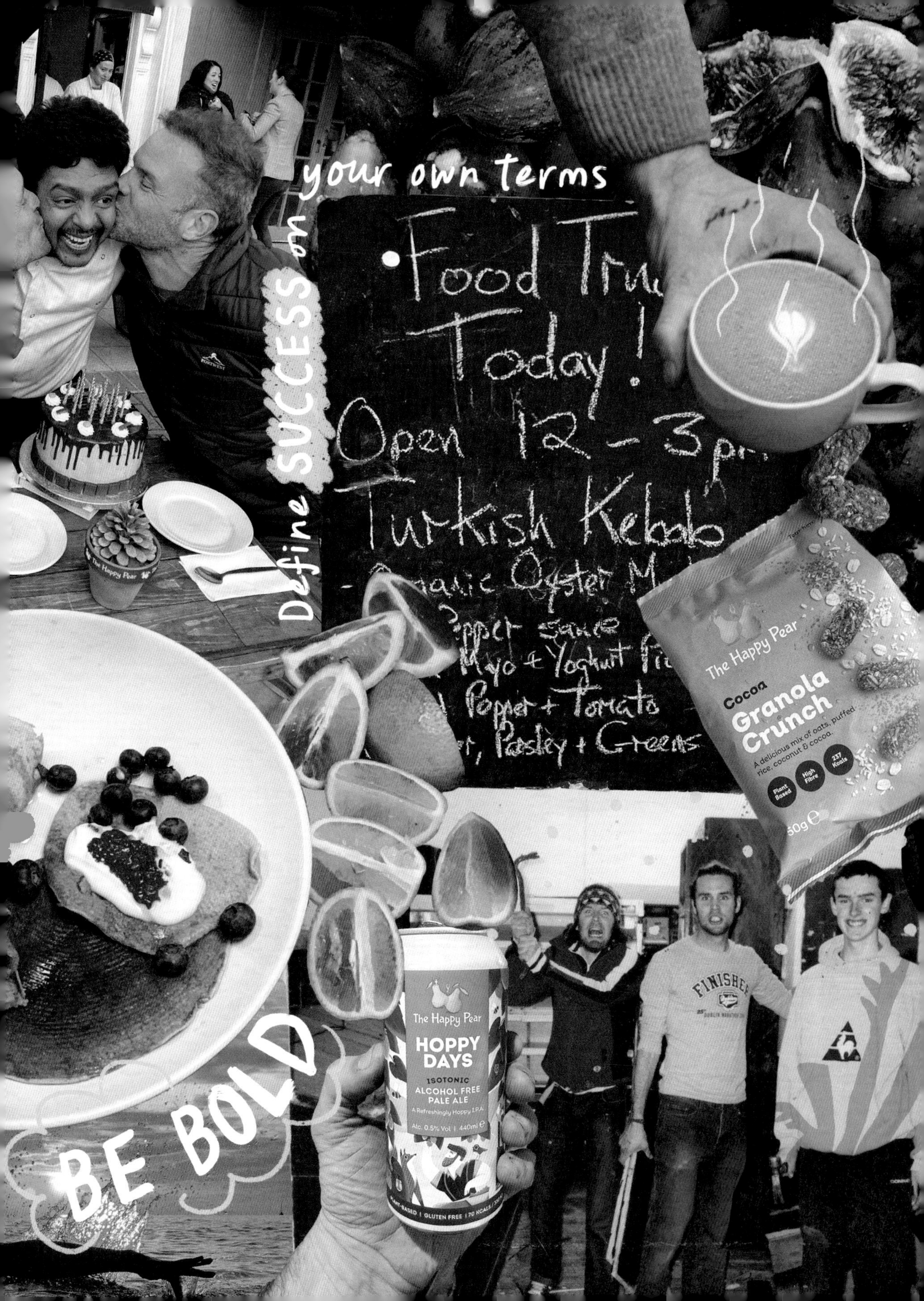
Define SUCCESS on your own terms
Food Tru
Today!
Open 12 - 3p
Turkish Kebab
Oyster
Pepper sauce
Mayo + Yoghurt
Pepper + Tomato
Parsley + Greens
The Happy Pear
Cocoa
Granola Crunch
A delicious mix of oats, puffed rice, coconut & cocoa.
Plant Based
High Fibre
237 Kcals
The Happy Pear
HOPPY DAYS
ISOTONIC
ALCOHOL FREE PALE ALE
A Refreshingly Hoppy I.P.A.
Alc. 0.5% Vol | 440ml
FINISHER
BE BOLD

5-INGR
CA

EDIENT
ES

5-INGREDIENT CARROT CAKE

Serves 12

Cake

400g self-raising flour
300g icing sugar
200g grated carrot
250ml neutral-tasting oil (sunflower or vegetable oil)
150ml water

Cream cheese icing

450g vegan cream cheese
150g icing sugar

Optional extras

100g raisins
100g chopped walnuts
1 tsp cinnamon
1 tsp allspice

This is a wonderful, delicious simplified version of the classic! To keep it to just five ingredients, we had to omit the walnuts, raisins and spices that would traditionally be in a carrot cake – we've included them as options here, if you want to add them for a more traditional touch.

Preheat the oven and prepare the tins: Preheat your oven to 180°C fan/400°F/gas 6. Grease and line two 20cm springform cake tins with baking parchment.

Combine the dry ingredients: Sieve the self-raising flour and icing sugar into a large mixing bowl. Add the grated carrot and any optional extras here and mix together.

Make the batter: Create a well in the centre of your dry ingredients. Pour in the oil and water. Stir the mixture until just combined using a spatula or hand mixer, taking care not to overmix.

Bake: Divide the cake mixture evenly between the two prepared tins. Bake in the preheated oven for 40 minutes, rotating the tins halfway through. Check for doneness with a skewer – it should come out clean.

Cool: Once baked, remove the cakes from the oven and place them on a rack to cool completely in the tins.

Make the icing: While the cakes are cooling, soften the vegan cream cheese with a fork, then sift in the icing sugar and whisk until smooth.

Assemble: Once the cakes have cooled, remove them from the tins, and spread half the cream cheese icing on the first cake. Top with the second cake and spread the remaining icing on top. If you want to take it to the next level top with some candied pecans or walnuts like in the photo!

5-INGREDIENT BANOFFEE PIE

*PLUS 1 HOUR CHILLING

Serves 12

Base

250g cashew nuts
150g pitted dates

Caramel

300g pitted dates
180g coconut oil
50ml water

Topping

3 bananas
2 × 400g tins of coconut milk (solid cream part only) or 300g vegan cream

To decorate (optional)

dark chocolate

This is such a winning dessert – it's super easy and quick to make and doesn't require any baking! We've made it in five minutes countless times when doing cooking demos at festivals. It's a fibre-rich dessert that's as good as the original, if not better!

Line the tin: Line a 24cm springform cake tin with baking parchment.

Prepare the base: Place cashew nuts in a food processor and blend to a breadcrumb-like consistency. Add 150g of dates and blend until the mixture begins to clump together. Press the mixture into the lined tin, creating an even base. Use the back of a spoon to firmly compress the mixture.

Make the caramel layer: Put 300g of dates, the coconut oil and the water into the food processor. Blend until the caramel is very smooth, which might take several minutes. Evenly spread the caramel over the prepared base.

Prepare the banana layer: Peel the bananas and slice into coins. Arrange the slices in a single layer on top of the caramel.

Add the cream: Open the tins of coconut milk and scoop out the solid cream, discarding the liquid. If using vegan cream, whip until you reach stiff peaks and spread over the banana layer. Use a fork to mash the coconut cream until it's smooth. Spread the coconut cream over the banana layer, smoothing the top.

Chill and serve: Place the pie in the fridge for at least 1 hour. Decorate with grated chocolate, if using, then slice and serve.

TIP: Leave the tins of coconut milk in the fridge beforehand to let the cream harden, particularly if you are in a warm climate!

5-INGREDIENT CHOCOLATE PEANUT-BUTTER CARAMEL TART

20* MINS PREP

*PLUS 30 MINUTES CHILLING

Serves 12

Base

250g cashew nuts
150g pitted dates
2 tablespoons coconut oil

Caramel

300g pitted dates
150g smooth peanut butter/ almond butter
120g coconut oil
6-10 tbsp water

Chocolate topping

300g chocolate
4 tbsp coconut oil

coarse salt flakes (optional)

Whenever we make this tart for cooking demos at festivals and events it's always a crowd pleaser. It's easy to make, healthier than most desserts and very satisfying. It's a popular choice in our cafés too and offers a healthier alternative to traditional salted caramel tarts, thanks to its higher fibre content.

Prepare the tin: Line a 24cm springform tin with baking parchment.

Make the base layer: Blitz the cashews in a food processor to a flour-like consistency. Add the 150g dates and coconut oil and blend until the mixture starts to come together. Transfer the base mixture to the tin, spread evenly and, using the back of a spoon, press firmly into the base to compact it.

Make the caramel layer: Without cleaning the food processor, add the 300g dates, peanut or almond butter, coconut oil and water. Blend until super smooth and caramel like – this may take from 5 to 10 minutes – adding more water if needed to achieve a smooth consistency. You can also add a pinch of salt to enhance the sweetness if you like. Spread the caramel evenly over the base layer – the best way to do this is to place some baking parchment on top of the caramel and then run the back of a spoon over the paper to smooth the caramel out.

For the chocolate layer: Melt the chocolate and coconut oil together in a bowl over a pan of simmering water or in a microwave, and stir well. Gently pour the melted chocolate over the caramel layer and spread it out to create an even topping.

Refrigerate and serve: Place the tart in the fridge for at least 30 minutes to allow the chocolate to set solid. To serve, sprinkle coarse salt flakes on top if desired. Use a hot knife to slice the tart, which helps to prevent the chocolate from cracking.

5-INGREDIENT CHOCOLATE GANACHE TART

*PLUS 60 MINUTES SETTING TIME

Serves 12

1 × 320g sheet of shortcrust pastry (defrosted if frozen)
350g dark chocolate
250g vegan cream
4 tbsp vegan butter
sea salt flakes, for garnish

This luxurious chocolate ganache tart is the epitome of simplicity meets elegance. Growing up, we always thought this type of cake was so posh and fancy – we only realised in recent years how easy it is to make and how incredibly delicious it is!

Preheat: Preheat your oven to 200°C fan/425°F/gas 7.

Roll out and blind bake the pastry: Roll out the pastry to fit a 23cm × 4cm (9 inch × 1½ inch) round tart tin, ensuring it covers the sides. Line the pastry with baking parchment and fill with baking beans or dried beans. Bake for 10 minutes, then remove the paper and beans and bake for a further 8 minutes, until golden and firm. Remove from the oven and let cool.

Make the ganache: Break the chocolate into small, even pieces and place in a bowl. In a saucepan, bring the plant-based cream and butter to a boil. Pour the boiling mixture over the chocolate and whisk until smooth and silky.

Assemble the tart: Pour the chocolate ganache into the cooled tart shell and level till smooth. Sprinkle sea salt flakes on top for a flavour contrast. Refrigerate until the ganache sets, around 60 minutes.

Serve: For smooth slices, heat a knife in hot water for 20 seconds, dry it, then cut. Clean the blade after each slice. Optionally, garnish with chopped pistachios or freeze-dried raspberries for an extra touch of luxury.

5-INGREDIENT COOKIES AND CREAM CHEESECAKE

*PLUS 2 HOURS CHILLING

Serves 12

Base

200g cashew nuts
200g pitted dates
2 tbsp coconut oil

Cheesecake layer

250g cashew nuts
250g vegan cream cheese
100g coconut oil
150g maple syrup

Optional extras

2 tbsp cacao powder (for the base)
seeds from ½ a vanilla pod and berries (for the cheesecake layer)

We were playing around with the 5-ingredient-cake theme for our YouTube videos when we came up with this. It's simple to make and really does taste like cookies and cream! It's also healthier than a traditional cheesecake, as instead of using crushed biscuits and butter as the base, we use cashew nuts and dates, and we also use cashews in the cream to increase the wholefood and fibre content.

Prep the tin: Line a 20cm springform tin with baking parchment.

Soak the cashew nuts: Place the 250g of raw cashew nuts for the cheesecake layer in a bowl and cover completely with boiling water. Set aside to soften. You don't need to soak the cashews for the base.

Make the base layer: In a food processor, blend the 200g of cashew nuts until they reach a breadcrumb-like texture. Next, add the pitted dates and coconut oil and blend till smooth and caramel-like. This should take about 2–3 minutes. If using cacao powder, add it here when blending to turn the base slightly brown and add a chocolatey note. Place the base mixture in the tin, and press it down firmly using the back of a spoon to ensure it's level, smooth and well compacted, so it holds together when the cake is cut and we get those lovely divisions of layers.

Drain and rinse the cashews, and make the cheesecake layer: Drain the cashew nuts and give them a good rinse to remove any acidic flavours arising from the soaking. Add them to a clean food processor along with the rest of the ingredients for the cheesecake layer. (If using the seeds from a vanilla pod, just scoop them in here.) Blend until super smooth – depending on your food processor, this may take 3–5 minutes. Pour on top of the base layer. Level and smooth and put in the fridge to set for 2 hours before serving (with some optional fresh berries!).

5-INGREDIENT MAPLE-GLAZED FRUIT PUFF-PASTRY SLICES

Serves 4

4 tbsp maple syrup
small handful of shelled pistachio nuts (unsalted)
4 small peaches or about 200g seasonal fruit of choice
1 × 320g sheet of vegan puff pastry, defrosted if frozen
30g icing sugar, to serve

A 5-ingredient delicious and super-simple fruity pastry slice that will leave you looking for more! You can use any seasonal fruit that you have to hand – we also love to make them with apricots or nectarines, and Steve's daughter May loves to make them with frozen raspberries and blueberries. We've made a great version with blood oranges too. If you are using citrus fruit, mangoes or bananas, just peel and slice them.

Preheat the oven and line the tray: Preheat the oven to 180°C fan/400°F/gas 6. Line a baking tray with baking parchment.

Drizzle the maple syrup and prep the fruit and nuts: Drizzle 4 × 1 tablespoon puddles of maple syrup on the baking parchment. Finely slice the pistachio nuts and sprinkle on top of the maple syrup. Slice each peach into 6 slices, and arrange the slices neatly on top of each maple-syrup puddle. If using other seasonal fruit, cut it into thin slices, or leave whole in the case of berries, and place on top of the maple syrup, spread out in a nice design, as this will be the top of the pastry.

Cut the pastry and position: Slice the sheet of puff pastry into 4 rectangles about 12cm × 6cm. Place one on top of each of the peach-covered maple syrup puddles, and press down lightly so the maple syrup covers the whole of the bottom side of the slice. If any excess maple syrup comes out the sides, spoon it on top of the pastry.

Bake and serve: Place in the preheated oven and bake for 25 minutes. Using a palette knife, remove them carefully from the baking parchment and turn over so the fruit side is facing up. Dust with some icing sugar using a sieve, and serve warm or cold.

5-INGREDIENT UPSIDE-DOWN PEAR TART

Serves 4–6

2 tbsp water
75g caster sugar or brown sugar
75g vegan butter
2 ripe pears
1 × 320g sheet of vegan puff pastry

You might think this is only a pear tart, as we once did, but it's a proper elegant, easy-to-make dessert. It started out as a quick-fire dessert – we were doing a crowdfunding video and wanted something with pears in it – but it ended up being so good that we couldn't leave it out of this book. We make a caramel, arrange the pears in it, put the pastry on top, then bake and flip before serving – which is always the exciting part!

Preheat: Preheat the oven to 200°C fan/425°F/gas 7.

Make the caramel: Take an oven-proof frying pan – we used a 20cm pan – and add 2 tablespoons of water along with the sugar and mix it till it all comes together with no clumps. Put the pan on a high heat and don't stir. Bring to a boil, then reduce to medium heat and leave to cook without stirring until the sugar starts to turn a light shade of gold. This will take about 4–5 minutes. Cut the butter into small cubes, add to the caramel and carefully mix through. Don't worry if the butter and caramel separate.

Slice and arrange the pears: Cut the pears into long slices the full length of the pear, and place a single layer of them on top of the caramel, so they lie flat and cover the caramel (be careful of your fingers with the hot pan and caramel). Do your best to arrange them into a nice pattern, as this will be the top of your tart.

Roll and fit the pastry: Roll out the pastry slightly bigger than the size of the pan. Place it on top of the pears in the pan, and carefully tuck it in around the edges. Pierce the pastry with a fork in a few spots to let steam evaporate.

Bake: Place the pan in the oven to bake for 20 minutes or until the pastry on top starts to turn golden, then remove.

Flip: This is the most fun bit! While the pan is still hot, place a board or flat plate that you want to serve the tart from on top of the pan, and carefully flip the pan over in a strong, confident manner. The pears and caramel will now be on the top and the pastry at the bottom. If any of the pears stick to the pan, carefully remove them and put them back on top of the tart. Cut and enjoy!

20 WAYS to PICK yourself UP when FEELING DOWN

1 Move! Engaging in some form of physical activity gets you out of your head and back in your body. It can be dancing, stretching, walking – whatever. Just move your body!

2 Do five minutes of breathwork or deep breathing to help bring you back to the present moment. Focus on a longer exhale than inhale, as this will take you down to your rest and restore state of being rather than your fight, flight or freeze state. Dave does five minutes of 5:7 breathing – a five-second inhale followed by a seven-second exhale when he is overwhelmed to bring him back to the present.

3 Listen to uplifting music or create a playlist of your favourite songs and move to them in whatever way feels right for you.

4 Sit with your eyes closed and focus on your breath without looking at your phone.

5 Go for a walk in nature and soak up any sunlight and the fresh air – try doing this without being plugged in (no headphones!).

6 Take a shower or have a warm bath where you light candles and use some nice oils and Epsom salts. A hot bath with salts is Dave's sanctuary of solace.

7 Practise gratitude by writing down five things you are thankful for today.

8 Do 15 minutes of yoga or stretching. Flexibility and balance are overlooked yet so important as we age.

May and Theo

9 Drink some water. A doctor specialising in hydration that we interviewed on our podcast estimates that 80 per cent of us don't drink enough water.

10 Journal – write down your worries or what is stressing you out. A blank sheet willingly accepts all.

11 Reflect on what you were hoping for five years ago and see how much of it has come true – quite often it's more than you expected.

12 Engage in a creative practice like painting, writing or playing a musical instrument, or cook something that you love to eat.

13 Smile at a stranger you pass on the street – by making someone else feel joy, you often feel it yourself.

14 Spend a few minutes petting an animal: it helps to relax your nervous system. If you can't do this, find a soft toy – research has found that cuddling can work in a similar way.

15 Do an old-school puzzle. It used to be a form of fun – now it is a mindfulness activity!

16 Reach out to a friend you have lost touch with – Steve calls lots of friends when doing long drives.

17 Take a break from social media and reconnect with hobbies you used to love when you were younger.

18 Look into volunteering or helping someone in need to shift your focus and feel a sense of purpose. People who volunteer are likely to be happier than those who don't.

19 Watch a funny movie or show to lighten your mood.

20 Create a vision board of what is important to you and what direction you want to take your life. Dave has his as the home screen on his phone, so he looks at it many times a day.

BRE

ADS

ALL ABOUT SOURDOUGH

WHAT IS SOURDOUGH?

Sourdough is an artisan method of creating bread using just three ingredients: flour, water and salt. It does not use commercial yeast to make it rise. A sourdough culture, or levain, is used as a mother culture to make the bread rise, and it also makes it lighter and easier to digest.

Sourdough bread has something magical and mystical about it – it's a wonderful organic process that works with nature to produce beautiful bread. Steve watched the 'Air' episode of Michael Pollan's *Cooked* series back in 2016 and decided to grow his own sourdough mother to try to really understand the process. He simply mixed flour and water and left it out, then it started to bubble and go sour, and after a few days he had a sourdough mother – a new pet that needed feeding and love! This was the birth of Steve's fascination with sourdough bread. It's so easy to get started, and he can't say enough positive things about the beauty of making fresh bread in your own home and having another mother to love and look after. He highly recommends you give it a go!

WHAT IS A SOURDOUGH STARTER/MOTHER/LEVAIN?

A starter is simply a mix of flour and water that, left exposed, over time naturally takes in wild yeasts and bacteria from the environment, as well as the yeast on the flour. These naturally occurring yeasts begin feeding on the sugars in the flour. After three days, lactic acid bacteria (also found in yoghurt, cheese and other fermented milk products) also start developing. This lactic acid, together with vinegary-smelling acetic acid, give sourdough its characteristic tangy taste.

By days 10 to 14, the starter will be stable, and the yeasts and lactic acid bacteria will grow vigorously. The yeasts will then be able to produce enough carbon dioxide to leaven and 'rise' a loaf of bread. Commercial yeast causes bread to rise quickly, whereas sourdough bread will be proofed typically over 6–12 hours and is characterised by its slightly tangy flavour, a soft, moist crumb or texture, a lovely burnt crust, and big open air pockets.

The invention of compressed yeast in the nineteenth century led to a major decrease in sourdough-style fermentation and its use as a leavening agent. As manmade yeast offered a much quicker, less time-consuming and more reliable way to leaven bread, it started to naturally dominate how bread was produced commercially and at home. As with many modern conveniences, commercial yeast offered speed but meant a loss of flavour and often a loss of quality.

How to make a sourdough mother

It's really easy to start your own sourdough mother – it's like growing your own pet that will require feeding and minding. It simply requires flour, time and of course love!

What flour to use

You can start a mother with most flours, but make sure to choose a flour that is easy to come by and is not that expensive, as the mother will require regular feeding. We use a white-flour-based mother culture in our bakery, and we also have a wholemeal spelt mother at home.

A white flour will have more sugars available and less fibre than a wholemeal flour, so the mother will grow quicker and therefore require more regular feeding. Wholemeal flour has a higher fibre content, so it will absorb more moisture and be slightly less active than white flour. If you can afford organic flour you are supporting better agriculture, and typically the grain is better and more nutritious when grown organically.

To start

Take a clean 400ml jam jar and add:

- **50g flour of choice (we prefer 100% wholemeal or wholemeal spelt)**
- **50ml water**

Mix well until homogenous. Cover with a tea-towel to stop flies from entering, while still allowing air and natural yeast through. Leave it to sit on the countertop for 3 days out of direct sunlight.

Once it smells yeasty and slightly beer-like and has small bubbles in it, it is ready for its first feed. You should always feed it with whatever flour your mother culture was created with – for example, if you used wholemeal spelt flour, then your mother culture needs to always be fed wholemeal spelt flour. You can change the type of flour over time, but it's a gradual process.

Establishing your new mother culture

Your sourdough culture will now need to be fed daily. First, pour out half of your mother culture (this is often called 'discard'). This half can be used to make a pancake or some crackers.

Now, to the same jar add:

- **25g flour (ensure it is the same flour your mother culture was created with)**
- **25ml water**

Mix well, **and leave. Repeat this process for 7 days, after which you will have an active sourdough mother ready to bake** bread!

How regularly should I feed my mother?

Generally, if your mother is kept on your kitchen counter, it should be fed once a day as above. If it's living in a warm environment, such as 20°C or over, it might need to be fed twice daily.

You can also keep it in the fridge, where it will need to be fed weekly or even, at a stretch, every second week (this is a good option if you're going on holiday or you only want to bake bread once a week or so). When starting to bake with your mother from the fridge, it will be cold and relatively inactive, so it will require one good feed before baking and to be left out of the fridge (in a warmer environment) to wake it up and get it active.

The easiest mother

The easiest way to get a mother is to simply call into your local sourdough bakery and ask them for some mother culture. Most bakeries are more than happy to share theirs. Alternatively, if a friend is a sourdough baker, they could give you some mother culture. As little as 50–100g is all you need. Make sure to find out what flour the culture is based on and what the current feeding cycle is.

Once you get some mother culture and feed it, you will now have the basis for some beautiful bread!

Building a levain – when is your sourdough mother ready to bake bread?

The levain is the mother culture that you create exclusively to bake bread – it's just another word to distinguish it from the mother culture that you never fully use. For example, when you feed your mother, you take the discard (the portion you have removed) and feed that separately to create a levain to use to bake bread.

Say your mother culture is 100g. When you go to feed it, you'll have 50g of discard. For your bread recipe, you need 150g of levain. So, to the 50g of discard, you add 50ml of water and 50g of flour, mix and leave until it is ready to pass the float test (see page 244).

The bell curve on the next page explains what happens once the levain has been fed and how, during the fermentation journey, it goes from underactive to overfed and inactive.

The vertical axis, or y axis, is the level of activity. The level of activity rises and falls like a bell curve. The width of this bell curve is dictated by temperature. This means that if you leave your levain to ferment in the fridge, it will slowly get active and you will have a longer window when your levain is ready for making dough with. Whereas if you store your fed levain at a room temperature of, say, 20°C, you'll have a much smaller window when your levain will be ready to make dough with. Neither is better or worse; both just give different results. Once you understand this, you can control the level of activity via temperature and ensure that your levain will be ready to suit your schedule. A famous expression in baking sourdough is that the bread should work for you, not you for the bread! So by understanding this cycle, you can control the level of activity so that it fits your lifestyle.

The longer you ferment your levain, the more acidic it becomes; and the more the microbes break down the gluten in the flour, the more the levain or dough loses its structure and becomes watery. So if you mix your dough when your levain is under- or over-fermented, your loaf will not have the optimum chances of a good rise.

The float test

The float test is the easiest method of knowing if your levain is ready for making dough. To do this, take about 1 tablespoon of levain, which should look light and aerated, and add it to a glass with at least 150ml of water in it.

- **If your levain is ready, it will float immediately and continue to float for a few minutes.**
- **If it is under-fermented and not yet ready, it will have no bubbles on the surface and will sink.**
- **If it is over-fermented, it will have bubbles on the surface and sink.**

UNDER-FERMENTED

If your levain is under-fermented, you need to leave it to ferment for longer and redo the float test until your levain floats.

OVER-FERMENTED

If your levain is over-fermented, you will need to feed it again, even just 100g of flour and 100ml of water, and go through the fermentation cycle again.

It is really vital to ensure that your levain passes the float test, as under- or over-fermentation of the levain is one of the most common reasons why sourdough bread doesn't rise. You can also use the float test to see if your dough is ready to bake – it works for mixed dough as well.

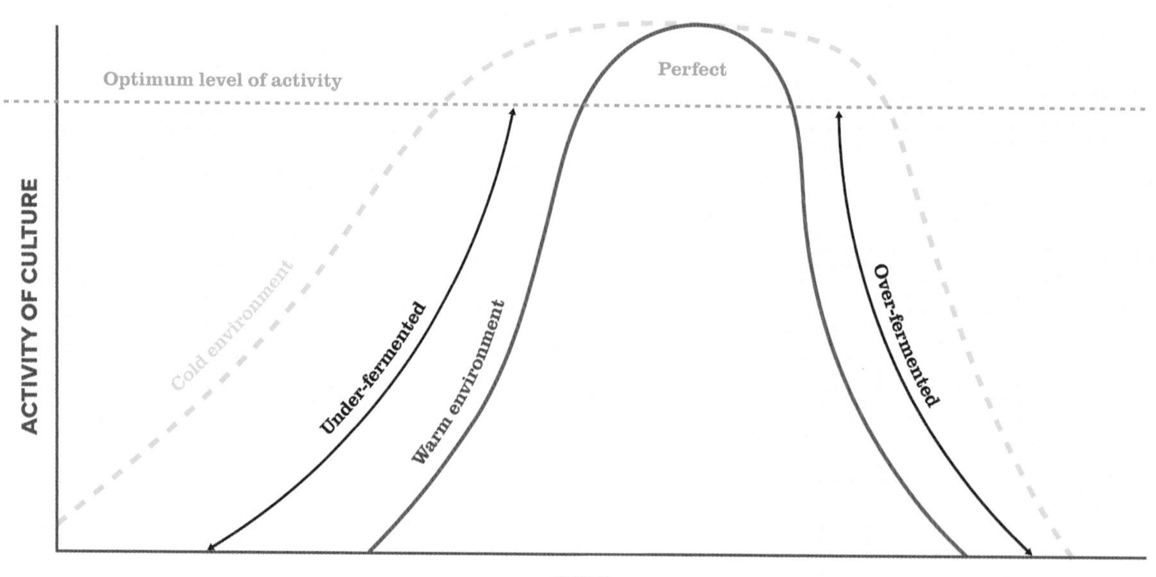

BASIC SOURDOUGH EQUIPMENT

Good-quality flour: ideally strong flour, as it is easier to develop gluten. If you can afford it, try to buy organic and support regenerative farms, as it is better for the environment and will typically result in better flour and, hence, better bread.

Water: ideally filtered water, but tap water will work fine.

Salt: try to use sea salt, as it has more minerals than table salt. A fine salt is easier to distribute throughout your dough than a coarse salt.

An oven

A Dutch oven (or cast-iron casserole dish with lid): not essential, but it will give you every chance of great bread at home. You can work around not having one, but they are worth the investment and can ensure you get great results most of the time.

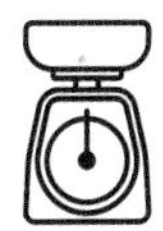

A weighing scales

A dough scraper: makes clean-up easier and means less waste – plastic dough scrapers are relatively inexpensive.

Mixing bowls

A 2lb loaf tin:
the one we use is 22cm × 13cm × 11.5cm.

A banneton basket or proving basket

Rice flour or semolina flour to dust your banneton basket to ensure your dough does not stick.

A sharp knife, scissors or razor blade to score your dough.

NO-KNEAD FREE-FORM SOURDOUGH LOAF

Makes 1 loaf

325ml lukewarm water
150g active levain
5g salt
400g strong white flour
100g wholewheat flour
rice flour, for dusting the banneton

This no-knead method allows gravity to develop the gluten, with the help of a couple of folds to add some structure. It's a universal method of baking great sourdough at home. We use 80 per cent strong white flour and 20 per cent wholemeal here, for added flavour, and it's 65 per cent hydration, which makes it easier to handle than some other sourdoughs.

Do the float test: First, make sure your levain is active and passes the float test (see page 244).

Mix the dough: Add the lukewarm water to a large mixing bowl and add the levain. With your hand, mix the levain through the water so it's well dispersed. Next, add in the two types of flour along with the salt, and bring it together to a shaggy dough. Leave it in the bowl at room temperature (15–20°C) for an hour or two.

Stretch and fold: When you come back to the dough, it will look similar but will have grown slightly due to fermentation and feel a little lighter and aerated. Using a dough scraper, carefully release the dough from the bowl onto the work surface. Don't use any flour. Stretch out the dough and fold from one side into the middle, then fold the other side right over to the opposite side, then catch the bottom and pull over to the top. This will help to develop structure.

Shape and prove overnight: Use your dough scraper to carefully flip the dough so the seam is facing down, and wet your hands a little to prevent the dough from sticking. Put your hands around the dough at the bottom and pull the dough back towards you. Repeat this a few times, moving around the dough, to develop surface tension till you have a nice round dough that looks a little like a taut balloon. Use the dough scraper to lift the dough off the work surface and put it back in the bowl. Cover with a damp tea towel or some cling film and put in the fridge overnight to proof.

Reactivate the dough and stretch and fold: The next morning, take the bowl with the dough out of the fridge and leave it for 60 minutes at room temperature (15–20°C) to warm up and get more active. Then, using your dough scraper, carefully remove the dough from the bowl onto the work surface. Again, avoid flouring the dough or the work surface. →

Carefully stretch out the dough and fold again as above to develop some structure. Be gentle, as you don't want to push out any of the air that the fermentation process has developed. Dust the banneton basket with rice flour, ensuring to get it into all the grooves.

Shape and prove: If the banneton is boule shaped (round), shape the dough into a ball by pulling it towards you from the bottom, as above, to develop surface tension. If it is batard shaped (rectangular), fold the square of dough over on itself so it is sausage shaped and, like above, pull towards you from the bottom carefully to develop surface tension. Using the dough scraper, lift the dough up and put it non-seam-side down into the floured banneton, so the seam-side is facing up.

Leave it to ferment, covered with a damp tea towel, at room temperature (15–20°C/59–68°F) for approximately 3–4 hours. When you press the dough with your finger, it should spring back slowly, and the loaf should have become convex or dome shaped.

Preheat and bake: Preheat the oven to 230°C fan/475°F/gas 9, with your Dutch oven inside with the lid on, for 20 minutes. Carefully take your Dutch oven out and remove the lid. Load in your dough, seam-side down, and score the top of the loaf using a scissors, very sharp knife or razor blade. Carefully put the hot lid on, and bake at 230°C for 20 minutes. Turn the temperature down to 180°C, remove the lid, and bake for a further 20 minutes until you have a lovely golden crust, or bake for longer if you prefer a darker crust. Carefully remove from the oven and leave on a cooling rack for an hour until cool, and enjoy!

NO-KNEAD WHOLEMEAL RYE WITH 100% HYDRATION

*PLUS C. 8 HOURS PROVING

Makes 1 2lb loaf

500ml lukewarm water
150g levain
500g wholemeal rye flour
5g salt
oil, for greasing

Rye is a variety of wheat that typically has lower levels of protein and which some gluten-intolerant people can eat and enjoy. It also has beautiful sweet, earthy tones. This bread is 100 per cent wholemeal, so it's really high in fibre and is a proper healthy bread. It goes great toasted with hummus, pickled cucumber, miso, kimchi or avocado.

This is a no-knead bread where we use a 2lb baking tin to support it, so there is no need to develop gluten by kneading or working the dough. It has equal quantities of water and flour (100 per cent hydration), so it results in a really wet, sticky dough that keeps well. If you prefer a drier bread, just reduce the water in the recipe below to 400ml.

Do the float test: First, make sure your levain is active and passes the float test (see page 244).

Mix the dough: Pour the lukewarm water into a large mixing bowl. Add the levain and, using a large wooden spoon, mix it through the water. Add in the rye flour and the salt, and mix just till the dough comes together. There's no need to work it.

Prep the tin and prove: Grease a 2lb loaf tin (22cm × 13cm × 11.5cm) with oil, ensuring to grease the sides and bottom well. Add in the mixed dough. It should come about halfway up the tin. Leave to prove until the dough has risen up to almost the lip of the tin – it should have doubled in size. The warmth of your environment will dictate how long it takes to rise – for example, we proved ours at 25°C, and it took 6–7 hours to prove.

Preheat and bake: Preheat the oven to 180°C fan/400°F/gas 6, then put in the loaf and bake for 60–70 minutes, until it's dark brown on top. Remove from the oven, take out of the tin, and place on a cooling rack. Tap the bottom of the loaf – it should sound hollow. If it doesn't, and it still feels heavy and dense, it needs to bake a little longer – just put it back into the oven without the tin for a further 10 minutes. Leave to cool fully. It should result in a sticky loaf with a tight, open crumb and a beautiful earthy, sweet tang.

EASY SESAME AND CORIANDER FLATBREADS

Makes 4

200g self-raising flour, plus extra for dusting
150ml natural soy yoghurt or coconut yoghurt
flour for dusting
3 tbsp black sesame seeds
1 tbsp oil, plus extra for brushing
10g fresh coriander
salt

These are surprisingly simple to make, and you can adapt this basic recipe to virtually any flavour you like. Here we've gone with sesame and coriander, but you could leave those out to make plain flatbreads.

Make the dough: In a mixing bowl, add the flour and a teaspoon of salt and stir together. Add the yoghurt and mix well until it's uniform in consistency. In the bowl, knead the mixture for 5 minutes till you get a soft dough.

Divide and roll out: Cut your dough into 4 equal pieces. Dust your work surface with flour, and roll out each piece of dough to about ½cm thick.

Cook: Put a large pan on a high heat. Once it's hot, reduce the heat to medium. Add a sprinkle of sesame seeds and 1 tablespoon of oil (use sesame oil if you want to increase the sesame flavour) then one of the rolled-out flatbreads. Cook till it starts to turn golden underneath – it may also start to form air pockets. Turn and cook on the other side till golden too. Repeat with the remaining flatbreads.

Serve: Brush with a little oil, then sprinkle with some freshly chopped coriander and coarse sea salt for one of our favourite types of flatbreads!

The Happy Pear

W DOLNE
GO W
DOLNEGO DOLNEGO
DOLNEGO

20 LEARNINGS from OUR PODCAST

Having a podcast has been like attending the magical university of life! We have learned so much through the conversations we've had with our guests – people from across a huge spectrum of the areas of health, well-being and life in general. Some of our favourite guests have been The Body Coach Joe Wicks, Bryan Adams (yes, that Bryan Adams!), Elle Macpherson (the former supermodel), Dan Buettner (the founder of Blue Zones) and Arthur C. Brooks (the Harvard professor of happiness) and so many more. We have recorded more than 150 episodes and had millions of listens. Here are some of the most important things we've learned.

1 **Life is like a game of snakes and ladders – some days you get a ladder up and feel like everything is going great, and other days you get a snake down and feel like you are going backwards, and there is often no rhyme or reason to it. A common theme which keeps coming up is that no one gets the 'full deck of cards', and perseverance, discipline, self-belief and faith can greatly influence your success. (Depending on how you define success, of course! We recorded two episodes with Manchán Magan, someone who has a very different definition of success to most, in the most refreshing way possible.)**

Us and Joe Wicks!

2 There is a degree of personal responsibility in terms of happiness. In talking to Harvard professor Arthur C. Brooks, we learned happiness can be a habit and a by-product of some core pillars, such as prioritising family, friends, faith and purpose and doing your best to ignore the four 'false gods or enemies of happiness': money, power, fame and pleasure.

3 Eat more veg – the theme of this book and The Happy Pear overall! We have had many doctors and consultants of all descriptions as podcast guests, including gastroenterologists Dr Alan Desmond and Dr Will Bulsiewicz, gynaecologist Dr Nitu Bajekal, neurologists Dr Oliver Bernath and Drs Dean and Ayesha Sherzai, cardiologists Dr Joel Kahn and Dr Kim Williams and urologist Dr Aaron Spitz. The message we heard consistently is that what you eat is one of the main contributing factors to your health and well-being. The more whole plant foods you eat the better for your microbiome and overall health. Regardless of whether you have cardiovascular or gut or skin or brain issues, whole plant foods will help in just about all cases!

4 The quality of your relationships directly impacts the quality of your life. How many times a week do you talk to a friend? Dan Buettner, founder of the Blue Zones, has featured twice on our podcast and is a huge advocate for prioritising real-world relationships.

5 Sleep is the cornerstone of health. If you don't get enough sleep, most aspects of your life will suffer. If you get six hours or less a night, you are likely to eat 300–500 more calories the next day than you normally would eat, and these are likely to be ultra-processed foods, not broccoli or kale! If you get poor sleep, you are much less likely to exercise or prioritise your mental health and relationships. Our podcast episode with Kathryn Pinkham is a great episode on this.

6 Menopause needs more light shone on it. As a society, we need to bring more attention and support to menopause and the women in our lives going through it. It will happen to approximately 50 per cent of the people on this planet, yet it is not as widely talked about as it should be. We learned from Dr Nitu Bajekal, senior consultant gynaecologist, that diet and lifestyle can greatly aid in a woman's journey through menopause – so we created our Happy Menopause course with her and some other medical experts. We also talked to Dr Louise Newson, founder of the Menopause Clinic in the UK, who believes that HRT is also worth considering in many cases.

7 We are an intrinsic part of nature, not separate from it. Nature feeds our spirits and souls in a way that a computer never can! How we live in terms of consumption, food, travel, fashion and refuse habits can greatly support or have devastating impacts on the natural world, and ultimately on ourselves. Dr Zach Bush visited us in person to talk about this.

8 Community and belonging is central to a good life. We did a series of 12 episodes on community, emphasising how important your relationships and community integration are to your overall sense of belonging, support and happiness.

9 Take time to contemplate and marvel at the sheer magnificence of life. Whether this is via journalling, meditating, mindfulness, manifesting, reading spiritual texts, watching a sunrise or sunset – whatever the practice, it's about making time to feel small and wonder at the larger awesomeness of life. This tends to make its woes easier to handle. Light Watkins's episode was a good reminder of this.

10 Your breath is an incredible tool to bring you into the present and help you destress. Considering you breathe about 25,000 times a day, a tiny optimisation could have significant benefits to your health and well-being. Our podcast conversations with international bestselling authors James Nestor and Patrick McKeown have us taping our mouths closed at night and doing breathwork most mornings! Try to focus most of your breathing through your nose, as it filters and compresses the air while also helping to dilate blood vessels to aid oxygen absorption.

11 We need to talk more openly about sex and bring it out of the shadows. We did a 10-episode podcast series on sex, talking to a range of experts. Sex is a balance between safety and excitement, connection and mystery – very much opposing forces. It is a space where many of us feel emotionally and physically exposed and vulnerable. It's essential that we actively work towards positive change in our conversations and societal norms surrounding sex.

12 **Shift your focus from the end result to the process itself.** Life is not about reaching specific destinations. The ideas we hold, like 'when I get married' or 'when I have a child' or 'when I achieve financial stability', are not endpoints in themselves. True fulfilment lies in the small, simple moments of our daily lives, rather than in the metaphorical 'I've made it' moments, where we imagine ourselves sipping cocktails on a beach in Ibiza. Our episode with Gary Gorrow was a great reminder of this.

13 **Failure is the greatest teacher of all.** As we heard in our episode with Elizabeth Day, we learn and typically grow far more from our failures than we do from our successes. Failure forms character and depth; success often does not.

14 **No matter how successful someone is, they still go through the same struggles that you and I go through.** Behind the shine of achievement and recognition, they grapple with self-doubt, face challenges and confront their own fears. Mo Gawdat, the former head of Google X, recorded a great episode with us on this topic. It's a reminder that our struggles are not unique, but rather a shared human experience that unites us all.

15 **'Success', material wealth and fame are what most of us are outwardly seeking more of.** Yet our relationships, physical health and sense of purpose are much bigger indicators of our long-term happiness and well-being. Dan Buettner, the founder of Blue Zones, was one Dave's favourite guests who spoke on this topic.

16 **Modern life is very demanding for most of us.** Make time for some quiet – whether that be meditation, mindfulness, walking in nature or looking at the stars. Our episode with Buddhist monk Gelong Thubten is a great reminder of this.

17 **The health of our soil is directly linked to human health.** Nicole Masters and Charles Dowding were both very inspiring on this topic. The microbial activity in the human gut and soil are very similar. The soil on planet earth is suffering greatly from industrial agriculture, deforestation and climate change. Your food choices directly impact this. Choose more organic and local plant-based foods.

18 **Manifesting is a genuine phenomenon!** Each of us emits a unique frequency, much like a tuning fork, and life responds accordingly. By cultivating gratitude and thanks for what we already have, we create an environment for attracting more abundance. Rather than worrying or stressing, do your best to relax, focus and nurture gratitude for what is here and now in the present. Roxie Nafousi's episode was great on this.

19 **In an inspiring episode, Matthijs Schouten showed us that we have the ability to address climate change by changing our mindset and facing our fears.** By coming together, we can make a real difference and find creative solutions to this pressing challenge. Let's remember that our collective actions inspire others, and together positive change can ripple further and wider than at any other time in history.

20 **The human spirit can overcome hardship and accomplish so much.** It can endure some of the toughest physical and emotional situations and grow from it – post-traumatic growth is a real thing. Damian Browne rowed the Atlantic ocean alone, which took him 112 days – his episode was seriously moving.

With Zach Bush

DIPS
SAV
DELI

AND
URY
GHTS

THE CREAMIEST HUMMUS EVER!

Makes about 800g

- 2 × 400g tins of cooked chickpeas
- ½ tsp baking soda
- 2–3 cloves of garlic, depending on your preference
- 4 tbsp lemon juice (about 2 lemons)
- 4 tbsp tahini
- 3–4 ice cubes
- 4 tbsp olive oil, plus extra to garnish
- 1½ tsp salt
- 1 tsp ground cumin
- pinch of sumac or sweet paprika, to garnish
- 1 tbsp sesame seeds, to garnish

We make literally tons of hummus every week in our factory in Pearville! Over the years, we have explored every trick and hack in search of the perfect hummus. Here are three simple tips to take your hummus to the next level:

1. **Boil your tinned chickpeas with baking soda for a few minutes, then remove the skins** – this makes the hummus creamier.
2. **Use ice instead of water** – it will help make the hummus lighter and fluffier.
3. **Blend for longer** – our friend from the Middle East blends his hummus for 30 minutes in his food processor!

Prepare the chickpeas: Drain and rinse the chickpeas and add to a pot. Add the baking soda, cover the chickpeas with just-boiled water and bring to the boil. Reduce to a simmer and cook for 10 minutes.

Remove the chickpea skins: Drain and rinse the cooked chickpeas. Set a small handful aside for garnish (if you'd like), then soak the rest in a large bowl filled with cold water. Try to get rid of the chickpea skins that came loose during the cooking by rubbing them together, or use a small sieve to help with this. Discard the skins.

Blend: Peel the garlic cloves. Add all ingredients for the hummus, except the sumac or sweet paprika and the sesame seeds, to a food processor and blend till super smooth – we recommend blending for 2–5 minutes, depending on your patience! Taste and adjust the seasoning to your palate. If it's too strong or too thick, add a little water to thin it out.

Serve: Serve with a glug of olive oil and a pinch of sumac or sweet paprika and a light dusting of sesame seeds.

BUTTERY HUMMUS

Makes 500g

2 × 400g tins of butter beans
½ tsp baking soda
1 lemon
6 tbsp light tahini
4 ice cubes
1½ tsp salt
5 tbsp water
2 small cloves of garlic
2 tbsp olive oil

To serve
1 ripe tomato
30g pickled red cabbage or red sauerkraut
10g fresh coriander
½ tsp sumac or Korean chilli powder
1-2 tbsp olive oil
4 slices of toast, flatbreads or fresh sourdough bread

This is insanely smooth and so easy to make – it really does feel like a top-quality hummus you've found on the streets of Lebanon. One of the keys to making it so smooth is using butter beans instead of chickpeas, as they are creamier and more buttery than chickpeas.

Prepare the butter beans: Drain and rinse the butter beans, add to a saucepan with the baking soda, and cover with just-boiled water. Boil for 5 minutes.

Remove the butter bean skins: Drain and rinse with cold water, and do your best to remove as many of the butter bean skins as possible. The easiest way to do this is to squeeze a cooked bean on its smaller side, and the bean should pop out of its skin. This isn't essential, but it does help produce a super-creamy texture.

Blend: Into a food processor, add the peeled butter beans, the juice of ½ the lemon, tahini, ice cubes, 1½ teaspoons of salt and 5 tablespoons of water. Peel the 2 garlic cloves and add. Blend for 2–3 minutes and slowly add in the olive oil. Taste and adjust the seasoning to your liking – if it tastes a bit flat or bland, add a little more salt; if it tastes thick and a bit stodgy, add more lemon juice; and if it tastes like it needs more base flavour, add ½ a clove of garlic.

Blend for a further 4–5 minutes until super silky-smooth and buttery. Taste and make any final adjustments by adding more salt or lemon juice. If you want it even smoother, just give it longer in the food processor.

Serve: Spoon out onto a plate and spread, making a hollow in the centre. Finely dice the tomato, the pickled red cabbage or sauerkraut and coriander, and mix together. Spoon the tomato, sauerkraut and coriander into the hollow in the hummus. Sprinkle with some sumac or chilli powder, drizzle with 1–2 tablespoons of oil, and serve with toast, flatbreads or fresh sourdough.

GUACAMOLE

Makes about 500g

2 ripe avocados
juice of 1 lime
1 clove of garlic – add extra if you love garlic
½ a medium-sized red onion (optional)
5 cherry tomatoes
½ tsp dried ground cumin
½ tsp fine sea salt
pinch of chilli powder
pinch of black pepper
10–15g fresh coriander

We love guacamole and could eat kilos of it in one go! It is so healthy and flavoursome, and it also looks so attractive with all its lovely colours and textures. Guacamole, like hummus, is a personal thing – this is our take on it, which we hope will bring as much joy to you as it does to us. It's a well-seasoned, full-flavoured guacamole, but feel free to adjust the seasoning to your liking!

Prep the avocados: Halve the avocados and remove the pits. Scoop the avocado flesh onto a chopping board and dice into small cubes. Transfer the diced avocado to a mixing bowl, and squeeze the lime juice over it.

Prep the rest of the veg: Peel the garlic and red onion, if using, then finely chop and add to the bowl. Quarter the cherry tomatoes and add them to the mixture. Sprinkle in the cumin, salt, chilli and black pepper. Chop the fresh coriander and add it to the bowl.

Mash and mix: Use a fork to mash some of the avocado, and bring everything together until well combined but still chunky. Adjust the seasoning to taste, adding more lime juice, salt, chilli, diced garlic or onion or black pepper if you like.

BABA GANOUSH

Makes 500g

2 medium aubergines
1 clove of garlic
2–3 tbsp tahini
juice of 2 lemons
1 tbsp olive oil
2 tbsp non-dairy yoghurt
salt and ground black pepper

To serve

½ cucumber
1 medium tomato
15g fresh coriander
olive oil, for drizzling
¼ tsp sumac (optional)
3 flatbreads (see page 253)

Baba ganoush, directly translated, means 'spoiled dad' – it's a smoky, creamy aubergine dip that's a beloved treat and a staple of Middle Eastern cuisine. It's also one of our all-time favourites! This easy-to-make recipe is perfect for a flavourful appetiser or snack.

Preheat: Preheat the oven to 220°C fan/475°F/gas 9.

Roast the aubergines: Cut the aubergines in half lengthways, lightly oil the flesh, and place them flesh-side down on a baking tray. Sprinkle with salt and roast for 40 minutes until charred and soft. Alternatively, char on an open gas flame for about 15 minutes, turning occasionally, until the skins are blackened and the insides are soft.

Prepare the dip: Let the aubergines cool slightly, then scoop out the soft flesh into a mixing bowl. Peel and finely chop or crush the garlic. Add the tahini, lemon juice, garlic, 1 tablespoon of olive oil, the yoghurt, 1 teaspoon of salt and a pinch of black pepper to the aubergine flesh. Mix well with a fork for a chunky texture, or blend in a food processor for a smooth consistency. Adjust the flavour with additional lemon juice, salt or a pinch of chilli as desired.

Prepare the garnish: Finely dice the cucumber and tomato. Chop the fresh coriander. Season the diced vegetables and coriander with a pinch of salt in a separate bowl.

Serve: Spread the baba ganoush on a large plate, creating a well in the centre. Add the cucumber, tomato and coriander mixture to the well. Drizzle with olive oil and sprinkle sumac around the sides for added flavour. Alternatively garnish with some sauerkraut or pickled red cabbage like the photo and some micro greens or chopped herb of choice. Cut the flatbreads into smaller pieces, serve and enjoy.

MUHAMMARA

Makes about 550g

50g walnuts
1 × 550g jar roasted red peppers
1 clove of garlic
juice of ½ lemon
2 tbsp oil
1 tsp chilli flakes
1 tsp ground cumin
1 tsp ground coriander
1 tbsp pomegranate molasses
50g breadcrumbs
¾ tsp sea salt

To garnish
small handful fresh coriander
small handful of pomegranate seeds

This beautiful dip based on roasted red peppers, walnuts and pomegranate molasses originates from Syria. It's sweet, smoky and acidic and goes wonderfully with flatbreads or toasted sourdough, some pickles and some hummus. It makes a mezze plate or dip plate pop with colour and a lovely acidic hit of flavour!

Toast the walnuts: Toast the walnuts in a dry pan over a medium heat for 4–5 minutes, tossing occasionally.

Prep the ingredients and blend the dip: Drain and rinse the red peppers, peel the clove of garlic, and add to a food processor along with half of the toasted walnuts, the lemon juice, oil, chilli flakes, ground cumin and ground coriander, pomegranate molasses, breadcrumbs and salt. Blend till super smooth. Taste and adjust the seasoning to your liking.

Prep the garnish: Roughly chop the remaining walnuts and some coriander leaves for garnish.

Serve: Carefully pour the muhammara into a bowl or onto a plate, and decorate with the walnuts, coriander and a pomegranate seeds or like the photo decorate with pomegranate seeds and some finely chopped coriander leaves.

TIP: If you can't source pomegranate molasses, replace with 1 tablespoon of maple syrup and a squeeze of lime.

Peanut
Rayu

PEANUT RAYU

Makes about 350g

- 100g raw peanuts
- 10 cloves of garlic
- 150ml oil
- 2 tbsp gochugaru or 1 tbsp smoked paprika and 1 tbsp chilli powder mixed together
- 1½ tbsp coconut sugar or brown sugar
- 3 tbsp sesame seeds
- 2 tbsp tamari or soy sauce
- salt and ground black pepper

This epitomises the phrase 'flavour bomb'! It is amazing served with noodles, as it has a wonderful fried garlic, roasted peanut note with an umami background and a lovely smoky spiciness, but it goes great with virtually all savoury foods – just mix before serving, as the oil separates. If you are allergic to peanuts, you can replace them with toasted almonds or even toasted sunflower seeds.

Preheat: Preheat the oven to 180°C fan/400°F/gas 6.

Roast the peanuts: Roast the peanuts for 15 minutes, then remove and leave to cool.

Prep and fry the garlic: Peel and finely dice the garlic, then add it to a medium saucepan with the oil. Heat on a medium–high heat till the garlic is lightly golden and crispy (if you overcook it, it will be bitter so be careful to stop it cooking before it gets any darker). This should only take a few minutes.

Mix the spices and garlic: In a medium bowl, mix the gochugaru or smoked paprika and chilli with the sugar and 2 teaspoons of salt. Pour the golden garlic and the hot oil over it and mix well.

Add the peanuts: Roughly chop the peanuts and add in, along with the sesame seeds and tamari or soy sauce, and mix well. Season with salt and pepper to taste.

VEGAN MAYONNAISE

Makes 600g

1 tsp garlic powder
300ml soy milk
2 tbsp lemon juice
½ tsp salt
¼ tsp ground black pepper
1 tbsp Dijon mustard
300ml olive oil or sunflower oil

This is so easy to make and so good – it's just like the real thing and goes splendidly with just about everything! You can use a light olive oil (better not to use extra virgin as the taste can be too dominant) or a neutral-tasting sunflower or vegetable oil. The main flavours you want to stand out here are the lemon, garlic and mustard, with the oil being the enricher.

Place all the ingredients in a blender or a food processor, except the oil, and blend for 1 minute. Next, while the blender is still running, slowly add the oil until the mix emulsifies. Blend until you reach a wonderful mayonnaise consistency – this should take about another minute. It will usually keep for about 2 weeks in the fridge.

EAT
MORE
VEG
Each meal is an opportunity
299

A better future
The POWER of COMMUNITY

SNA

CKS

CHOCOLATE CARAMEL MINI BITES

*PLUS 15 MINUTES SETTING TIME

Makes 24 bites

- 200g dark chocolate
- 150g peanut butter (smooth or chunky)
- 100g mixed nuts
- 100g pitted dates
- 2 tbsp coconut oil
- pinch of salt

A friend makes a raw-food version of these, and they're so pretty and such a great way to make a healthy dessert look so desirable that we had to make our own version. They look super indulgent, but they're actually made of mostly wholefoods, and they require no baking and are gluten-free. We sometimes make nut-free versions using tahini instead of peanut butter and seeds in place of the nuts so the kids can take them to school. You will need a silicone mould to shape them – ours has 24 squares, each 2.5cm × 2.5cm × 1cm.

Melt the chocolate, mould and freeze: Chop the chocolate into small pieces and melt in a bowl over a pan of simmering water or in a microwave. Divide the melted chocolate between all the squares in the mould. Fill each square about ⅓ full with chocolate, and use a small spoon to bring the chocolate up the sides a bit so it forms little cups. Put the chocolate-filled moulds into the freezer for 15 minutes so the chocolate hardens.

Make the peanut-butter layer: Once the chocolate is set, spoon a small amount of peanut butter onto each square. Again, it should fill about ⅓ of each cup, so now, with the chocolate and peanut butter, the cups in the mould should be ⅔ full.

Blend nuts and dates: In a food processor, blend the mixed nuts until they reach a breadcrumb-like consistency. Add the pitted dates, coconut oil and a pinch of salt, and blend until it comes together. This should take 2–3 minutes.

Fill and chill to set: Carefully divide the date-and-nut mixture between the squares, filling each one. Put in the fridge to set for 20 minutes before removing from the moulds. These will last for 2 weeks once they're kept out of sunlight and away from warmth.

CHOCOLATE CHIP COOKIE DOUGH BALLS

Makes 12

90g cashew nuts, raw or roasted
pinch of salt
90g chopped pitted dates
1 tsp vanilla extract
3 tbsp cacao nibs, dark chocolate chips or chopped chocolate

A great healthier take on cookie dough, based mostly on wholefoods and easily made gluten-free. Dave came up with these years ago and whenever we make them at a cooking demo people are always amazed at how simple, yet how tasty, they are. If you want them to be sugar-free, you can use cacao nibs instead of the chocolate chips or chopped chocolate. They're a great snack that will satisfy any sweet cravings.

Blend salt and cashews: In a food processor, blend the cashew nuts with a pinch of salt for a couple of minutes, till they form fine crumbs.

Add the dates: Add the chopped dates and blend for a further 2 minutes. You may need to scrape down the sides of the processor.

Add vanilla: Add the teaspoon of vanilla extract, and process. You may have to stop your food processor and scrape down the sides a few times to make sure it blends properly. If it's too crumbly to form a dough, add a couple of teaspoons of water and process again.

Fold in chocolate chips or cacao nibs, roll into balls: Transfer the mixture to a large mixing bowl. Add the cacao nibs or chocolate and fold them through. It should form a big cookie-dough ball! Break off pieces and roll into balls. Store at room temperature for a few days, or refrigerate or freeze for a few weeks.

TIP: These can also be made into bars if you prefer.

CHEWY CARROT AND ALMOND FLAPJACKS

25 MINS PREP

30 MINS COOK

55 MINS TOTAL

Makes 16

100g carrot
pinch of salt
200g jumbo oats
75g almond flour
125g brown sugar
150g flaked almonds
125g vegetable oil
50ml maple syrup
½ tsp almond extract

These are a great way to sneak some extra veg into little and big kids alike! Carrot is the second sweetest of all veg, and when it's baked like this, it goes a little crispy and adds beautifully to the chewy sweetness.

Preheat the oven and line the tin: Preheat the oven to 160°C fan/350°F/gas 4. Line a 28cm × 18cm brownie tray with baking parchment..

Grate the carrot: Finely grate the carrot into a bowl, add a tiny pinch of salt and mix. Then transfer to a sieve and squeeze out any juice.

Mix the dry ingredients: In a bowl, mix the oats, flour, brown sugar and flaked almonds together (reserve a handful of flaked almonds to sprinkle on top). Mix and make a well in the middle.

Mix the wet ingredients: In another bowl, mix the oil, maple syrup, almond extract and grated carrot together.

Combine the wet and dry ingredients: Add the wet ingredients to the well in the dry ingredients and mix thoroughly.

Bake: Spoon the flapjack mixture into the tin and sprinkle on the remaining flaked almonds. Press the mixture into the corners and flatten with the back of a spoon so it is compacted, but not too well-compacted. Bake for 30 minutes.

Leave to cool: Remove from the oven, allow to cool for 10 minutes, then, while still in the tray, portion using a knife while still warm into 16 rectangles, or the size you prefer, then allow to cool fully before removing from the tray. Store in an airtight container for 7 days – we don't know how long they'd last beyond that, as they are always eaten before then!

TIP: For crispier flapjacks, bake at 180°C fan/400°F/gas 6 for 30 minutes.

EASY 'SAUSAGE' ROLLS

Makes 4 large rolls

- 1 × 400g tin of cooked lentils
- 2 cloves garlic
- 1 medium red onion
- 1 tbsp oil
- 3 tbsp maple syrup
- 3 tbsp balsamic vinegar
- 2 tbsp tamari or soy sauce
- 100g cashew nuts
- 1 × 320g sheet of vegan puff pastry, defrosted if frozen
- 50ml oat milk or non-dairy milk of choice
- 2 tbsp sesame seeds
- salt and ground black pepper

Steve's kids adore these and don't even realise they're eating lentils – pastry is a great way to disguise them! These are so good – sweet, earthy, crispy and chewy. They make a perfect healthier snack.

Preheat the oven and line the tray: Preheat the oven to 200°C fan/425°F/gas 7. Line a baking tray with baking parchment.

Prep the lentils and veg: Drain and rinse the lentils. Peel and finely chop the garlic, and peel and cut the onion into thin slices

Caramelise the onion and add the lentils: Add 1 tablespoon of oil to a pan over a high heat. Once hot, add the sliced onion, a pinch of salt and a pinch of black pepper and cook on a medium heat for 5 minutes, stirring occasionally, until the onions are nicely browned and softened. Add the chopped garlic, maple syrup and balsamic vinegar, mix well to coat the onions, reduce to a low heat, and cook for 3–4 minutes, stirring regularly, until the onions are nice and soft and sticky. Add the drained lentils and tamari or soy sauce and cook for 3–4 minutes, stirring occasionally, to evaporate any extra moisture. Remove from the heat.

Pulse in a blender or food processor and season to taste: In a food processor or blender, add the cashews, and pulse until they reach a rough breadcrumb consistency. Add the onion-and-lentil mixture and ½ teaspoon of ground black pepper, and pulse until the mixture comes together but is not too smooth. You want to ensure there's a slight bite to the filling. Taste and season with salt and pepper to your liking. Remove from the food processor and divide into 4 × 80g chunks, and then roll each into a sausage shape about 12–13cm long.

Roll out puff pastry: Roll out the puff pastry and cut into four even rectangles, about 12cm × 16cm. Place a sausage at one side of a pastry rectangle, 2–3cm in from the edge. Brush some oat milk along the other side, then roll the sausage up in the pastry until it overlaps and press gently along the seam to seal. Then place the sausage roll seam-side down and gently press down on it with the palm of your hand to help seal it more and to ensure it stays rolled when you bake it. Repeat with the remaining sausages and pastry.

Brush with oat milk and bake: Using a pastry brush, brush each sausage roll with a light coating of oat milk (this will help them to brown), then sprinkle with the sesame seeds, place on a parchment-lined baking tray and bake for 20 minutes, or until the pastry is golden brown.

IKEA

20 FOODS we couldn't LIVE WITHOUT

1 Tamari: Dave's number 1! A by-product of miso production, it's concentrated umami flavour in a bottle. We use it in everything: as the epitome of the fifth flavour profile, it's a great way to add instant deliciousness to any dish.

2 Fresh figs: One of our all-time favourite foods. One of Steve's happiest memories is finding wild fig trees laden with fresh figs while on holidays. The first time this happened we were in Italy for our friend Katie's wedding. We spotted a wild fig tree and climbed through the bushes to get some ripe figs – we ruined our fancy wedding clothes but, wow, was it worth it. Figs were also two of Dave's daughters' first food!

3 Sundried tomato pesto: Steve came up with a recipe for this over 20 years ago, and it was one of our first products. His boys eat about a kilo a week – he actually has to restrict how much they eat! It's still one of our favourites and a great way to add instant flavour to any savoury dish. A girl once stopped us at a festival to say she came home late one night and was craving something savoury – she had nothing to put our sundried tomato pesto on so she had it with chocolate digestive biscuits and said it went down a treat!

4 Tahini: We love to add some maple syrup to tahini, and a little sunflower oil, and drizzling it on fruit salads! Tahini is one of the core ingredients in hummus and the basis of tahini cream, which turns any vegetable dish into a centrepiece.

5 Oats: We eat so much porridge that we reckon it could be swimming around in our blood! Steve has porridge at least once a week for dinner, as his kids are always happy to eat it and it's a really easy meal.

6 **Hummus:** Our love of hummus has grown so much that we actually have a hummus factory! With our great team, we have been making hummus and its variations for two decades and still adore it.

7 **Almond butter:** Many years ago, Steve was living in France and fell in love with a nut butter called Jean Hervé. He would often eat a jar a day and developed a small nut-butter gut! Since then, we have both adored nut butters, with almond butter being our favourite. Monki is our go-to brand that we eat most days and sell in our shop.

8 **Dates:** Nature's toffees! There are so many varieties, with medjool being the most readily available in Ireland. We use dates most for desserts and when making a date caramel, where we blend them with almond or peanut butter. Dave loves to make date burgers, stuffing medjool dates with walnuts or almonds for a healthy snack.

9 **Sauerkraut:** We didn't like this as kids – the idea of sour, salty cabbage was too much for us. But we have developed a love for it after realising the benefits of eating probiotic foods like sauerkraut for our immune systems. By adding salt to sliced cabbage and submerging it under water, you are transforming one of the cheapest vegetables, pound for pound, into a super-healthy food (see page 296).

10 **Chocolate:** Steve has always had a love of chocolate. In the early days of the café, Steve and Michael, a fellow twin and chocolate lover, could often be found up late at night learning how to properly temper chocolate – they'd have eaten so much chocolate they'd have to have a bag of crisps before going home to bed to balance out all that sweetness! Over the last decade, Steve has developed a near-obsessive love of craft bean-to-bar chocolate. He makes his own and dreams of opening a small bean-to-bar production facility and launching a range of speciality chocolate.

11 **Kimchi:** Korean women have one of the longest life expectancies in the world, and one of the many contributing factors is that they eat a lot of fermented foods such as kimchi. Kimchi is like a spicy sauerkraut, originating in Korea and using a distinctive dried red chilli powder known as gochugaru (see page 300).

12 **Chia seeds:** We sometimes feel like we're cheating on porridge having chia pudding for breakfast, but over recent years we've both begun to have it quite often. Chia seeds are a superfood that, when soaked with oat milk and flax seeds and topped with lots of different fruit, coconut yoghurt and almond butter, make the most wonderful breakfast (see page 22).

13 **Avocados:** In 2001 we first read about the health properties of avocados, and only tried them for the first time in our early twenties, as they weren't widely available in Ireland. We expected to get superpowers after eating them but found them rubbery and awful (at the time we didn't know what a ripe one looked like!). But now they're one of our favourite foods, and it's hard to beat our sourdough breakfast toasties with smashed avocado, tomatoes and olives (page 40).

14 **Mangoes:** We never tried mango growing up, as it wasn't easily found in Ireland at that time. We both remember trying it in our early twenties and thinking it tasted like sunshine. When we travel, we love nothing more than finding a fruit market that has ripe mangoes, then sitting down at the side of the road, peeling it and just getting stuck in, like wild animals, happily making a mess of ourselves!

15 **Sea salt:** No amount of fancy cooking techniques can make up for an under-seasoned dish – one that doesn't have enough salt. Salt, as one of the five base flavours, accentuates the other four flavours when added.

Our favourite type of meal – sharing fruit at the side of the road!

16 **Garlic and ginger:** We've joined these to help squish in more of our favourite foods. They form the foundation flavours of loads of our dishes – so many of our recipes start with 'peel and finely dice the ginger and garlic'! Both ferment really well too (see page 307).

17 **Potatoes:** We felt if we left potatoes out here we couldn't call ourselves Irish! Potato will always be in our favourite foods – we eat the Spanish chickpea, potato and pesto bake most weeks, as it's such a crowd--pleaser at home (see page 143).

18 **Coffee:** When we first started the café in 2005, Steve didn't want to serve coffee, and he definitely was not going to serve any cakes with sugar – this was going to be a fun-free zone (it was back in our righteous, puritanical days). Of course, we had to sell coffee – we were opening a café! A few years into it, a friend from our childhood, Paul Grimes, came along with a wild passion for the diversity of flavour in speciality coffee. As chefs, we were intrigued, and since then we've bought a coffee roastery and roast our own specialty coffee, which we serve in our café and sell. There is such a wide range of flavour profiles in coffee, depending on where in the world the beans were grown, at what altitude and how it was processed, roasted and brewed. We love having an early morning coffee with Raj, Harold and whoever else is around – we're always grateful for this simple ritual that enriches our lives.

19 **Oyster mushrooms:** Our favourite type of mushroom, they are meaty and chewy and amazing. We love to cook them using a simple compression technique – we place a clean saucepan on top of them while cooking to enhance the grilling and caramelisation, and then add a little tamari. Our friend Steffan, who works with us, grows incredible oyster mushrooms locally, which we use and sell. Of the commercially available mushrooms, they have the most meat-like texture.

20 **Coriander:** Steve remembers being introduced to this for the first time as cilantro in Canada, and he absolutely hated it – he thought it tasted like soap. Now it's our favourite herb, and we grow kilos and kilos of it on our farm. About 10 per cent of the population have a gene that may cause coriander to taste like soap to them!

FERMEN
Fermented
Garlic

TATION
kimchi
carrot
ribbons
PREMIER

WHAT IS FERMENTATION?

Fermentation is like alchemy: it transforms simple veg into living, delicious homemade probiotics.

Traditionally, it was a means of preserving veg so they would last the winter. However, the fermentation process not only helps to extend the shelf life of produce, but it also creates lots of beneficial bacteria and microorganisms that are good for gut health.

According to our friend Dr Alan Desmond, an expert in gut health, consuming these simple fermented foods is far more likely to benefit your gut microbiome than using costly probiotic supplements.

The fermentation process that we discuss here is based on lactic acid fermentation, which is relatively straightforward. This type of fermentation occurs underwater in the absence of oxygen. We use a 2 per cent salt solution, which acts like a bouncer, keeping out harmful or unwanted bacteria and ensuring we get the healthy ones that we want to proliferate.

Lacto-fermentation brings acidity, fruitiness and umami to produce, so it's a great way to develop flavour and also make beneficial healthy probiotics.

What happens is lactobacillus bacteria transform sugar into lactic acid – they're the magic ingredient behind sauerkraut, kimchi, sourdough, yoghurt and even beer! They're anaerobic, meaning they can flourish without oxygen. Lactobacillus are present on the leaves and skins of just about all fruit and veg, waiting patiently for the right environment to start fermenting.

2% salt solution

The basis of most lactic acid fermentation, including making sauerkraut, is to use a 2% salt solution: take the total weight of the veg you want to ferment, multiply it by 2% or .02, and that is the amount of salt needed. You slice the veg into bite-sized pieces, add the salt and mix well. Get a sterilised jar, add this salted veg, cover with water until the veg is submerged, then leave it to ferment for a few days at room temperature for the microbes to work their magic! Once the veg reaches a level of acidity you're happy with, it's ready to eat and store in the fridge to halt fermentation.

NATURAL FERMENTING AND PICKLING

Fermenting and pickling are easy to do and a vital skill to help you add flavour to your food. One of the keys to being a good chef is the ability to layer flavours and learning to combine flavours that contrast. By mastering fermenting and pickling, you massively increase your capacity to play with acid, colour and texture, and you give yourself a vital component with which to layer on flavour.

Ferments and pickles are a great way to bring acidity to a dish, which may not sound that desirable, but let us make our case! Increasing acidity accentuates sweetness, which is typically the opposite flavour profile to acid, while also bringing vibrancy, which can help cut through a stodgy or heavy dish with a high fat content. Acidity is vital, and when used correctly it really improves your capacity to increase flavour and diversity. The most common pickle in the world is the pickled cucumber or gherkin, possibly better known for being removed from burgers throughout the world!

Spiced Carrot ribbons
Fermented Garlic

SAUERKRAUT

We love sauerkraut and find that its tangy flavour goes great with savoury dishes. We eat it with virtually all meals except breakfast! It's especially perfect on sandwiches and with curries.

SAUERKRAUT VERSUS NATURALLY FERMENTED CABBAGE

When making sauerkraut, once the salt has been added, the cabbage is typically mashed with a saucer or by hand until the cabbage releases its juices. The cabbage is then submerged under these juices for fermentation. This results in a stronger, more intense flavour – and also broken-down cabbage that can lose its shape. Naturally fermented cabbage excludes the mashing of the cabbage, so it's easier and quicker to make. The flavour can be more diluted, as water is used instead of cabbage juice for fermentation. However the finished fermented cabbage holds its shape better, as it wasn't subjected to a good bashing!

PINK SAUERKRAUT

*PLUS ABOUT 1 WEEK FERMENTATION TIME

400g red cabbage
8g salt
water to cover

This makes a beautiful garnish and makes any dish pop with its vibrant pink colour. The acidity complements most dishes as well as giving your food a probiotic hit.

Prep the jar: Sterilise a 1-litre jar with a lid by putting it through the dishwasher or filling it with boiling water and leaving to sit for a few minutes.

Prep the cabbage: Remove the outer leaves of the cabbage and set aside. These will be used as a plug to keep the cabbage submerged underwater and stop mould developing. Slice the cabbage thinly, using a very sharp knife, into nice long strips. Alternatively, grate the cabbage using the largest grater size or a food processor with a grater attachment.

Mix the cabbage and salt: Add the sliced or grated cabbage and the salt to a large metal bowl, and either bash it with a saucer to release the cabbage juices to make sauerkraut or skip this step to make naturally pickled cabbage. Both work fine.

Add to the jar and submerge in water: Add the cabbage and salt mixture and any juices to the jar, and press down with a wooden spoon to make sure that the cabbage is really compacted. If you haven't enough juices to cover the cabbage, add enough water so that the liquid just covers the cabbage, and then compress again with your wooden spoon, leaving a little room at the top of the jar as more moisture will be released. →

You want to ensure the cabbage is fully submerged. Then cover the cabbage with one of the outer leaves that you set aside earlier. Use a clean stone, or even a lemon or lime, to weigh down the outer cabbage leaf so that all the cabbage is kept submerged under water. Any part of the cabbage that is not submerged fully may develop yeast or mould.

Ferment the cabbage: Close the lid of your jar and leave to ferment at room temperature for about 1 week to a month. The longer you ferment it for, the more acidic it will become. Every few days burp the jar – open the lid to release any build up of gases then put the lid back on. (The lid is to stop any insects from getting in.)

Transfer to the fridge: Once the cabbage has turned a light, bright pink, is soft to the bite and tastes acidic to your liking, transfer it to the fridge to stop fermentation, and it's ready to enjoy! It will last for months in the fridge.

TIP: Date your jar so you remember when you started fermentation – trust us! We all typically live busy lives and can easily forget about the sauerkraut ...

Carrot Ribbons
Spiced 24/8/25

EASY KIMCHI

*PLUS ABOUT 1 WEEK FERMENTATION TIME

Makes 1½ litres

1kg mixed veg (carrot, pak choi, Chinese cabbage, radish, leeks)
20g salt (2% salt ratio)

Sauce

5 cloves of garlic
1 tsp maple syrup
25g rice flour
200ml water
large thumb-sized piece of ginger
½ a small onion
4 tbsp tamari or soy sauce
½ tsp kelp powder or seaweed of choice (optional)
2½ tbsp gochugaru, or 1 tbsp sweet paprika and 1½ tbsp chilli powder or cayenne powder

Kimchi is definitely one of our favourite condiments! It's like a Korean-style sauerkraut with a wonderful spicy, gingery flavour. It goes great with virtually everything, if you like strong savoury flavours, and it's packed full of probiotics. Traditionally, kimchi is made using Chinese cabbage and takes hours to make, but we've adapted it using simple lactic acid fermentation, so it's quicker and easier yet still tastes fab!

Sterilise the jar: Sterilise a jar with a lid that holds at least 1½ litres by putting it through the dishwasher or filling it with boiling water and leaving it to sit for a few minutes.

Prepare the veg: Roughly chop the mixed veg into bite-sized pieces. Put in a large bowl or saucepan, add the salt and mix well.

Make the sauce and mix with the veg: Peel the garlic cloves. Add all the ingredients for the sauce (apart from the kelp powder and gochugaru) to a blender or food processor and blend till smooth. Pour over the already salted veg, then add the gochugaru or paprika and chilli mix and mix well.

Add to the jar and submerge: Add everything to the sterilised jar. Ensure all the veg is submerged under the liquid (if there is not enough, add more water so that all the veg is under the water). Add a plug or outer leaf of cabbage followed by a clean stone or weight to weigh down the veg so that it stays under the water. Close the lid to stop small insects or flies getting in. Write the date on your jar so you know when you started fermenting.

Ferment: Leave to ferment at room temperature, which is ideally around 15–25°C, for 3–7 days, until it starts to become slightly bubbly. You will need to burp the jar every 2 days by opening the lid and releasing the gas that has built up then putting the lid back on.

Taste: After a few days taste the kimchi. If you prefer it to be more acidic and sharper, leave it to ferment for longer. Once you are happy with the level of acidity, put it in the fridge to stop fermentation and enjoy for many months, or even years, to follow.

TIP: When fermenting your kimchi, make sure that the veg stays submerged under the liquid. If not properly submerged, the top layer that is exposed to the air can start to go off slightly and suffer a mould or yeast infection. Don't worry about this – the veg with the mould can simply be discarded, and the underneath layer should still be perfectly fine to eat. Just ensure to remove all mould and any infected areas.

HOMEMADE LACTO-FERMENTED CHILLI SAUCE

*PLUS 7–10 DAYS FERMENTATION

Makes 1 litre

Chilli ferment

500g assorted fresh chillis
12g ginger
75g carrot
4 cloves of garlic
12g salt
water to cover

Hot sauce

fermented chillies, garlic and ginger
320ml chilli brine (from fermentation)
7 tbsp apple cider vinegar
7 tbsp maple syrup
1 tsp salt
½ tsp ground black pepper
2 roasted carrots (optional)
1 tbsp tamari or soy sauce

We were never really into chilli sauce, but when we got really into fermentation we decided to trial a fermented chilli sauce and found we absolutely adored it. It's simple to make and is a great way to preserve a large chilli harvest. This sauce is perfect for adding flavour to any dish and makes a delightful homemade gift.

Sterilise the jar: Sterilise a 1-litre jar with a lid by putting it through the dishwasher or filling it with boiling water and leaving to sit for a few minutes.

Prepare the ferment: Remove the stalks from the chillies, slice them open lengthwise on one side, and place them in the sterilised jar. Peel and roughly chop the ginger. Finely slice the carrot. Peel the garlic cloves. Add the garlic, ginger, carrot and salt to the jar with the chillies. Pour water over to cover the ingredients. Place a lid or saucer inside the jar to keep everything submerged, adding a weight if necessary. Put the lid on to keep insects out and label with the date.

Ferment the chillies: Ferment at room temperature for 7–10 days, burping the jar every 2 days. To do this, simply open the lid for a second and close it; this will release any excess gas build up.

Drain the fermented chillies: After fermentation (7–10 days), drain the chillies, reserving the brine.

Blend the hot sauce: Add the fermented chillies, garlic, ginger, chilli brine, apple cider vinegar, maple syrup, salt, black pepper, optional roasted carrots and tamari or soy sauce to a blender. Blend until smooth.

Strain and season: Pass the sauce through a sieve for a finer texture. Taste and adjust seasoning with additional salt, maple syrup, vinegar or tamari or soy sauce as desired.

Bottle and store: Use a funnel to pour the sauce into sterilised bottles. Store in the fridge for up to 3 months.

TIP: If you want to make it less spicy just increase the amount of carrot in the recipe from 75g up to 150g.

PICKLED CUCUMBERS

*PLUS 2 WEEKS FERMENTATION

Makes 500g

350g cucumber
12.25g salt (3.5% of weight of the cucumber)
water to cover

Optional seasoning
2 bay leaves
2 sprigs of fresh thyme
1 tbsp pink peppercorns
1 clove of garlic
3 blackcurrant leaves
30g fresh horseradish

Steve helps his Polish mother-in-law to make ogórek kiszony, or pickled cucumber, every year with small ridgeback cucumbers from their garden. They ripen at the same time as blackcurrants and horseradish so they're always put together, which makes a beautiful pickle. Typically a ridgeback cucumber or cucumber with a thick skin is used, but an ordinary cucumber will work fine too. Here we use 3.5 per cent salt to prevent the cucumber going soggy.

Sterilise the jar: Sterilise a 1-litre jar with a lid by putting it through the dishwasher or filling it with boiling water and leaving to sit for a few minutes.

Prepare the ferment: Chop the cucumbers lengthwise into quarters and add to the sterilised 1-litre jar, ideally filling the jar. Add any of the optional seasoning (slice the horseradish if using). Add the salt and mix. Cover with water so that all the cucumbers are submerged.

Ferment the cucumbers: Leave to ferment at room temperature for 2 weeks. Once they are nicely softened and acidic tasting (taste them!), transfer them to the fridge to halt fermentation. They will last for a couple of months in the fridge.

LACTO-FERMENTED GARLIC

*PLUS 3-4 WEEKS FERMENTATION

Makes 200g

200g peeled cloves of garlic
4g salt
water to cover

This is a probiotic-health flavour bomb! The idea of eating full cloves of garlic can sound crazy, but once pickled or naturally fermented, the harsh raw garlic taste transforms into a sweet delicate taste with a crunchy texture. Garlic contains a strong antibiotic called allicin that is released when it's chewed. By fermenting garlic, you are also introducing a probiotic health element to super charge it as well as a beautiful flavour bomb!

Sterilise the jar: Sterilise a 300g jar with a lid by putting it through the dishwasher or filling it with boiling water and leaving to sit for a few minutes.

Ferment the garlic: Add the garlic cloves and salt and cover with water until they are submerged. Give it a good mix. Use a weight to ensure the cloves stay submerged, such as the lid of a smaller jar. Make sure to write the date on the lid or on a label so you know when you started this ferment. Loosely add the lid, and leave on the counter away from direct sunlight to ferment for approximately 1 month. The garlic will need to be burped each day, which simply means to remove the lid and put it back on, this will release the build up of gases (which are a natural part of fermentation) and means that the lid won't fly off!

Taste it and move to the fridge: After a few weeks, taste the garlic (the longer it ferments at room temperature the more acidic it will become), and once it reaches a taste you are happy with, transfer it to the fridge, where it will last for months.

3 QUICK VINEGAR-BASED PICKLES

A quick pickle is when you slice up a veg or fruit and submerge it in a vinegar solution, such as 50 per cent vinegar and 50 per cent water, season it with salt and herbs and spices, and leave it for a short time to pickle. It's quick, very easy and you can flavour it to your liking. We most often use this method to quickly pickle red onions. Other veg we like to pickle are radish, cucumber and fennel. We often use some pink sauerkraut brine and vinegar to turn these veg, which are typically white or clear on the inside, a bright pink colour, as well as transform them into beautiful carriers of acid! By using a potato peeler or a mandolin, you can change the shape of any veg, and once pickled it takes on a different acidic personality.

PICKLED RED ONIONS

*PLUS 15 MINUTES PICKLING

Makes 200g

1 red onion (approx 200g)
½ tsp salt
60ml clear vinegar of choice
60ml of water

Pickling red onions helps to remove the strong raw-onion-like taste and transform the colour from red to pink, thus making a super-pretty, tasty garnish that also brings a little acidity.

Peel and finely slice the red onions into thin strips. Add to a jar along with the salt, cover with the vinegar and water, and mix well. Leave to pickle for 15 minutes and they are good to use. The longer they pickle for, the pinker they will become. They will keep for a week in the fridge with the lid on. They will last longer, however the onions will start to disintegrate over time.

PINK CUCUMBER

5
MINS
PREP

*PLUS 10 MINUTES PICKLING

Makes 150g

½ a cucumber
80ml pink sauerkraut brine (see page 296)
80ml clear vinegar
½ tsp salt

Red sauerkraut brine is simply the water from making red cabbage sauerkraut. It will have its own salty acidity to it and a vibrant red colour which will turn these cucumbers pink on the inside. We love these as a garnish and pop of acid. They go great with the easy dhal recipe on page 148. Only leave them to pickle for 10 minutes – any longer and the cucumber slices start to break down.

Slice the cucumber in half lengthwise and cut into ½ cm slices. To a jar, add the sliced cucumber along with the sauerkraut brine, vinegar and salt and mix well. Leave to pickle for 10 minutes for them to turn pink. They will last a week in the fridge with the lid on, and because cucumbers are more delicate, after 2–3 days they will start to lose their shape so ideally use them within 3 days.

SPICED CARROT RIBBONS WITH CHILLI AND GINGER

5
MINS
PREP

*PLUS 15 MINUTES PICKLING

Makes 300g

1 carrot
1 clove garlic
½ a thumb-sized piece of ginger
1 red chilli
100ml vinegar of choice
100ml water
½ tsp salt
1 tsp ground turmeric

Use a potato peeler to peel some long strips of carrot – they should start to fold in on themselves like a yoyo string. Peel and finely dice the garlic, and finely dice the ginger and chilli (remove the seeds from the chilli if you like it less spicy). Add all the ingredients to a jar, except the carrot, and mix together. Add in the carrot and ensure it's submerged under the brine. Leave to pickle for 15 minutes. They will last a week in the fridge with the lid on.

GINGER BUG

*PLUS 5 DAYS FERMENTATION

Makes 2 litres

To make the ginger bug

100g fresh ginger (ideally organic, as it works better!)
4 tsp brown sugar
2 litres water

To feed the ginger bug (each day for 5 days)

10–15g fresh ginger
1 tsp brown sugar

A ginger bug is a culture of beneficial bacteria made from fresh ginger root and sugar. The yeast on the ginger and in our environment feeds off the sugar and converts it into probiotic bacteria through the fermentation process. It takes about a week to make a ginger bug, and then this concentrated source of fermented ginger is used as a base to make beautiful iced tea or other fermented drinks such as our Hay Fever Probiotic Iced Tea on page 326. It's easy to make and great for gut health!

Sterilise the jar: Sterilise a 3-litre jar with a lid by putting it through the dishwasher or filling it with boiling water and leaving to sit for a few minutes.

Make the ginger bug: Cut the 100g ginger up finely, and add it to the sterilised jar with the sugar and water. Mix well, seal with the lid and label it with the date. Leave it to ferment at room temperature till the next day.

Burp and feed the ginger bug every day for 5 days: Finely cut up 10g–15g of fresh ginger and add to the jar, along with 1 teaspoon of brown sugar. Mix well and leave to ferment. Repeat each day for 5 days. By feeding it daily you will be letting the gas out (burping it)!

At the end of 5 days you will have a ginger bug. It should smell yeasty, like beer or bread, indicating that it's ready to use. You can use it straight away (just remove the bits of ginger) or store it in the fridge (leaving the ginger in it), where it will live for about 1 week; otherwise it needs to be fed regularly to keep it active. Add it to fizzy water or soda water with some maple syrup and lemon juice for a delicious fizzy probiotic hit!

GINGER-BUG ICED TEA

Makes about 1 litre

50ml ginger bug (strained of ginger pieces)
50g frozen raspberries (in place of ice)
6 sprigs of fresh mint
1 lemon, cut in wedges
1½ tbsp maple syrup
1 litre water, still or sparkling

Add all the ingredients to a jug, taste and adjust the sweetness to your liking for a beautiful gut-healthy treat!

Kombucha Scoby

KOMBUCHA

*PLUS 10-15 DAYS FERMENTATION (THE WARMER THE TEMPERATURE, THE QUICKER THE FERMENTATION)

Makes 3 litres

2½ litres water
6 teabags of your preferred flavour (e.g. green tea, ginger tea, black tea – it doesn't need to be caffeinated)
150g white sugar (see page 314 for alternatives)
1 active SCOBY (see page 314)
300ml previously brewed, or store bought, kombucha

Kombucha, a fermented tea with origins in China, is believed to be naturally probiotic and beneficial for gut health while also tasting like a fizzy drink. It is much lower in sugar than traditional soda or mineral drinks. Two decades ago, a friend of our mother's introduced us to a SCOBY – the collection of microbes that convert the sugar in kombucha into probiotic bacteria and carbon dioxide, creating the natural carbonation. It piqued our interest and, before long, we were brewing our very own. Making kombucha at home is straightforward, and you can tailor it to your taste preferences. We've simplified the usual two-step process to a single fermentation, using teabags for added flavour.

Sterilise the jar: Sterilise a 3-litre jar with a lid by putting it through the dishwasher or filling it with boiling water and leaving to sit for a few minutes.

Brew the tea: Boil 500ml of water. In a large bowl, steep the teabags and dissolve the sugar in the hot water, allowing the flavours to infuse for about 5 minutes. Discard the teabags. Allow the water to cool to below 37°C (body temperature).

Combine the ingredients: Add the remaining 2 litres of water to the jar. Mix in the brewed tea once it has cooled to avoid harming the SCOBY.

Ferment: Place the SCOBY and the 300ml of live kombucha into the jar. Don't seal the jar, instead cover with a tea-towel and ferment for 10–15 days at room temperature, away from direct sunlight. After the fermentation period, remove the SCOBY. Your kombucha is now ready for consumption. This is your first fermentation.

OPTIONAL SECOND FERMENTATION

For increased carbonation and flavouring, you can ferment the kombucha a second time. Transfer the kombucha into smaller jars or bottles, adding a pinch of sugar and additional teabags for different flavours, such as mixed berry or lemongrass and ginger. Seal the jars and let them sit for another day, then burp them to release excess gas. Leave for 1–3 more days before drinking. Longer fermentation will increase carbonation.

KOMBUCHA Q&A

How long should I ferment kombucha?

The ideal fermentation time is about 10–14 days at 20°C. Variables like SCOBY size and ambient temperature can affect this. Taste your kombucha to determine readiness – it should be bubbly and not overly sweet. The longer you ferment for, the more acidic it will become. Extended fermentation can lead to a more vinegar-like taste and more carbonation.

What should I use to ferment my kombucha?

Glass jars are best, but BPA-free plastic works too. Avoid metal containers and utensils, as they can damage the SCOBY.

Where can I get a SCOBY?

You can purchase them online or acquire one from a friend who brews kombucha. As you continue brewing, you'll have extra SCOBYs to share.

How do I grow a SCOBY from scratch?

Begin with an unpasteurised store-bought kombucha. Brew a small cup of tea with 1 tablespoon of sugar, matching the tea type in the kombucha. Once cooled below 37°C, combine with the kombucha in a jar, cover with a cloth, and ferment at room temperature out of direct sunlight for 2–4 weeks. A SCOBY should develop, becoming thicker over time. You can use this SCOBY to start your first batch of kombucha.

Why does kombucha require sugar?

Sugar is essential for fermentation, serving as food for the SCOBY. During the process, sugar is converted into probiotics and carbon dioxide, leaving minimal sugar in the final product.

What type of sugar is best for brewing kombucha?

- **White sugar:** easiest for the SCOBY to consume
- **Brown sugar:** May alter the flavour and is harder for the SCOBY to digest
- **Honey:** can be used, but ensure it's pasteurised to maintain SCOBY balance
- **Agave syrup:** best mixed with another sugar type to maintain culture health

Remember, the sugar is primarily for the SCOBY, not for consumption. Properly fermented kombucha contains significantly less sugar compared to other sweetened drinks.

Kombucha Scoby
PREMIER

20 DREAMS we HAVE

Our dreams hold the power to shape a reality that surpasses boundaries and limitations. They are the manifestations of our imagination, offering us endless possibilities. With our dreams, we become co-creators of a visionary future. So let's dare to dream big, embracing the joy and freedom that comes with knowing that dreams are priceless gifts, ready to be explored and realised.

1 To start an annual health and wellness super-fun festival called 'Pear-fest' in Greystones or close by to bring more awareness to health and wellness and, of course, to celebrate life!

2 To open a hostel with an event space near The Happy Pear in Greystones and host lots of fun retreats and community events.

3 To open a cooking school along with the hostel and event space.

4 To open a fresh juice bar again in our Greystones Happy Pear like the first one we opened over 18 years ago.

5 To open a bean-to-bar chocolate shop in The Happy Pear, where we are making amazing craft bean-to-bar chocolate.

6 To open The Happy Pear in Greystones at night four to five times a week with an amazing restaurant that uses mostly produce from our farm, so our food is literally 'farm to fork'.

7 To have a local meal delivery service that would support and make it easier for our community and customers to eat delicious wholefood plant-based meals by delivering them to their door.

8 To open a community skills warehouse in Greystones where the older and more experienced members of our community could share their skills with the young – a hub of life, creation and craft. Individuals could rent it out too, and there would be shared tool usage.

9 To build some sort of structure with our own hands – we both love DIY. Maybe we could start with building a shed on the farm!

10 To have our delicious range of food products widely available in the UK, USA and beyond.

11 To continue enhancing our amazing Happy Pear team spirit and culture by increasing team engagement across our entire business, including benefits like healthcare and pensions. Think of it like fermentation: the mother culture spreads and flourishes, but it requires the right conditions to thrive.

12 To work more with schools and educating kids, inspiring them about growing and cooking and the importance of nature, food and health and how it is all linked.

13 To start a school focused on practical life skills that is more child-led and less curriculum-based – maybe this is part of our retreat centre, but who knows?

14 To film a fun and inspirational transformational TV show, telling the stories of amazing people who are changing their lives via health, eating a more plant-based diet and adopting habits that help them to shine and inspire others to follow suit.

15 To film a TV show in search of the Middle East's best hummus! We've always wanted to go on a hummus expedition and filming it would be even more fun.

16 To write books on happiness, community and the deeper aspects of life, moving beyond food.

17 To write at least one poetry book.

18 To take our families on a trip to Canada, where we were born, and another one to the USA.

19 To help inspire Greystones, our home town, to become a blue zone of sorts, where the healthy choice is the easier choice.

20 That our farm continues to become a model that others copy, and that Ireland starts to support and encourage more veg growers. The Netherlands is 69 per cent smaller than Ireland, yet it grows about 28 times more produce than we do.

CHOOSE LOVE

CHOOSE LOVE

Steve dreams of opening a bean-to-bar chocolate shop

O
NUM
ON

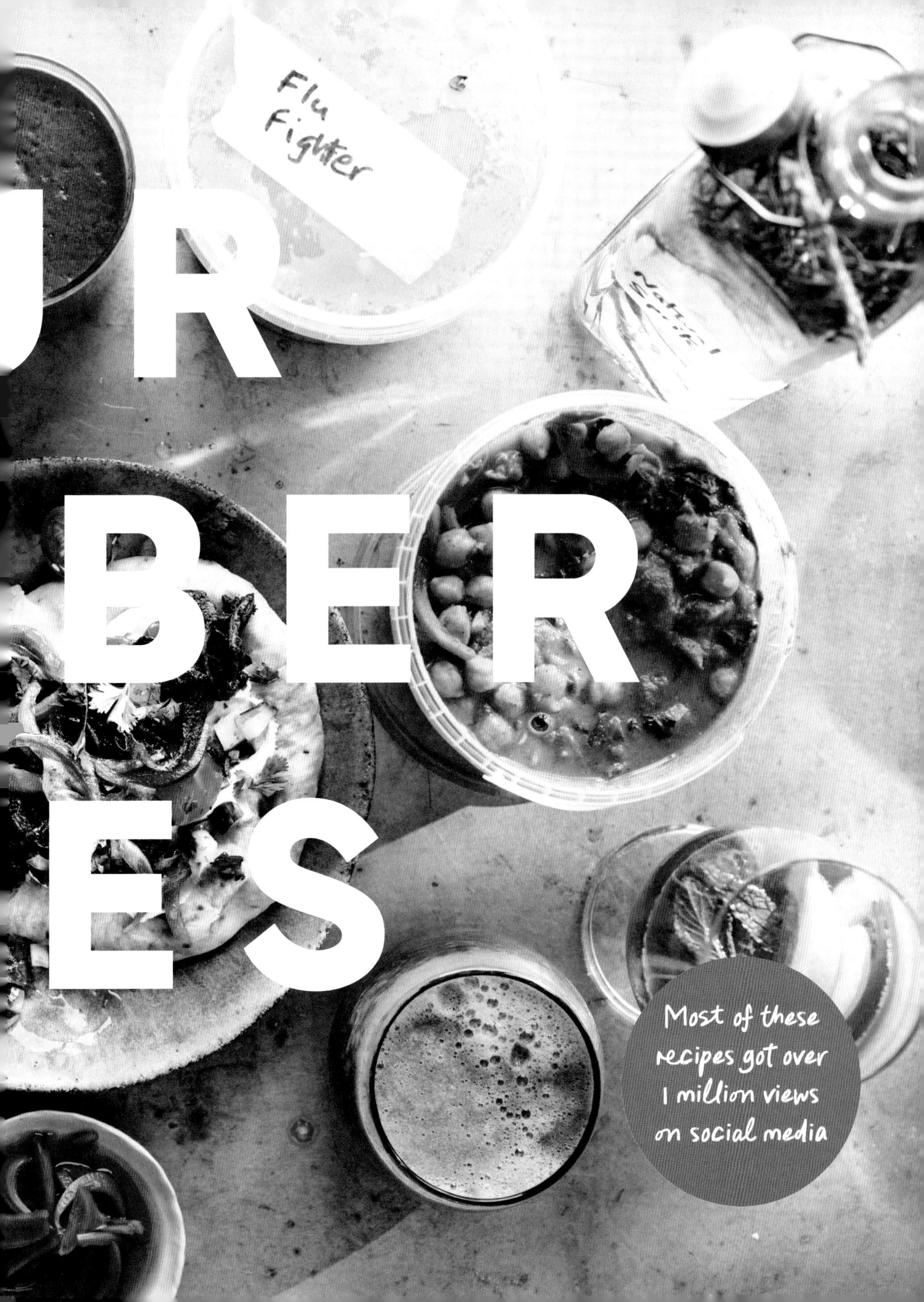
Flu
Fighter
JR
BER
ES
Most of these
recipes got over
1 million views
on social media

COLD KILLER

Makes about 1 litre

2 limes
1 grapefruit
10g fresh turmeric
½ a thumb-sized piece of ginger
1 green apple
½ a cucumber
10 fresh mint leaves
50g baby spinach
120ml water

This delicious smoothie is a great way to get more greens into you. It also has turmeric, which can be great for reducing inflammation, and is packed with vitamin C. The video for this has gotten over 3 million views on Instagram – it really is worth trying!

Prepare the ingredients: Peel the limes and grapefruit, ensuring to remove as much of the white pith as possible, as it's bitter. Peel the turmeric and ginger if not using organic, and cut into small pieces. Cut the apple and cucumber into small pieces. Remove the mint leaves from the stalks.

Blend: Add all the ingredients to a blender, and blend till super smooth. If it's a little thick, add some more water or ice cubes to thin it out.

TIP: We normally drink 250ml per day to help keep colds at bay!

Daisy and Steve

FLU FIGHTER GOLDEN SHOTS

Makes 1 litre

35g fresh turmeric
100g fresh ginger
2 oranges
2 lemons
½ tsp ground turmeric
pinch of black pepper/5 whole peppercorns
400ml water
½ tsp coconut oil

Like drinking liquid sunshine with a nice fiery hit, these fresh turmeric and ginger golden shots are a great immune booster. Often they're strained, but we've left in all the fibre goodness, which will help you absorb the nutrients as well as fill you up! The ground black pepper and coconut oil help with the absorption of the curcumin in the turmeric. When we first shot a video of this recipe, it got over 2.5 million views on Instagram.

Prep the ingredients: Cut the turmeric and ginger into small pieces (peel them if they are not organic). Peel the oranges and lemons.

Blend: Add all of the ingredients into a blender. Pop the lid on and blend on high until super smooth. Store in the fridge for 5 days, and have a good shot of it each day to give you a boost and help keep colds and flu at bay!

HAY-FEVER PROBIOTIC ICED TEA

*ASSUMING YOU HAVE A GINGER BUG!

Makes about 1 litre

50ml ginger bug (see page 311)
50g frozen raspberries/strawberries in place of ice
6 sprigs of mint
1 lemon, cut in wedges
1 tbsp maple syrup
1 litre water
50ml ginger bug (strain the ginger pieces)

We got over 1 million views of the video recipe for this delicious drink. We use a ginger ferment as the basis for it, which makes the iced tea naturally probiotic. We make it look pretty by adding frozen raspberries, lemon wedges and some mint leaves, and we sweeten it with maple syrup. This is very tasty on a warm day – or any day, really!

Add all the ingredients to a jug, taste and adjust the sweetness to your liking!

TIP: You can use sparkling water instead for a fizzier treat!

MIDDLE EASTERN 'MEATY' MUSHROOM FLATBREADS

Serves 2

200g oyster mushrooms
1 tbsp oil

Seasoning
1 tbsp sumac
½ tsp ground turmeric
1 tbsp paprika
½ tsp chilli powder
½ tsp ground black pepper
3 tbsp tamari or soy sauce
1½ tbsp maple syrup

Salad
⅓ of a cucumber
15g fresh coriander
10 cherry tomatoes
pinch of salt

Tahini cream
50 ml light tahini
100 ml soy yoghurt
1 tsp garlic powder
juice of 1 lemon
pinch of salt

To serve
2 flatbreads (see page 253)
pickled red onions (see page 308)

This has almost 500k views, is surprisingly easy to make and definitely one of our favourite meals to eat, as it's so tactile and deliciously messy!

Prepare the mushrooms: Tear the oyster mushrooms into thin shreds. In a bowl, combine the mushrooms with all the seasoning ingredients, and mix well to ensure even coating.

Cook the mushrooms: Heat 1 tablespoon of oil in a wide pan over a high heat. Place the mushrooms in a single layer in the hot pan, making sure they have enough room to spread out. Use another pan (with a clean base) to compress the mushrooms while cooking – this adds weight to help draw out the water. Cook for 1–2 minutes, remove the pan on top and flip over the mushrooms, and compress and cook again on the other side for 1–2 minutes until they are well charred and have a meaty texture. Remove from the pan and roughly chop the cooked mushrooms.

Prepare the salad: Dice the cucumber finely. Chop the fresh coriander. Halve the cherry tomatoes. In a bowl, mix together the cucumber, coriander, cherry tomatoes and a pinch of salt. Set aside.

Make the tahini cream: In a separate bowl, combine the tahini, yoghurt, garlic powder, lemon juice and a generous pinch of salt. Mix well, until the mixture reaches a creamy consistency. Taste and adjust the seasoning if necessary.

Assemble and serve: Spread a generous layer of tahini cream on each flatbread. Add some cucumber, tomato and coriander salad on top of the cream. Place a portion of the cooked mushroom mixture over the salad, and top with pickled red onions. Roll up the flatbreads, serve immediately and enjoy!

5-MINUTE CHICKPEA CURRY

Serves 2–4

2 cloves of garlic
1 bunch of scallions
½ a thumb-sized piece of ginger
½ a red chilli
10 cherry tomatoes
2 × 400g tins of chickpeas
small bunch of coriander
1 tbsp oil
2 tbsp curry powder
1 × 400g tin of chopped tomatoes
1 × 400g tin of coconut milk
2 tbsp tamari or soy sauce
1 tsp salt
½ tsp ground black pepper
juice of ½ a lime
50g baby spinach

Serving suggestions
pickled red onion (see page 308)
cooked brown rice
toasted nuts, for garnish

Our most popular recipe on YouTube, with over 3 million views! We call this 5-minute chickpea curry, but it might take you 10 minutes depending on your knife and cooking skills. It's a wholesome, nourishing and easy-to-make dish, delicious served with brown rice or any grain of your choice. To make it lower in calories, you can use a tin of low-fat coconut milk instead of full fat.

Prepare the vegetables: Peel the garlic. Finely chop the scallions and garlic. Peel and grate or finely chop the ginger. Thinly slice the chilli, removing seeds and membrane, if desired, for less heat. Halve the cherry tomatoes. Drain and rinse the chickpeas. Finely chop the coriander, keeping the leaves and stalks separate.

Sauté the base flavours: Heat a large pan over high heat with 1 tablespoon of oil. Add the chopped scallions, chilli, ginger and garlic. Sauté for 2–3 minutes, stirring regularly.

Deglaze the pan and the spice: If anything starts to stick to the pan, add a bit of water (1–2 tablespoons) to deglaze it, scraping the bottom with a wooden spoon or silicone spatula. Stir in the curry powder and cook for another 30 seconds to allow the spices to release their flavours.

Bring to the boil: Add the chopped tomatoes, coconut milk, chickpeas, coriander stalks, tamari or soy sauce and halved cherry tomatoes to the pan and bring to the boil. Then reduce to a simmer and season with the salt and black pepper.

Final touches: Stir in the lime juice and baby spinach. Adjust the seasoning to taste. Cook just until the spinach wilts.

Serve: Serve the curry with your choice of grain, such as cooked brown rice. Garnish with the coriander leaves and some pickled red onions and toasted nuts, if desired.

EASY CREAMY ROASTED RED PEPPER PASTA

Serves 3–4

300g wholemeal pasta (use gluten-free pasta if desired)

Red pepper sauce

100g cashew nuts
500ml oat milk
1½ tsp salt
¼ tsp ground black pepper
1 tsp garlic powder
juice of ½ a lemon
100g roasted red peppers (from a jar)

To serve

75g roasted red peppers (from a jar)
20g fresh basil

A simple yet flavourful dish, this pasta is enhanced with the sweetness and slightly charred flavour of roasted red peppers, perfect for a quick and satisfying meal. This recipe has had over 1 million views on our YouTube channel and can be easily adapted for gluten-free needs.

Cook the pasta: Cook the pasta according to the package instructions in well-salted water.

Make the red pepper sauce: Blend the cashew nuts, oat milk, salt, black pepper, garlic powder, lemon juice, and 100g of roasted red peppers until silky smooth.

Drain the pasta: Once the pasta is cooked, drain it, reserving some of the pasta water.

Mix the pasta and sauce: Return the pasta to the pot and pour in the red pepper sauce. Stir over medium heat until everything is well combined and warmed through. If the sauce is too thick, add a few tablespoons of the reserved pasta water till it reaches your desired consistency. Simmer until the sauce thickens to your liking.

Taste and serve: Taste and adjust the seasoning if necessary. Slice the 75g of roasted red peppers and add. Serve the pasta hot, garnished with chopped fresh basil leaves.

VEGAN BUTTER

*PLUS OVERNIGHT TO SET

Makes 400ml

200ml odourless coconut oil
150ml non-dairy milk, oat milk preferred for creaminess
1 tbsp white miso paste
2 tbsp lecithin, soy-based recommended
juice of 1 lemon
¾ tsp salt

We played around with making our own plant-based butter for a long time – we used shea butter and cacao butter, but it just never seemed to be quite right. But when we started using lecithin and coconut oil, we finally cracked it, and the video got over 1 million views on YouTube! Lecithin is an emulsifier that binds the milk and coconut oil together to form that wonderful creamy texture so it melts like butter and tastes like butter! Lecithin is widely available in most health food stores and also online.

Melt the coconut oil: Place the coconut oil in a saucepan. Heat the saucepan on high until the coconut oil is fully melted.

Blend the ingredients: Into a blender, add the melted coconut oil, non-dairy milk, white miso paste, lecithin, lemon juice and salt. Blend the mixture until it becomes super smooth, ensuring the lecithin is fully incorporated.

Pour and set: Once the mixture is blended and smooth, pour it into a large bowl or divide it into a few smaller butter bowls. Place the mixture into the refrigerator and leave to set overnight.

Enjoy your vegan butter: After the setting time, remove the vegan butter from the fridge. It's now ready to use! Enjoy it on toast, in your cooking or as a base for other flavourful spreads.

(More than) 20 PEOPLE who have made THE HAPPY PEAR what it is

Our mom and dad, Ismay and Donal Flynn. They have changed our points of view more than anyone else and helped us to see sense so many times – for instance, that it was not OK to cut the roof off an old limo and drive it across the US. They have been the true founders of The Happy Pear and always support us.

Our granny – the great May Flynn. Steve named his daughter after Granny May. She was always so kind and open-minded, even as she got older, and she was a great athlete who was always humble. We may not be as humble, but we definitely strive to be more like our granny! Check out Granny's Irish stew on page 147.

Our families and kids. To our wives and kids: you help challenge and temper our dreams and realise that ideals are called ideals because we strive towards them, but we don't necessarily get there. You help us to be more realistic and to ground our often slightly crazy ideas and bubbling enthusiasm!

Some of the team in Pearville after our AA food safety accreditation

Us and Nana Evelyn

Our parents, Ismay and Donal

Orna Murphy. Orna was the first member of our team and is one of the kindest, nicest people you could ever meet. She indirectly helped us to set up The Happy Pear culture.

Tommy Kelly. When we were 21, our friend Tommy was turning 40 and we all said we'd run a marathon to celebrate. We forgot to train and a month beforehand gave up alcohol and went on a 'detox' – and that was the start of our health journey!

Adrian from Australia. In 2002 Steve was in Whistler and met a fella from Australia called Adrian, who was a vegetarian. Before then he had never met a man that was a vegetarian – as stupid as it sounds, he didn't think a man could be. Steve asked Adrian if he could eat the same food as him for a week and that was that: we've been plant-based since!

Our brothers. We have two brothers, **Mark and Darragh.** Darragh is the managing director of The Happy Pear, and he follows a very similar lifestyle to us in that he went plant-based more than 20 years ago and loves to run and meditate. Mark used to live in Berlin and travelled the world as a DJ (the drifter). His lifestyle was quite different to ours for many years, but now he has come back home and joined us at The Happy Pear. Both our brothers have been rocks of support for us in so many ways.

Our team. We have had and have so many amazing people that we got to and get to work beside. In reality, they have made all this possible, as business is a team sport! Our team continues to balance our perspectives and help us bring our dreams to life.

Dorene Palmer – our chef mother. When we first started The Happy Pear, Dorene was our head chef – she preferred to be called a cook! She worked with us for nearly a decade, taught us how to cook professionally and the importance of organic produce and good sourcing, and really helped to shape our approach to food in general.

Matt, Leanne and Ciaran Butler from the Dublin fruit market. When we first started going to the Dublin fruit market, it had a strong culture of hard workers and it took a while for us to become accepted – we had to prove ourselves via showing up and hard work. Matt, Ciaran and Leanne were like family to us: they inspired us in so many ways. They were all very hardworking, fun and really believed in supporting local veg farmers.

Niall Meehan and our swim-rise family. We never thought we'd be those crazy people who swim in the sea all year round. But we went for that one swim with Niall, and we just kept coming back – not only for the benefits of cold exposure but also for the fun and craic from facing this common enemy of the cold sea together and collectively getting over it. Our group has grown in so many ways and we've made so many wonderful friends – big shout out to Jay for being the queen of birthdays and to Eric for increasing the cheer by playing his guitar on special occasions!

Angela Chambers. Angela kindly agreed to measure blood pressure, weight and cholesterol for our first Happy Heart Course, which led to the birth of our app, where we now have eight different health courses with medical professionals and have helped over 100,000 people from all over the world.

Seanie and Steve

Darragh and his son Fionn

Rossa Crowe. Rossa loves the romance of food production – when we first met him, while meditating, he was moving to France to find a sourdough baker to teach him the traditional method of baking sourdough bread in wood-fired ovens. He opened a beautiful bakery and now is into bean-to-bar chocolate making. Steve has a similar love for making food.

Simon Pratt. Simon started Avoca with his family and has always been a huge role model for us. Dave asked him one day if he would help to mentor us, and we ended up having amazing conversations about life, work and everything in between. He's become a good friend who we are very grateful for.

Damien Rice and Mark Lawlor. They are two of our dearest friends – both true artists in their own ways. Damien always challenges any fixed views we have and opens us up to new ways of looking at things, while also having amazing attention to detail. Mark is one of a kind, a fellow idealist and Virgo, and someone who really practises what he preaches.

A summer staff party

Linda and Detty. Both in their seventies, they swim with us most days at sunrise and are two of the most youthful people we know. They are so kind and up for life and adventure and always remind us how lucky we are to be alive and to make the most of what we have.

T. Colin Campbell. We read *The China Study* years ago, and Colin was always a hero of ours. He came to visit us once, and we put on an event together in Dublin in 2012. People often say you shouldn't meet your heroes as you will likely be disappointed, but Colin was such a gem and really reminded us that you should do your best to uphold your ideals, but not to beat yourself up if you fall short.

Raj, Harold, Sara and Seanie. The importance of the second yes. If you have a crazy idea, all you need is someone to back you up and support you to get it going – thanks for always being there for us!

Michael O'Loughlin and Patricia Deevy from Penguin Ireland. When we first started to explore writing a cookbook in 2010 we were very intimidated by the idea and grappled with imposter syndrome. Michael and Patricia from Penguin Ireland were such a joy to work with and so professional – they inspired us in many ways!

Yury Dubin. Yury, who was from Belarus, came in looking for a job one day with a sparkle in his eyes, and Dave said, 'He's a true lover of veg!' He became a core member of the founding culture of The Happy Pear. He worked with us for over a decade and had the driest sense of humour and such strong integrity. He died in a paragliding accident but will always be a part of us.

Dan Buettner. The man behind Blue Zones research, a kindred spirit who has inspired and encouraged us in so many ways. Blue Zones' messages about eating predominantly a wholefood plant-based diet, prioritising your relationships and having a purpose are vitally important.

Jamie Oliver. We were honoured to be asked to join his FoodTube family in 2012, and we flew to London once a month to film and work with his team creating healthy plant-based video recipes for YouTube, for which we now have nearly 50 million views!

Steve and Ned

The late Yury Dubin

Elsie, May, Izzy
and Dave in 2014

INDEX

A

almond butter
  Overnight Oats 3 Ways 18, 21
  Raspberry Ripple Pancakes 28
almond flour, Chewy Carrot and Almond Flapjacks 284
almonds
  Chewy Carrot and Almond Flapjacks 284
  Easy Bakewell Tart 214
  Mushroom and Pumpkin Wellington with Redcurrant Jus 176, 178
  Raspberry Bakewell Breakfast Muffins 39
  Red-Pepper Pesto and Bean Salad 84
almonds (ground)
  Apple and Berry Crumble 212
  Easy Bakewell Tart 214
  Raspberry Bakewell Breakfast Muffins 39
Apple and Berry Crumble 212
apples
  Apple and Berry Crumble 212
  Beetroot, Spinach and Apple Salad with Toasted Seeds 79
  Cold Killer 322
  Raspberry Caramel Apple Pie 210
aquafaba, Portuguese Chocolate Mousse Cake 202
Asian-Style Rainbow Crunch Salad 74
aubergines
  Baba Ganoush 269
  Creamy Harissa Aubergine with Zhoug 184
  Creamy Roasted-Veg Pasta Bake 140
  One-Pot Creamy Tomato Pasta 124
  Quinoa Tabbouleh Salad 87
avocados
  Black Bean, Roasted Sweet Potato and Avocado Salad 76
  Creamy Harissa Aubergine with Zhoug 184
  Creamy Spiced Black Bean Quesadillas 117
  Easy Burritos with Guacamole 138
  Guacamole 267
  Mexican Breakfast Bowl 10, 12
  Smashed Avocado, Tomato and Olive 40

B

Baba Ganoush 269
bananas
  Caramel Chocolate Banana Cake 198
  Caramelised Bananas 35
  5-Ingredient Banoffee Pie 223
basil, 10-Minute Lower-Fat Basil Pesto Pasta 123
beans
  Black Bean, Roasted Sweet Potato and Avocado Salad 76
  Cauliflower Curry Bake 120
  Creamy Spiced Black Bean Quesadillas 117
  Easy Burritos with Guacamole 138
  Ikarian Longevity Stew 150
  Mexican Breakfast Bowl 10, 12
  Quinoa Tabbouleh Salad 87
  Red-Pepper Pesto and Bean Salad 84
  Shepherdless Pie 162
  'Steak' and Kidney Pie 161
beetroot
  Beetroot, Spinach and Apple Salad with Toasted Seeds 79
  Beetroot, Walnut and Feta Burgers 107
  Shawarma Skewers with Oyster Mushrooms and Beetroot 100
Beetroot, Spinach and Apple Salad with Toasted Seeds 79
Beetroot, Walnut and Feta Burgers 107
berries
  Apple and Berry Crumble 212
  Fruit Compote 35
Black Bean, Roasted Sweet Potato and Avocado Salad 76
breadcrumbs
  Beetroot, Walnut and Feta Burgers 107
  Ultimate Mac and Cheese 114
broccoli
  Cream of Broccoli, Celeriac and Roasted Hazelnut Soup 59
  Ikarian Longevity Stew 150
Brownie Overnight Oats 21
Buttery Hummus 264
Buttery Hummus with a Pop 40

C

cabbage
  Asian-Style Rainbow Crunch Salad 74
  Happy Pear Farmhouse Salad with Roasted-Pumpkin-Seed Pesto 80
  Sauerkraut 296, 298
  Sticky Sesame Tofu Burgers with Charred Pineapple and Kimchi Mayo Slaw 105
cacao powder
  Chocolate Coffee Caramel 3-Tiered Cake 204
  Portuguese Chocolate Mousse Cake 202
capers, Kale Caesar Salad 83
Caramel Chocolate Banana Cake 198
Caramelised Banana 35
Caramelised Red Onion and Mushroom Tart Tatin 128
carrots
  Asian-Style Rainbow Crunch Salad 74
  Chewy Carrot and Almond Flapjacks 284
  Cream of Mushroom and Lentil Soup 62
  5-Ingredient Carrot Cake 220
  Roasted Carrot Falafel with Tahini Drizzle 157
  Roasted Veg Lasagna 144
  Soul-Nourishing Lentil Soup 67
  Spanish Chickpea, Potato and

Pesto Bake 143
Spiced Carrot Ribbons with Chilli and Ginger 309
'Steak' and Kidney Pie 161
cashew nuts
Beetroot, Walnut and Feta Burgers 107
Chocolate Chip Cookie Dough Balls 283
Creamiest Vegan Butter 'Chicken' 154
Creamy Mushroom Linguine 112
Creamy Spiced Black Bean Quesadillas 117
Easy Creamy Roasted Red Pepper Pasta 333
Easy 'Sausage' Rolls 286
Easy Spanakopita - Spinach and Filo Pastry Pie 153
5-Ingredient Banoffee Pie 223
5-Ingredient Chocolate Peanut-Butter Caramel Tart 224
5-Ingredient Cookies and Cream Cheesecake 228
Roasted Veg Lasagna 144
10-Minute Lower-Fat Basil Pesto Pasta 123
Ultimate Mac and Cheese 114
cauliflower
Cauliflower Curry Bake 120
Golden Roasted Cauliflower Steaks with Tahini Cream 174
Cauliflower Curry Bake 120
celeriac
Cream of Broccoli, Celeriac and Roasted Hazelnut Soup 59
Cream of Mushroom and Lentil Soup 62
Soul-Nourishing Lentil Soup 67
Chana Masala with Easy Gram Flour Dosa 188
Chewy Carrot and Almond Flapjacks 284
Chia Pudding with Fruit 22
chia seeds
Healthy Chia Pudding 3 Ways 22, 24
Overnight Oats 3 Ways 18, 21
chickpeas
Chana Masala with Easy Gram Flour Dosa 188
Creamiest Hummus Ever! 262
Easy 10-Minute Indian Dhal 118
5-Minute Chickpea Curry 330
Ikarian Longevity Stew 150
Real Falafel with Tahini Cream and Chilli Sauce 102
Roasted Carrot Falafel with Tahini Drizzle 157
Spanish Chickpea, Potato and Pesto Bake 143
chillies, Homemade Lacto-Fermented Chilli Sauce 303
chocolate
Caramel Chocolate Banana Cake 198
Chocolate Caramel Mini Bites 280
Chocolate Chip Cookie Dough Balls 283
Chocolate Coffee Caramel 3-Tiered Cake 204
Chocolate Hazelnut Loaf Cake 201
Chocolate Orange Pancakes 31
5-Ingredient Chocolate Ganache Tart 226
5-Ingredient Chocolate Peanut-Butter Caramel Tart 224
Super-Chewy Chocolate Chip Cookies 206
Chocolate Caramel Mini Bites 280
Chocolate Chip Cookie Dough Balls 283
Chocolate Coffee Caramel 3-Tiered Cake 204
Chocolate Hazelnut Loaf Cake 201
Chocolate Orange Pancakes 31
Chunky Spanish Lentil and Veg St-Oup 65
Cinnamon Swirls in 30 Minutes 36
citrus fruit, Flu Fighter Golden Shots 325
cocoa powder, Chocolate Coffee Caramel 3-Tiered Cake 204
coconut, Apple and Berry Crumble 212
coconut cream/milk
Cauliflower Curry Bake 120
Chocolate Coffee Caramel 3-Tiered Cake 204
Creamiest Vegan Butter 'Chicken' 154
Easy Heart-Warming Red Lentil Dhal 148
5-Ingredient Banoffee Pie 223
5-Minute Chickpea Curry 330
Mushroom Steak and Pepper Sauce 182
Raspberry Caramel Apple Pie 210
coffee
Chocolate Coffee Caramel 3-Tiered Cake 204
Tiramisu 209
Cold Killer 322
community 190–4
courgettes, Easy Heart-Warming Red Lentil Dhal 148
Cream of Broccoli, Celeriac and Roasted Hazelnut Soup 59
Cream of Mushroom and Lentil Soup 62
Creamiest Hummus Ever! 262
Creamiest Vegan Butter 'Chicken' 154
Creamy Harissa Aubergine with Zhoug 184
Creamy Mushroom Linguine 112
Creamy Mushroom Puff Pastry Pie 159
Creamy Roasted-Veg Pasta Bake 140
Creamy Spiced Black Bean Quesadillas 117
Crispy Tofu and Mushroom Ramen 164
Crispy Tofu Thai Noodle Soup 53
croutons, Kale Caesar Salad 83
cucumbers
Cold Killer 322
Middle Eastern 'Meaty' Mushroom Flatbreads 328
Pickled Cucumbers 304
Pink Cucumber 309
Quinoa Tabbouleh Salad 87
Real Falafel with Tahini Cream and Chilli Sauce 102

Shawarma Skewers with Oyster Mushrooms and Beetroot 100
curry paste, Crispy Tofu Thai Noodle Soup 53

D
Date and Vanilla Velvet Chia Pudding 24
dates
Chocolate Caramel Mini Bites 280
Chocolate Chip Cookie Dough Balls 283
Date and Vanilla Velvet Chia Pudding 24
5-Ingredient Banoffee Pie 223
5-Ingredient Chocolate Peanut-Butter Caramel Tart 224
5-Ingredient Cookies and Cream Cheesecake 228
Overnight Oats 3 Ways 18, 21
Downtown Flavour Bomb! 40
dried fruit
5-Ingredient Carrot Cake 220
Granola 3 Ways 15–16
Overnight Oats 3 Ways 18, 21

E
Easy 10-Minute Indian Dhal 118
Easy Bakewell Tart 214
Easy Burritos with Guacamole 138
Easy Creamy Roasted Red Pepper Pasta 333
Easy Heart-Warming Red Lentil Dhal 148
Easy Kimchi 300
Easy Miso Soup 50
Easy 'Sausage' Rolls 286
Easy Sesame and Coriander Flatbreads 253
Easy Spanakopita - Spinach and Filo Pastry Pie 153
Easy Tomato and Basil Soup 61

F
failure, learning about 130, 132–3
farm, the 88, 90–1
Fennel and Carrot Sauerkraut 298
fermentation 294
5-Ingredient Banoffee Pie 223
5-Ingredient Carrot Cake 220
5-Ingredient Chocolate Ganache Tart 226
5-Ingredient Chocolate Peanut-Butter Caramel Tart 224
5-Ingredient Cookies and Cream Cheesecake 228
5-Ingredient Maple-Glazed Fruit Puff-Pastry Slices 230
5-Ingredient Upside-down Pear Tart 232
5-Minute Chickpea Curry 330
flaxseeds
Caramel Chocolate Banana Cake 198
Chocolate Hazelnut Loaf Cake 201
Chocolate Orange Pancakes 31
Healthy Chia Pudding 3 Ways 22, 24
Portuguese Chocolate Mousse Cake 202
Raspberry Bakewell Breakfast Muffins 39
Super-Chewy Chocolate Chip Cookies 206
Vegan Hoisin 'Duck' Pancakes 187
Flu Fighter Golden Shots 325
food philosophy 42–7
food production 92
fruit, Healthy Chia Pudding 3 Ways 22, 24
Fruit Compote 25

G
ginger
Flu Fighter Golden Shots 325
Hay-Fever Probiotic Iced Tea 326
Ginger Bug 311
Ginger-Bug Iced Tea 311
Golden Roasted Cauliflower Steaks with Tahini Cream 174
gram flour
Chana Masala with Easy Gram Flour Dosa 188
High-Protein Pancakes 31
Granny's Irish Stew 147
Granola 3 Ways 15–16
Guacamole 267

H
Happy Pear Farmhouse Salad with Roasted-Pumpkin-Seed Pesto 80
harissa paste, Creamy Harissa Aubergine with Zhoug 184
Hay-Fever Probiotic Iced Tea 326
hazelnuts
Chocolate Hazelnut Loaf Cake 201
Cream of Broccoli, Celeriac and Roasted Hazelnut Soup 59
Healthy Chia Pudding 3 Ways 22, 24
High-Protein Pancakes 31
hoisin, Vegan Hoisin 'Duck' Pancakes 187
Homemade Lacto-Fermented Chilli Sauce 303
hummus
Beetroot, Walnut and Feta Burgers 107
Buttery Hummus 264
Buttery Hummus with a Pop 40
Creamiest Hummus Ever! 262

I
Ikarian Longevity Stew 150
Irish Root Vegetable Soup 54

J
jam, Easy Bakewell Tart 214

K
kale, Super-Greens Pesto Pasta 126
Kale Caesar Salad 83
kimchi
Downtown Flavour Bomb! 40
Sticky Sesame Tofu Burgers with Charred Pineapple and Kimchi Mayo Slaw 105
King Oyster Mushroom 'BLT' Sandwich 99
Kombucha 313–14

L
Lacto-Fermented Garlic 307
Leek and Potato Soup 56
leeks
Cauliflower Curry Bake 120

Easy Spanakopita - Spinach and Filo Pastry Pie 153
lentils
Chunky Spanish Lentil and Veg St-Oup 65
Cream of Mushroom and Lentil Soup 62
Easy 10-Minute Indian Dhal 118
Easy Heart-Warming Red Lentil Dhal 148
Easy 'Sausage' Rolls 286
Ikarian Longevity Stew 150
Shepherdless Pie 162
Soul-Nourishing Lentil Soup 67
lettuce
Kale Caesar Salad 83
King Oyster Mushroom 'BLT' Sandwich 99
liqueur, Tiramisu 209
Love Letter to Porridge 32, 35

M
Mexican Breakfast Bowl 10, 12
Middle Eastern 'Meaty' Mushroom Flatbreads 328
miso paste
Easy Miso Soup 50
Vegan Hoisin 'Duck' Pancakes 187
Muhammara 270
Mushroom Bourguignon with Pumpkin and Mash 181
Mushroom and Pumpkin Wellington with Redcurrant Jus 176, 178
Mushroom Steak and Pepper Sauce 182
mushrooms
Caramelised Red Onion and Mushroom Tart Tatin 128
Cream of Mushroom and Lentil Soup 62
Creamiest Vegan Butter 'Chicken' 154
Creamy Mushroom Linguine 112
Creamy Mushroom Puff Pastry Pie 159
Crispy Tofu and Mushroom Ramen 164
Granny's Irish Stew 147
King Oyster Mushroom 'BLT' Sandwich 99
Middle Eastern 'Meaty' Mushroom Flatbreads 328
Mushroom Bourguignon with Pumpkin and Mash 181
Mushroom and Pumpkin Wellington with Redcurrant Jus 176, 178
Mushroom Steak and Pepper Sauce 182
One-Pot Creamy Tomato Pasta 124
Plant-Based Philly Cheesesteak 96
Roasted Veg Lasagna 144
Shawarma Skewers with Oyster Mushrooms and Beetroot 100
'Steak' and Kidney Pie 161
Vegan Hoisin 'Duck' Pancakes 187

N
No-Knead Free-Form Sourdough Loaf 246, 248
No-Knead Wholemeal Rye with 100% Hydration 250
noodles
Crispy Tofu and Mushroom Ramen 164
Crispy Tofu Thai Noodle Soup 53
nuts
Chocolate Caramel Mini Bites 280
5-Ingredient Maple-Glazed Fruit Puff-Pastry Slices 230
Granola 3 Ways 15–16
Mushroom and Pumpkin Wellington with Redcurrant Jus 176, 178
Overnight Oats 3 Ways 18, 21
see also cashew nuts; hazelnuts; walnuts

O
oats
Apple and Berry Crumble 212
Chewy Carrot and Almond Flapjacks 284
Chocolate Chip Cookie Dough Balls 283
Granola 3 Ways 15–16
Love Letter to Porridge 32, 35
Overnight Oats 3 Ways 18, 21
Raspberry Bakewell Breakfast Muffins 39
olives, Smashed Avocado, Tomato and Olive 40
One-Pot Creamy Tomato Pasta 124
oranges, Chocolate Orange Pancakes 31
Overnight Oats 3 Ways 18, 21

P
Pancakes 3 Ways 28, 31
pasta
Creamy Mushroom Linguine 112
Creamy Roasted-Veg Pasta Bake 140
Easy Creamy Roasted Red Pepper Pasta 333
Ikarian Longevity Stew 150
One-Pot Creamy Tomato Pasta 124
Super-Greens Pesto Pasta 126
10-Minute Lower-Fat Basil Pesto Pasta 123
Ultimate Mac and Cheese 114
pastry
Caramelised Red Onion and Mushroom Tart Tatin 128
Creamy Mushroom Puff Pastry Pie 159
Easy Bakewell Tart 214
Easy 'Sausage' Rolls 286
Easy Spanakopita - Spinach and Filo Pastry Pie 153
5-Ingredient Chocolate Ganache Tart 226
5-Ingredient Maple-Glazed Fruit Puff-Pastry Slices 230
5-Ingredient Upside-down Pear Tart 232
Mushroom and Pumpkin Wellington with Redcurrant Jus 176, 178
Raspberry Caramel Apple Pie 210
'Steak' and Kidney Pie 161

peaches, 5-Ingredient Maple-Glazed Fruit Puff-Pastry Slices 230
peanut butter
- Chocolate Caramel Mini Bites 280
- 5-Ingredient Chocolate Peanut-Butter Caramel Tart 224

Peanut Rayu 273
pears, 5-Ingredient Upside-down Pear Tart 232
peppers
- Asian-Style Rainbow Crunch Salad 74
- Creamy Roasted-Veg Pasta Bake 140
- Easy Creamy Roasted Red Pepper Pasta 333
- Easy Tomato and Basil Soup 61
- Muhammara 270
- Plant-Based Philly Cheesesteak 96
- Quinoa Tabbouleh Salad 87
- Red-Pepper Pesto and Bean Salad 84

pesto
- Creamiest Vegan Butter 'Chicken' 154
- Red-Pepper Pesto and Bean Salad 84
- Spanish Chickpea, Potato and Pesto Bake 143
- Super-Greens Pesto Pasta 126
- 10-Minute Lower-Fat Basil Pesto Pasta 123

Pickled Cucumbers 304
Pickled Red Onions 308
pickles
- Buttery Hummus 264
- Crispy Tofu and Mushroom Ramen 164
- Downtown Flavour Bomb! 40
- Real Falafel with Tahini Cream and Chilli Sauce 102
- 3 Quick Vinegar-Based Pickles 308–9

pineapples, Sticky Sesame Tofu Burgers with Charred Pineapple and Kimchi Mayo Slaw 105
Pink Cucumber 309
Pink Sauerkraut 296, 298
Plant-Based Philly Cheesesteak 96
Podcast 256–8
pomegranates, Shawarma Skewers with Oyster Mushrooms and Beetroot 100
Portuguese Chocolate Mousse Cake 202
potatoes
- Chunky Spanish Lentil and Veg St-Oup 65
- Creamy Mushroom Puff Pastry Pie 159
- Easy Tomato and Basil Soup 61
- Granny's Irish Stew 147
- Leek and Potato Soup 56
- Spanish Chickpea, Potato and Pesto Bake 143

pumpkins
- Mushroom Bourguignon with Pumpkin and Mash 181
- Mushroom and Pumpkin Wellington with Redcurrant Jus 176, 178

Q

Quick and Easy Porridge 32
Quinoa Tabbouleh Salad 87

R

radicchio, Happy Pear Farmhouse Salad with Roasted-Pumpkin-Seed Pesto 80
raspberries
- Easy Bakewell Tart 214
- Ginger-Bug Iced Tea 311
- Hay-Fever Probiotic Iced Tea 326
- Raspberry Bakewell Breakfast Muffins 39
- Raspberry Caramel Apple Pie 210
- Raspberry Ripple Pancakes 28

Raspberry Bakewell Breakfast Muffins 39
Raspberry Caramel Apple Pie 210
Raspberry Ripple Pancakes 28
Real Falafel with Tahini Cream and Chilli Sauce 102
red onions
- Caramelised Red Onion and Mushroom Tart Tatin 128
- Creamy Roasted-Veg Pasta Bake 140
- Pickled Red Onions 308

Red-Pepper Pesto and Bean Salad 84
redcurrants, Mushroom and Pumpkin Wellington with Redcurrant Jus 176, 178
rice
- Black Bean, Roasted Sweet Potato and Avocado Salad 76
- Easy Heart-Warming Red Lentil Dhal 148

Roasted Carrot Falafel with Tahini Drizzle 157
Roasted Veg Lasagna 144
rye flour, No-Knead Wholemeal Rye with 100% Hydration 250

S

Salted Caramel Overnight Oats 18
Sauerkraut 296, 298
- Buttery Hummus with a Pop 40

SCOBY, Kombucha 313–14
seaweed
- Crispy Tofu and Mushroom Ramen 164
- Easy Miso Soup 50

seeds
- Apple and Berry Crumble 212
- Asian-Style Rainbow Crunch Salad 74
- Beetroot, Spinach and Apple Salad with Toasted Seeds 79
- Creamiest Hummus Ever! 262
- Creamy Spiced Black Bean Quesadillas 117
- Granola 3 Ways 15–16
- Happy Pear Farmhouse Salad with Roasted-Pumpkin-Seed Pesto 80
- *see also* flaxseeds; sesame seeds

sesame seeds
- Easy 'Sausage' Rolls 286
- Easy Sesame and Coriander Flatbreads 253
- Peanut Rayu 273
- Sticky Sesame Tofu Burgers with Charred Pineapple and

Kimchi Mayo Slaw 105
Shawarma Skewers with Oyster Mushrooms and Beetroot 100
Shepherdless Pie 162
Smashed Avocado, Tomato and Olive 40
Soul-Nourishing Lentil Soup 67
Sourdough 240, 243–5
sourdough
No-Knead Free-Form Sourdough Loaf 246, 248
No-Knead Wholemeal Rye with 100% Hydration 250
soy milk, Vegan Mayonnaise 275
Spanish Chickpea, Potato and Pesto Bake 143
Spiced Carrot Ribbons with Chilli and Ginger 309
spinach
Asian-Style Rainbow Crunch Salad 74
Beetroot, Spinach and Apple Salad with Toasted Seeds 79
Chana Masala with Easy Gram Flour Dosa 188
Chunky Spanish Lentil and Veg St-Oup 65
Cold Killer 322
Easy 10-Minute Indian Dhal 118
Easy Heart-Warming Red Lentil Dhal 148
Easy Spanakopita - Spinach and Filo Pastry Pie 153
Happy Pear Farmhouse Salad with Roasted-Pumpkin-Seed Pesto 80
Mexican Breakfast Bowl 10, 12
Soul-Nourishing Lentil Soup 67
sprouted beans
Asian-Style Rainbow Crunch Salad 74
Happy Pear Farmhouse Salad with Roasted-Pumpkin-Seed Pesto 80
'Steak' and Kidney Pie 161
Sticky Sesame Tofu Burgers with Charred Pineapple and Kimchi Mayo Slaw 105
Strawberries and Cream Chia Pudding 24
Super-Chewy Chocolate Chip Cookies 206
Super-Greens Pesto Pasta 126
sweet potatoes
Black Bean, Roasted Sweet Potato and Avocado Salad 76
Cauliflower Curry Bake 120
Creamy Mushroom Puff Pastry Pie 159
Roasted Veg Lasagna 144

T

tahini
Baba Ganoush 269
Buttery Hummus 264
Creamiest Hummus Ever! 262
Creamy Harissa Aubergine with Zhoug 184
Golden Roasted Cauliflower Steaks with Tahini Cream 174
Middle Eastern 'Meaty' Mushroom Flatbreads 328
Real Falafel with Tahini Cream and Chilli Sauce 102
Roasted Carrot Falafel with Tahini Drizzle 157
Shawarma Skewers with Oyster Mushrooms and Beetroot 100
Vegan Hoisin 'Duck' Pancakes 187
tea, Kombucha 313–14
tempeh, Kale Caesar Salad 83
10-Minute Lower-Fat Basil Pesto Pasta 123
3 Quick Vinegar-Based Pickles 308–9
Tiramisu 209
Tiramisu Overnight Oats 21
Toasties 3 Ways 40
tofu
Crispy Tofu and Mushroom Ramen 164
Crispy Tofu Thai Noodle Soup 53
Easy Burritos with Guacamole 138
Easy Spanakopita - Spinach and Filo Pastry Pie 153
Mexican Breakfast Bowl 10, 12
Sticky Sesame Tofu Burgers with Charred Pineapple and Kimchi Mayo Slaw 105
tomato purée
Ikarian Longevity Stew 150
One-Pot Creamy Tomato Pasta 124
Roasted Veg Lasagna 144
tomatoes
Black Bean, Roasted Sweet Potato and Avocado Salad 76
Creamy Harissa Aubergine with Zhoug 184
Creamy Spiced Black Bean Quesadillas 117
Easy 10-Minute Indian Dhal 118
Easy Burritos with Guacamole 138
5-Minute Chickpea Curry 330
Guacamole 267
King Oyster Mushroom 'BLT' Sandwich 99
Middle Eastern 'Meaty' Mushroom Flatbreads 328
Real Falafel with Tahini Cream and Chilli Sauce 102
Red-Pepper Pesto and Bean Salad 84
Shawarma Skewers with Oyster Mushrooms and Beetroot 100
Smashed Avocado, Tomato and Olive 40
10-Minute Lower-Fat Basil Pesto Pasta 123
tomatoes (tinned)
Chana Masala with Easy Gram Flour Dosa 188
Chunky Spanish Lentil and Veg St-Oup 65
Creamy Roasted-Veg Pasta Bake 140
Easy Heart-Warming Red Lentil Dhal 148
Easy Tomato and Basil Soup 61
5-Minute Chickpea Curry 330
Ikarian Longevity Stew 150

Mushroom Bourguignon with Pumpkin and Mash 181
One-Pot Creamy Tomato Pasta 124
Roasted Veg Lasagna 144
Shepherdless Pie 162
Soul-Nourishing Lentil Soup 67
Spanish Chickpea, Potato and Pesto Bake 143
20 Dreams we have 316–18
20 Foods we couldn't live without 288–91
20 Learnings from our Podcast 256–8
20 People who have made the Happy Pear what it is 336–338
20 Things we've learned after 20 years 68–70
20 Ways to eat more vegetables 166, 168
20 Ways to pick yourself up 234, 236–7

U
Ultimate Mac and Cheese 114

V
Vegan Butter 334
vegan cheese
Beetroot, Walnut and Feta Burgers 107
Caramelised Red Onion and Mushroom Tart Tatin 128
5-Ingredient Carrot Cake 220
5-Ingredient Cookies and Cream Cheesecake 228
Plant-Based Philly Cheesesteak 96
vegan cream
5-Ingredient Chocolate Ganache Tart 226
Tiramisu 209
Vegan Hoisin 'Duck' Pancakes 187
vegan mayo
King Oyster Mushroom 'BLT' Sandwich 99
Plant-Based Philly Cheesesteak 96
Sticky Sesame Tofu Burgers with Charred Pineapple and Kimchi Mayo Slaw 105
Vegan Mayonnaise 275
vegan sausages
Cauliflower Curry Bake 120
Mexican Breakfast Bowl 10, 12
vegetables, 20 ways to eat more 166, 168
vegetables (mixed)
Chunky Spanish Lentil and Veg St-Oup 65
Crispy Tofu Thai Noodle Soup 53
Easy Miso Soup 50
Easy Tomato and Basil Soup 61
Granny's Irish Stew 147
Ikarian Longevity Stew 150
Irish Root Vegetable Soup 54
Mushroom Bourguignon with Pumpkin and Mash 181
Sauerkraut 296
Shepherdless Pie 162

W
walnuts
Beetroot, Walnut and Feta Burgers 107
Caramel Chocolate Banana Cake 198
5-Ingredient Carrot Cake 220
Muhammara 270
White Sauerkraut with Caraway Seeds 298
wine
Cream of Mushroom and Lentil Soup 62
Mushroom Bourguignon with Pumpkin and Mash 181
Mushroom and Pumpkin Wellington with Redcurrant Jus 176, 178
Mushroom Steak and Pepper Sauce 182

Y
yeast (nutritional)
Creamy Mushroom Linguine 112
Creamy Mushroom Puff Pastry Pie 159
Easy Burritos with Guacamole 138
Easy Spanakopita - Spinach and Filo Pastry Pie 153
One-Pot Creamy Tomato Pasta 124
Roasted Veg Lasagna 144
Ultimate Mac and Cheese 114
yoghurt
Baba Ganoush 269
Creamy Harissa Aubergine with Zhoug 184
Easy Sesame and Coriander Flatbreads 253
Golden Roasted Cauliflower Steaks with Tahini Cream 174
Middle Eastern 'Meaty' Mushroom Flatbreads 328
Real Falafel with Tahini Cream and Chilli Sauce 102
Shawarma Skewers with Oyster Mushrooms and Beetroot 100
Strawberries and Cream Chia Pudding 24

Z
zhoug, Creamy Harissa Aubergine with Zhoug 184